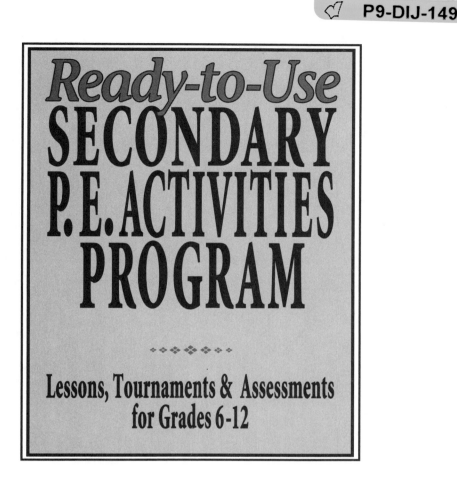

Ready-to-Use
SECONDARY
P.E. ACTIVITIES
PROGRAM

❖ ❖ ❖ ❖ ❖

Lessons, Tournaments & Assessments
for Grades 6-12

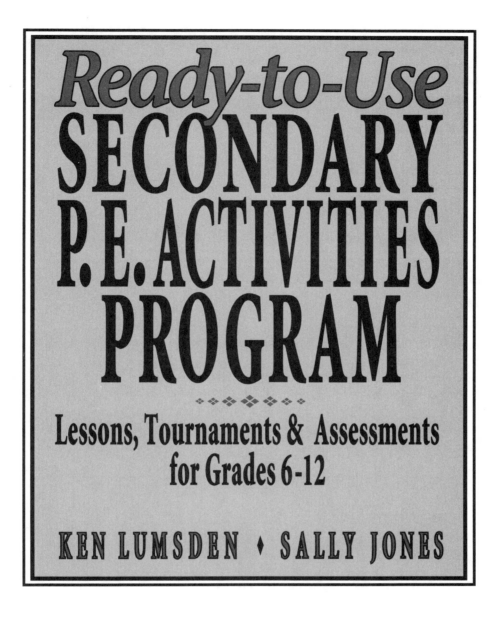

Ready-to-Use SECONDARY P.E. ACTIVITIES PROGRAM

Lessons, Tournaments & Assessments for Grades 6-12

KEN LUMSDEN ◆ SALLY JONES

PARKER PUBLISHING COMPANY
West Nyack, New York 10994

Library of Congress Cataloging in Publication Data

Lumsden, Ken.
    Ready-to-use secondary P.E. activities program : lessons,
tournaments & assessments for grades 6-12 / Ken Lumsden and Sally
Jones.
      p.   cm.
    ISBN 0-13-470007-4
    1. Physical education and training—Study and teaching
(Secondary)—United States.   2. Physical fitness—United States—
Testing.   I. Jones, Sally Donna, 1942-   . II. Title.
GV365.L85   1996
795'.071'2—dc20   95–52156
                                     CIP

Printed in the United States of America

10 9 8 7 6 5 4

ISBN 0-13-470007-4

ATTENTION: CORPORATIONS AND SCHOOLS

Parker Publishing Company books are available at quantity discounts with bulk purchase for educational, business, or sales promotional use. For information, please write
to: Prentice Hall Career & Personal Development Special Sales, 113 Sylvan Avenue,
Englewood Cliffs, NJ 07632. Please supply: title of book, ISBN number, quantity, how
the book will be used, date needed.

PARKER PUBLISHING COMPANY
West Nyack, NY 10994

On the World Wide Web at http://www.phdirect.com

PRENTICE-HALL INTERNATIONAL (UK) LIMITED, *LONDON*
PRENTICE-HALL OF AUSTRALIA PTY. LIMITED, *SYDNEY*
PRENTICE-HALL CANADA INC., *TORONTO*
PRENTICE-HALL HISPANOAMERICANA, S.A., *MEXICO*
PRENTICE-HALL OF INDIA PRIVATE LIMITED, *NEW DELHI*
PRENTICE-HALL OF JAPAN, INC., *TOKYO*
PEARSON EDUCATION ASIA PTE. LTD., *SINGAPORE*
EDITORA PRENTICE-HALL DO BRASIL, LTDA., *RIO DE JANEIRO*

ABOUT THE AUTHORS

Ken Lumsden has been a secondary physical education teacher and coach at Ashland Middle School in Ashland, Oregon since 1976. He received his Masters degree in Physical Education and Health from Southern Oregon State College in 1981. Ken has had articles published in two national journals, been a guest lecturer for college methods classes, and spoken at both state and national physical education conferences. He has also created several games, a method of organizing students, and a procedure for success-oriented grading. In his spare time, Ken enjoys fishing, agate hunting, and developing his inventions.

    Sally Jones is Professor of Health and Physical Education at Southern Oregon State College where her primary assignments are in the areas of health promotion/fitness management and teacher education. Prior to instructing at SOSC for twenty years, she taught in public schools for ten years in Oregon, California, and Texas. Sally received her B.S. and Ph.D. degrees from the University of Oregon, and M.Ed. degree from North Texas State University. Collaboration with colleagues is important to Sally, and she has worked with others on presentations and workshops at the state, northwest, and national levels. As a former coach, she continues to be active in women's sports issues. In her spare time, Sally enjoys playing tennis, jogging, and her house!

ACKNOWLEDGMENTS

We would like to thank our many colleagues and students for their time, ideas, and feedback about this program. Our special thanks to Don McClure, retired physical education teacher, for his inspiration, and to Deanna Arthur, Dick Copple, John Lefler, Kathy Pauck and Diane Paulsen, physical education teachers, for their insight, creativity, and assistance in this undertaking.

ABOUT THIS RESOURCE

Ready-to-Use Secondary P.E. Activities Program focuses on modifying and expanding many of the existing curriculum activities and games in any middle, junior high, or high school as a way to motivate your students by making physical education interesting and fun as they are learning. The book is also developed to invoke success, self-confidence, and enthusiasm for each and every student within each activity or unit. Many of the tournament formats, activities, activity variations, and assessments are unique. The information should be used as a follow-up after the students have learned the basic rules, court and field dimensions, skills, and strategies of the many games and activities included in this book.

Section 1, **Activity Variations,** encompasses a wide range of activities and interests, be they individual, team, competitive, noncompetitive, or creative in structure. Each game and activity lists its objectives, essentials needed, how to play, student tasks and variations that will challenge the students at any secondary level. Safety is always a concern and should be covered by you in a prudent manner before any activity or game begins. Activities list additional safety precautions when necessary. You may alter any activity to fit the needs, interests and skills of each age group in grades 6–12. Easy-to-read diagrams, student forms, and lay-outs are provided. All of the forms and information can be copied, placed on a clipboard, and used during class.

Section 2, **Tournaments,** along with its unique "Mix 'n Match" format, was created to enhance the organizational aspects of grouping students for team play. Allowing students to be with and against all members of a class, to give more time for skills and games, and to aid in solving the problems with absenteeism are a few of the important benefits realized. All of the necessary forms are provided, along with illustrated, easy-to-read samples, and can be easily copied and used year after year.

Section 3, **Assessments,** offers a fascinating method of grading where the student is totally responsible for the grade he or she receives. This section also includes detailed charts and easy-to-follow explanations, and gives you a simple, effective, and fair method to evaluate, follow, and inform all of the individuals concerned.

It is hoped this book will allow participants to explore physical education, experience a vast variety of activities, set individual goals, enjoy more opportunities for success, and benefit from its many life-long resources. With this innovative program approach, it is our goal that students will be motivated to **want** to be active, rather than the teacher attempting to **make** them.

Ken Lumsden and Sally Jones

CONTENTS

Bowling—35

Create a Game—39

Cross Country—41

Darts—58

Dodgeball—71

Section 2:

TOURNAMENTS—285

Section 3:

ASSESSMENTS—309

Section 1

◆◆◆◆◆

STUDENTS' CHOICE ACTIVITIES

The following section is a compendium of many of the more popular activities that can be offered in any physical education curriculum. It is by no means a complete and comprehensive curriculum guide, but we have included here the winners—those activities that students most often want to do. Each activity is broken down into objectives, essentials, how to play, student tasks, and variations. Safety is always a concern and should be covered by each teacher in a prudent manner before any activity or game begins. Activities that might require additional safety precautions will list them when necessary.

Each activity has been designed and written so that it takes little time to cover the rules and regulations. Activity guidelines and forms can be easily copied, placed on a clipboard, and utilized during class.

Each section of the activity guidelines can be changed, altered, or modified to fit the age or class being taught. Using volleyball as an example, it would not be of great interest to allow high school juniors and seniors to serve the ball from anywhere on the court; however, this would be an advantage for sixth, seventh, and eighth graders. Instructors have the freedom to create and conjure up new ideas and methods that will further challenge and enhance student successes. Again in volleyball, older students must be involved in five hits during a game, while the younger students would only need to be involved in two. We encourage instructors to be enterprising, resourceful, and imaginative. Do not be afraid to listen to the students, for sometimes they often have great new ideas because of their lack of a fixed mind set.

It is hoped that student interest and participation is enhanced since the same activities can be changed to add variety and excitement. A softball unit, for example, can now have four or five different games and a collection of variations to play each game.

LINE AEROBICS

Objectives:

- ◆ To allow students to be leaders.
- ◆ To allow students to be creative.
- ◆ To develop cardiovascular fitness.

Essentials:

- ◆ Large room
- ◆ Mats for the floor (optional)
- ◆ Music source

How to Play:

1. Allow the students to bring in the music.
2. Use the **Mix 'n Match** form and divide the students into 9 or 11 teams.
3. Combine new teams each day.
4. Create rows of teams on the floor. (This is the time to stretch and loosen up.)
5. The team in front leads the first session of exercises.
6. Each person on that team attempts to do a different exercise for 15 to 20 seconds. If a student does not know what to do, have him/her do something as simple as jumping jacks.
7. After all of the students have led, return to the first student and start over.
8. After all of the first-row students have had two turns at leading, have them rotate to the back row. All other lines move toward the front one row.
9. Row two is now up front and leads the class in the same manner as the first group did.

Student Tasks:

1. Bring in some great music.
2. Create a couple of new or interesting movements.

Variations:

1. Allow a group of students to lead the class for the entire period.
2. Have an outside aerobics instructor lead the class for one or more days.
3. Use a video and have the students follow along.
4. Form a large circle around the room. Allow different individuals or groups to step to the middle and lead.

Safety:

1. Remember to cover the exercises that could cause possible injury so that students do not attempt them while leading.

2. Allow plenty of time for warming up and cooling down.

3. Low impact aerobics are highly recommended.

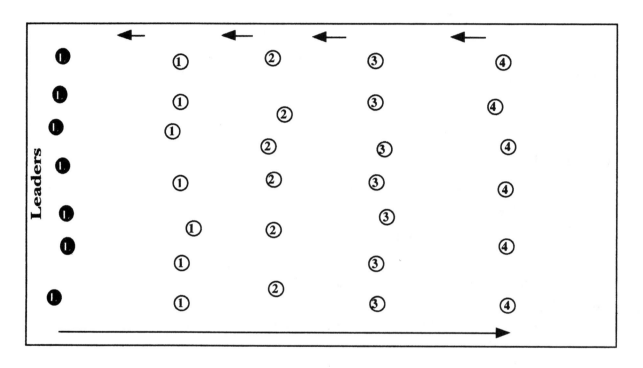

ABOUT "AQUATICS"

Objectives:

- ◆ To develop and improve beginning, intermediate, and advanced swimming skills.
- ◆ To increase cardio-respiratory endurance.
- ◆ To acquaint students with safety factors pertaining to aquatic activities.
- ◆ To develop swimming skills so that students will feel confident in the water.

Essentials:

- ◆ 20- to 25-yard swimming pool
- ◆ Videotape recorder
- ◆ Fins, masks, snorkels
- ◆ Life jackets

How to Play:

1. Sport workouts.
2. Fitness lap swimming with stroke improvement through time and laps.
3. Skin diving and snorkeling.
4. Safety skills such as throwing and reaching rescues, life jacket skills, disrobing, and drownproofing.
5. Water carnival with games and relays.
6. Warm-up activities such as diving for coins.
7. Creativity project such as a new stroke, design a pool, or create a game.
8. Make an aquatics dictionary.
9. Interview someone connected with aquatics.
10. Read a book related to aquatics.

Student Tasks:

1. Improve one swimming skill level: from beginner to advanced beginner to intermediate to advanced.
2. Present a game or relay.
3. Demonstrate a safety skill.
4. Do a creative project.
5. Complete a 20-minute swim.

Safety:

1. Do not enter the pool until the instructor gives directions.
2. Remove all jewelry, bandages, adhesive tape, etc., before leaving the shower room.

3. No person shall run or engage in horseplay in or around the pool.

4. Be certain no one is using the diving board when there are swimmers in the diving vicinity. The diver is responsible for seeing that the area is clear under the board.

5. No food, gum, or drink is allowed in the pool area.

AQUA AEROBICS

Objectives:

- ◆ To allow students to be creative.
- ◆ To develop cardio-respiratory endurance.

Essentials:

- ◆ 20- to 25-yard swimming pool
- ◆ Music source

How to Play:

1. All participants are in the water.
2. Five individuals stand on the side of the pool.
3. The first person in line leads the entire class in water aerobics. After leading for approximately 20 seconds, he/she jumps into the pool and follows the next leader.
4. As someone goes into the pool, another future leader exits and waits for her/his turn.

Student Tasks:

1. Try not to touch the bottom.
2. Create a new exercise.

Variations:

1. Allow everyone to stand in the shallow end.
2. Follow the same format as in **Line Aerobics.**
3. Lead from the diving board and then dive into the pool when finished leading.

Safety:

1. Do not enter the pool until the instructor gives directions.
2. Remove all jewelry, bandages, adhesive tape, etc., before leaving the shower room.

3. No person shall run or engage in horseplay in or around the pool.

4. Be certain no one is using the diving board when there are swimmers in the diving vicinity. The diver is responsible for seeing that the area is clear under the board.

5. No food, gum, or drink is allowed in the pool area.

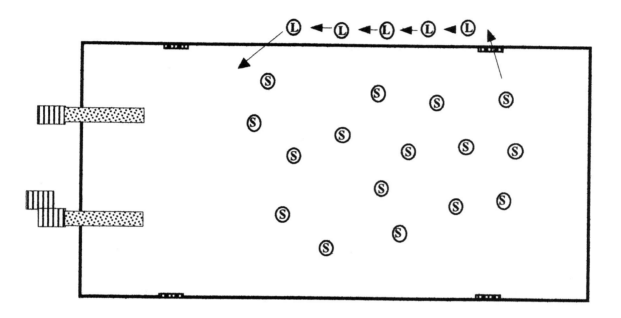

SYNCHRONIZED SWIMMING

Objectives:

◆ To create a 2-minute synchronized routine with two participants.

◆ To demonstrate and video record the routines.

Essentials:

◆ 20- to 25-yard swimming pool

◆ Video recorder

◆ Music source

How to Play:

1. Allow the students to choose pairs.

2. Give enough time for each team to choreograph a routine.

3. Video each routine as the rest of the class watches.

Student Tasks:

1. Attempt a skill that no other group accomplished.
2. Conjure up a new skill.
3. Add music to the routine.

Variations:

1. Make larger groups.
2. The entire class must develop a routine.
3. Allow students to stand in the shallow water.

Safety:

1. Do not enter the pool until the instructor gives directions.
2. Remove all jewelry, bandages, adhesive tape, etc., before leaving the shower room.
3. No person shall run or engage in horseplay in or around the pool.
4. No food, gum, or drink is allowed in the pool area.

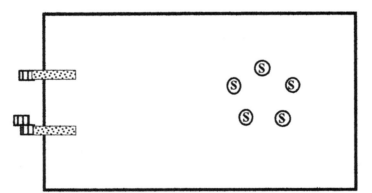

20-MINUTE SWIM

Objectives:

- To increase cardio-respiratory endurance.
- To develop swimming skills so that students will feel confident in the water.
- To continuously swim for 20 minutes without stopping.

Essentials:

- 20- to 25-yard swimming pool
- Timing device

AQUATICS

How to Play:

1. Allow all students to spread out on the side of the pool.
2. On the start of the time, all students will swim from side to side for 20 minutes. Any strokes can be used.

Student Tasks:

1. Finish the 20-minute swim.
2. Use three or more different strokes.

Variations:

1. Shorten the time.
2. Lengthen the time.
3. Swim in a circle around the edge of the pool.
4. Every time a whistle is blown, all participants must change direction.

Safety:

1. Do not enter the pool until the instructor gives directions.
2. Remove all jewelry, bandages, adhesive tape, etc., before leaving the shower room.
3. No person shall run or engage in horseplay in or around the pool.
4. No food, gum, or drink is allowed in the pool area.

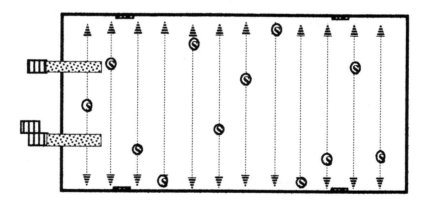

MIRROR IMAGE

Objective:

◆ To get the highest score possible by hitting one side of the target and then the other.

Essentials:

◆ Large field

◆ Large room with back stop net

◆ Bows, arrows, targets, finger and arm guards

◆ Pencils and scratch paper for scoring

◆ Field cones to mark scratch lines

◆ Tape or string

How to Play:

1. Archers should spread out evenly at each target.
2. The distance is 30 feet.
3. Attach the tape or string down the middle of the target.
4. Each participant shoots two arrows in a row, trying to get one on the right side and one on the left side of the tape. If this is achieved, then the student may add the scores of the two arrows. If the target is missed or both arrows are on the same side, no score is recorded.
5. After the completion of the fifth session, scores are tallied.
6. Winner is that person with the highest total of points.

Student Tasks:

1. Win the tournament.
2. Finish in the top five.
3. Hit the right and left three consecutive times.

Variations:

1. Change the scratch line distances to:
    a. 40 feet
    b. 50 feet
    c. 60 feet
2. Make teams of two or more and combine the scores of all players on a team.

3. Cut the target into four sections with players shooting four arrows in a row.

4. Have the opponent tell the shooter in which section the arrow must hit.

NAIL IT DOWN

Objective:

◆ To shoot two arrows in a high arc and have them land in the nail box.

Essentials:

◆ Large field

◆ Bows, arrows, targets, finger and arm guards

◆ Field cones

How to Play:

1. Archers make four lines at the end zone of a regulation football field.

2. Each nail gun has two arrows (nails) that are recognizable or different from the rest.

3. The first four archers step to the line and lob two arrows into a nail box at the other end of the field. (See the diagram on next page.)

4. After the completion of the last four shooters, all competitors go to the nail box to see how many landed inside.

5. Retrieve the individual arrows and return to the scratch line. Do this until each player has had ten chances.

6. Winner is that person with the highest total of nails in the box.

Student Tasks:

1. Win the tournament.

2. Finish in the top five.

3. Put more than four nails in the box.

Variations:

1. Make teams (of the four lines) and combine the totals of each player.
2. Change the size, distance, or shape of the nail box.

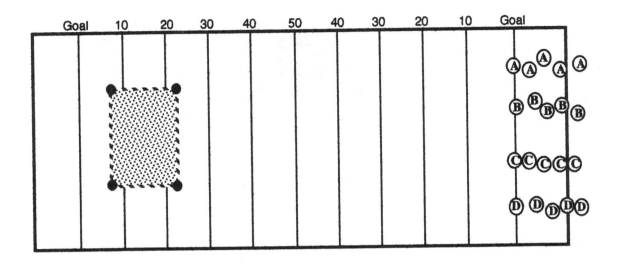

STICK-TAC-TOE

Objective:

◆ To capture three squares in a row, either horizontally, vertically or diagonally.

Essentials:

◆ Large field
◆ Large room with back stop net
◆ Bows, arrows, targets, finger and arm guards
◆ Pencils and scratch paper for scoring
◆ Field cones to mark scratch lines
◆ Tape or string

How to Play:

1. Archers spread out evenly at each target.
2. The distance is 30 feet.
3. Attach the tape or string to form a tic-tac-toe grid on the target.
4. Each participant shoots one arrow and then rotates.
5. If and when a square has been taken, mark it on a piece of scratch paper.

6. Go until three in a row are captured or the cat (nobody) has won.

7. Winner is the best two out of three matches.

Student Tasks:

1. Win a match in three shots.

2. Win a match in four shots.

3. Defeat three different opponents.

Variations:

1. Change the scratch line distances to:

    a. 40 feet

    b. 50 feet

    c. 60 feet

    d. 70 feet

2. Play in teams of two.

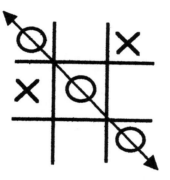

TEN ARROWS

Objective:

◆ To get the highest score possible by combining the scores of ten shots.

Essentials:

◆ Large field

◆ Large room with back stop net

◆ Bows, arrows, targets, finger and arm guards

◆ Pencils and scratch paper for scoring

◆ Field cones to mark scratch lines

How to Play:

1. Archers spread out evenly at each target.

2. The distance is 30 feet.

3. Each participant shoots two arrows in a row, records the score, and rotates with the next shooter.

4. After the completion of the fifth session, scores are tallied.

5. Winner is that person with the highest total of points after ten shots.

Student Tasks:

1. Win the tournament.

2. Finish in the top ten.

3. Come from behind and win on last two shots.

Variations:

1. Change the scratch line distances to:
   a. 40 feet
   b. 50 feet
   c. 60 feet
   d. 70 feet

2. Make teams of two or more and combine the scores of all players on a team.

TURKEY SHOOT

Objective:

◆ To score the most points possible in a predetermined number of shots.

Essentials:

◆ Large field

◆ Large room with back stop net

◆ Bows, arrows, targets, finger and arm guards

◆ Markers, crayons, or colored paint

◆ Large pieces of butcher paper to hang on the target

◆ Field cones to mark scratch lines

ARCHERY

How to Play:

1. Group students into three or four teams.
2. Pass out the paper and markers and allow the students to draw a picture of something. Give them just a few minutes to do this task.
3. Give point values to the features, then tape it to the target.
4. First player to score 100 points is the winner.
5. Save the drawings and post them in the halls or gymnasium.

Student Tasks:

1. Win at two different turkey targets.
2. Hit the same counter two times in a row.

Variations:

1. Allow only 10 shots to determine a score.
2. After a short time, approximately five minutes, have each team rotate one target to the left. Start a new game at a new turkey.
3. Teams compete against the other teams by keeping records of their scores at each of the different targets.

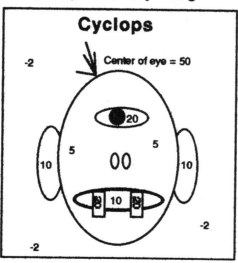

Sample Turkey Target

WILLIAM TELL

Objective:

◆ To hit the apple sitting on top of William Tell's head.

Essentials:

◆ Large field
◆ Large room with back stop net
◆ Bows, arrows, targets, finger and arm guards
◆ Apple-sized balloons
◆ Field cones to mark scratch lines

How to Play:

1. Archers spread out evenly at each target.
2. The distance is 30 feet.
3. Each student inflates two balloons to about the size of an apple, then attaches them to the target.
4. Each participant shoots two arrows in a row, records his/her number of hits, and rotates with the next shooter(s).
5. After the completion of the fifth session of shooting at the apples, scores are tallied.
6. Winner is that person with the highest total of broken apples.

Student Tasks:

1. Win the tournament.
2. Finish in the top ten.
3. Hit three balloons in a row.

Variations:

1. Change the scratch line distances to:
   a. 40 feet
   b. 50 feet
2. Make teams of two or more and combine the scores of all players on a team.

© 1996 Parker Publishing Company

ABOUT "BADMINTON"

Objective:

◆ To be the first person/team to score 11 (singles) or 15 (doubles) first.

Essentials:

◆ Gymnasium or field
◆ Birds
◆ Rackets
◆ Net

How to Play:

1. SINGLES: One player is on each side, play to 11 points, win by two.

   a. If your score is even, serve from the right-hand court.

   b. If your score is odd, serve from the left-hand court.

2. DOUBLES: Two players on each side, play to 15 points, win by two.

   a. Always start an inning by serving from the right-hand court to the opponent's diagonal court.

   b. Racket head must be lower than the wrist and waist on the serve.

   c. When serving keep both feet stationary.

   d. Bird must land inside serving boundary and may not hit the net.

   e. Only the serving side may score.

   f. Must alternate service courts after each point.

   g. Except for the first inning, each player has a chance to serve before the opposition gets to serve.

3. FAULTS: Breaking of rules by which the bird goes to the next server or a point is scored, depending on who broke the rule.

   a. Hitting the bird out of bounds.

   b. Serving faults.

   c. Hitting the wall or ceiling.

   d. Carry or sling: Not hitting the bird but just pushing it.

   e. Hitting the bird to the wrong service court.

   f. Wrong receiver hitting the serve.

   g. Reaching over the net to hit the bird.

   h Hitting the net during play.

4. GENERAL:

   a. A bird that hits the net and falls into the proper court is good.

   b. A bird falling on a boundary line is good.

   c. A shot that is disputed should be replayed.

Student Tasks:

1. Use several different strokes during play.

2. Win a game that is tied at 15 points.

Variations:

1. Serve and score as in:

   a. Volleyball.

   b. Table tennis.

   c. Tennis.

2. See **Table Tennis** and **Tennis** for a list of the many different games that can be adapted for the game of badminton.

3. Use a volleyball court and play the game just like volleyball, using six or more players on a side. *Note:* Be aware of other players when swinging the racquet.

Floor Diagram for Doubles Play

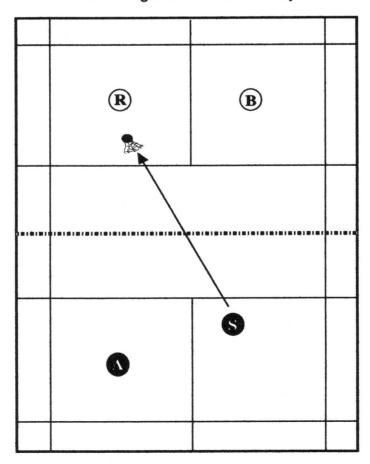

AROUND THE WORLD

Objective:

- Be the first player to make all the shots from the different spots.

Essentials:

- Basketball floor
- 1 basketball per group
- Tape with letters "A" through "R" written on each and located on the floor

How to Play:

1. Two or three players per group.
2. Players may attempt two shots from each letter.
3. If a player makes a designated shot, he/she will move to the next letter and continue shooting.
4. If a player misses her/his first attempt, she/he may elect to stop at that spot and give up the ball to the next shooter. She/he would start at this spot when it is her/his next turn. If she/he elects to shoot the second shot and misses it, she/he gives up the ball and on her/his next possession will start over at letter "A."

Student Tasks:

1. Move up four or five spots without a miss.
2. Come from behind to win.

Variations:

1. After going all the way to the top letter, return in reverse letter order.
2. Use the right, then the left, arm every other shot.
3. Use the off arm only.
4. The backboard must be used when possible.

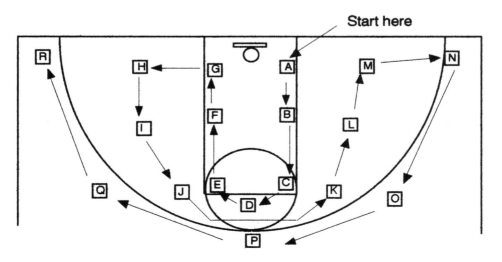

BASKETBALL TOP GUN

Objective:

◆ To win two or three games in a row at the **Top Gun** court.

Essentials:

◆ Basketball court with four to six baskets
◆ 1 ball for each court
◆ Pinnies

How to Play:

1. All basketball rules apply.
2. Can have up to five players on a team.
3. All games are played on a half-court floor.
4. Winners move to the next court. Losers stay and play the challengers.
5. The first team to score a certain number of baskets wins. Six to ten points is usually best so that the games are short. If a team finishes ahead of the others, give them a rest, since a lot of games will be played.
6. No player may score more than two baskets in a row.
7. Any team that loses at the **Top Gun** court starts over at court number one.
8. When a team wins two or three games at the **Top Gun** court, this team—along with the vanquished—returns to the first court and attempts to work their way back up.

Student Tasks:

1. Score two baskets in a row.
2. Get two or more assists.
3. Get three or more rebounds.
4. Beat a team that has already been "top gun."

Variations:

1. **Make It, Take It:** When a team scores a basket, they get the ball again.
2. No dribbling is allowed during the game.
3. Play the games until a certain amount of time has expired.

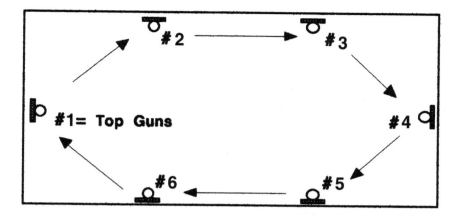

BUMP OUT

Objectives:

◆ To make a shot before the player behind the first shooter makes his/hers.

◆ To be the last player.

Essentials:

◆ Basketball floor

◆ 2 basketballs per 8 to 10 players

How to Play:

1. Players line up in single file at the free throw line.

2. The first two players in line each have a basketball.

3. The first shot attempt must be from behind the free throw line.

4. First player shoots and:

   a. If the shot is made, quickly gets the ball and throws it to the third person in line, then returns to the end of the line.

   b. If the shot is missed, she/he quickly gets the ball and attempts to score from anywhere. If the second player makes a basket **before** the first player does, then the first player is eliminated.

5. The second player may shoot as soon as the ball is released from the first shooter's hand.

6. As soon as the third person in line gets the ball from the first shooter, she/he may shoot, and so on.

Student Tasks:

1. Eliminate a past winner.
2. Win two games in a row.

Variations:

1. Allow students to use their ball to bump or hit another player's ball that is attempting to score. No hitting it out of their hands, though. This creates a challenging game but can take longer to determine a winner.
2. First shot attempt must be with the off hand.
3. First shot attempt must be from behind the three-point line.

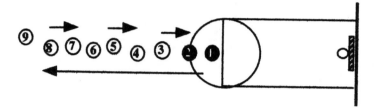

DRIBBLE TAG

Objective:

◆ Avoid getting tagged by *IT.*

Essentials:

◆ Full court or half court
◆ 1 ball for each player on the court

How to Play:

1. Any number of players can be on the floor with a basketball.
2. While dribbling the ball, *IT* attempts to:
   a. Cause a player to go out of bounds.
   b. Force a player to lose control of her/his ball.
   c. Tag a player anywhere on her/his body.
   d. If and when *IT* is successful, then that player now becomes *IT.*
3. Choose a new *IT* if a tag is not completed in 20 to 30 seconds.
4. *IT* may not retouch the player that tagged her/him.

Student Tasks:

1. Avoid being tagged the entire game.

2. Tag a player who has never been *IT*.

Variations:

1. Only the left or right hand may be used when dribbling.

2. Have more than one *IT*.

3. *IT* does **not** have a ball and must touch another player's ball, force her/him out of bounds, or cause her/him to lose control. If any of these happen, then the dribbler must give his/her ball to *IT*.

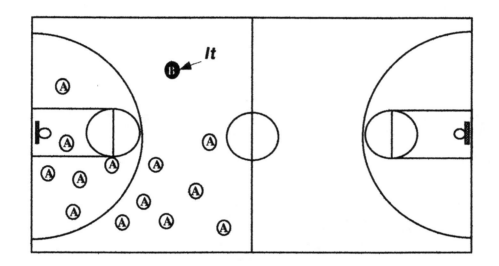

DUNK HOOPS

Objective:

◆ To allow students to add a new dimension (the dunk shot) to their game.

Essentials:

◆ Open area on the playground
◆ 1 backboard, 1 **double** ring rim, 1 net, and 1 post

How to Play:

1. Rim heights:

   a. Middle school should be around 7′ to 8′ high.

   b. Junior high school should be around 7′6″ to 8′6″ high.

   c. High school should be around 8′ to 9′ high.

2. Play any game that is played on a regulation court.

Student Tasks:

1. Develop a trick shot.
2. Do a trick dunk.
3. Dunk two basketballs simultaneously.

Variation:

Create a dunk tournament that is judged as in the NBA.

Safety:

1. Do not allow participants to hang on the rims. Paint this message on the backboard.
2. The playing surface is best if it is cement or asphalt. Sand or soil is not recommended since players could slip when jumping.

FOUR-THREE-TWO-ONE

Objective:

◆ To make the shot.

Essentials:

◆ 1 basketball court

BASKETBALL

- ◆ 2 basketballs
- ◆ Floor cone

How to Play:

1. Nine to ten players line up behind where a floor cone has been placed. This location is changed with each new game.

2. The first two players in line possess a basketball.

3. The first player shoots at the basket.

   a. If the shot is made, she/he will go to another basket and get some free shooting time.

   b. If the shot is missed, she/he will go to the end of the line and work to the front for another attempt.

4. Continue this format until there are only four participants left.

5. These four players shoot for free throws or something predetermined. The first player (of these four) to make the shot goes to another basket and must stay there until she/he makes one free throw. The second player to make the shot goes to another basket and must make two free throws, and so on.

6. Start the second game by changing the cone location and reversing the order of finish with the last four players. The individual who had to make four free throws starts the second game.

Student Tasks:

1. Make your first shot attempt.
2. Make your first shot attempt in three games.
3. Never finish in the last four places.
4. Never finish in third or fourth place.

Variations:

1. Shoot with the off hand only.
2. Must shoot backboard shots when possible.
3. Shoot a shot that does not hit the rim.

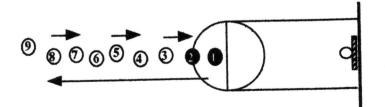

© 1996 Parker Publishing Company

H-O-R-S-E

Objectives:

- ◆ To make various shots that the other contestants cannot duplicate.
- ◆ To avoid receiving the letters that spell "H-O-R-S-E."

Essentials:

- ◆ Basketball court
- ◆ 1 basketball for each group of 2 to 3 players

How to Play:

1. Competitors determine a shooting order.
2. The first player shoots any shot of his/her choice.
3. If the shot is made, the next player must duplicate the same shot.
4. If the second player:
   a. Misses the shot, she/he will now have the letter "H." The next shooter now attempts the shot of her/his choice.
   b. Makes the shot, the next shooter (other than the person who made the original shot) must also duplicate it.
5. If that shot is missed, the next player has a choice, and so on.
6. Any player to acquire the letters to spell "H-O-R-S-E" is out.

Student Tasks:

1. Invent a trick shot.
2. Perform a regular or trick shot with the off hand.
3. Defeat a past winner.
4. After getting the letter "S" first, defeat your opponent.

Variations:

1. **Prove It:** If a player is on the last letter, she/he may ask the shooter to make the same shot again. If it is duplicated the second time, the shooter wins. If the shooter misses, then the other person is still in. The shooter continues with the next turn though.
2. **Tricks of the Trade:** Shooters may call such things as "no rim," "backboard," or "do spectacular trick shots."
3. **O-X** or **P-I-G:** Same game as **H-O-R-S-E** but only a shorter version.
4. Set up a tournament by using a single, double elimination, or round robin format. Games can be based on a time limit.
5. Base all games on a set amount of time.

HUNCH

Objectives:

- ◆ To get to a predetermined number of points first (usually 11, 15, or 21).
- ◆ To compete with or against the other two players.

Essentials:

- ◆ Basketball court
- ◆ 1 ball for every 3 players

How to Play:

1. The rules for basketball apply.
2. Form groups of three people and play a regulation game of basketball.
3. The game is played at only one basket.
4. Two points are awarded for a made basket and that player then goes to the free throw line and shoots free throws (worth one point) until she/he misses. Play resumes on any missed free throw.
5. The person with possession of the ball must try and score against the other two players.
6. All missed shots that hit the rim or backboard must be brought back out to the free throw line by the defensive player who got the rebound.
7. All steals, turnovers and air ball shots can be immediately taken to the basket for a score.

Student Tasks:

1. Score a certain number of free throws in a row.
2. Rebound a certain number during a game.
3. Block a shot.

Variations:

1. Any three-point shot that is made gives that player two chances to make the first free throw shot.
2. Play a game with four players. Do not allow any double teaming of the ball.

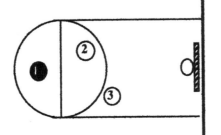

MONKEYBALL

Objectives:

◆ To be the first, second, or third person in line.

◆ To shoot the basketball and make the basket.

Essentials:

◆ Basketball court

◆ 2 basketballs

◆ 8 to 10 floor marking cones

How to Play:

1. Set the cones at a desired distance from the rim in a large arc.

2. All of the players line up behind the cones and spread out from one end to the other.

3. The first two players in line get a ball.

4. The last person in line is always the **monkey** and must rebound the shots from the various players in line. She/he must pass the ball to the next person in line.

5. The first person shoots the ball. If the shot is made, she/he stays in that #1 spot. If the shot is missed, then the **first** player to make a shot goes to the #1 spot. The second player to make a shot goes to the #2 position, and so on.

6. After the monkey has shot, round two begins. If the monkey was the fourth person to make a basket, then she/he goes to the #4 spot. The last person in line is now the new monkey.

7. Players next to the shooter may not interfere with the shot.

8. Play six or seven complete rotations. The participants in the top two or three positions are the winners.

Student Tasks:

1. Go from being a monkey during the game to a first, second, or third position when it is finished.

2. Stay in the #1 position three times in a row.

Variations:

1. Set a time limit of five or more minutes.

2. Set a time limit but do not tell the players how long or how much time is left.

3. Shorten the distance to the rim for the players nearer the end of the line.

4. Players must use their off hand when shooting.

5. Allow players a second attempt. If it too is missed, they automatically trade places with the monkey.

6. After a game has been completed, flip the shooting order so that the past winner is now the monkey.

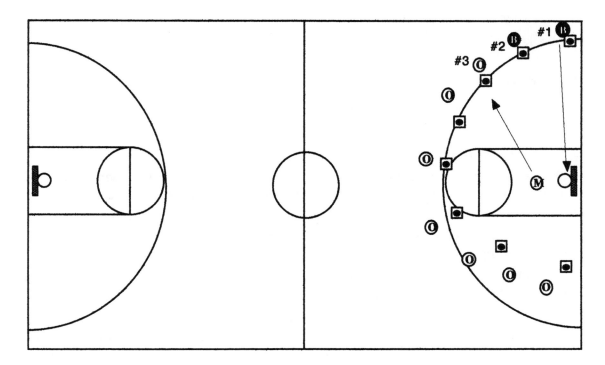

Key:

1. Player with a ball ---------- **Ⓑ**

2. Player without a ball ----- **Ⓞ**

3. Monkey (Rebounder) ---- **Ⓜ**

4. Floor marking cone ------ **▣**

PIN 'EM DOWN

Objectives:

◆ To score a set number of points (30 to 50) before the other teams do.

◆ To make free throws and lay ups.

◆ To knock the pin down.

Essentials:

- Gymnasium with 4 backboards
- 1 bowling pin or object to knock down
- 4 basketballs

How to Play:

1. Divide the class into four equal teams.
2. Place a pin at center court.
3. Have each team line up behind the bowling line.
4. On a command, each team tries to knock over the pin by rolling their basketball at it. Only the first player may retrieve **any** rolled ball and give it to the next player in line.
5. The first team to knock down the pin goes to the nearest basketball hoop and shoots lay-ins. One point is scored for each lay-in made.
6. The other three teams recover a basketball and shoot free throws. The first team to make three free throws causes all action to stop. They receive three points.
7. The four teams then return back to the bowling line and wait for the next command to begin. This continues until a team has accumulated the projected number.

Student Tasks:

1. Knock down the pin.
2. Make a certain number of lay-ins in a row.
3. Make a certain number of free throws in a row.

Variations:

1. Shoot lay-ins from the left side.
2. Teams must go to the across court basket.
3. Teams must shoot three point shots instead of free throws.
4. Make four teams, combine two different teams, and add their scores for a best of two out of three. Can a team go undefeated by winning each of the three series?
   a. Series #1 = A + B vs. C + D. Best two out of three.
   b. Series #2 = A + C vs. B + D. Best two out of three.
   c. Series #3 = A + D vs. B + C. Best two out of three.

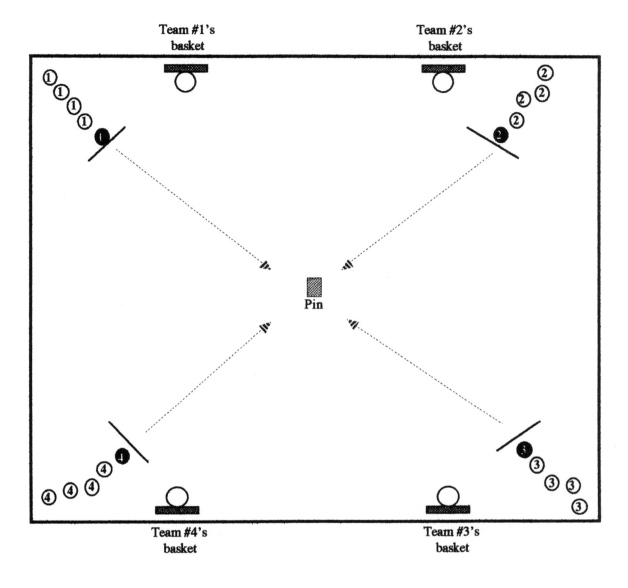

TEAM SHOOTING RELAYS

Objectives:

◆ To be the first team to make a predetermined number of shots.

◆ To be the first team to win a predetermined number of games.

Essentials:

◆ Full court or two half courts

◆ 1 ball for each team

◆ 1 floor marking cone for each team

How to Play:

1. Choose six to eight teams. Four or five players each is recommended.

2. Place the marker cones at various spots on the floor.

3. The first player in line has a ball and attempts to make a shot. If the shot is made, then all of the team members must yell out the number **ONE.** This lets the instructor and all of the other players know what number the various teams are at. Along with this added pressure, it also adds a lot of excitement. If the shot is missed, she/he must quickly get the rebound, pass it to the next person in line, and go to the end of the line.

4. Rebounders are not allowed to interfere with the other basketballs.

5. After a team wins, rotate all teams clockwise to a new location.

6. First team to win five games is the winner.

Student Tasks:

1. Make three of the team's total shots.

2. Come from behind and win the contest.

Variations:

1. Allow only backboard shots to count.

2. Players must use their off hand.

3. Combine two teams. Both teams must make the given number to win.

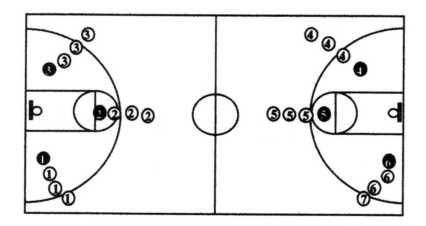

THUNDERBALL

Objectives:

- ◆ To score more points than the other team in a given time.
- ◆ To get rebounds.
- ◆ To play defense.

Essentials:

- ◆ Basketball court
- ◆ Pinnies
- ◆ Score-keeping device
- ◆ Basketball

How to Play:

1. All of the rules of regulation basketball apply except for the scoring.
2. Scoring:
   a. Each shot attempt that hits the rim is worth one (1) point . Points are not awarded for a ball bouncing around on the rim two or three times. If a player grabs several offensive rebounds in a row and hits the rim each time, then a point is awarded for each time the ball initially touches the rim.
   b. A shot made from inside the lane is worth two (2) points.
   c. A shot made from inside the regulation three-point line is worth three (3) points.
   d. A shot made from behind the free throw line while inside the half circle is worth four (4) points.
   e. A shot made from outside the regulation three-point line is worth (5) points.
3. First team to reach 15 points is the winner.

Student Tasks:

1. Get a set number of rebounds.
2. Block a shot attempt.
3. Get an assist.
4. Make a shot using the off hand.

Variations:

1. Put a time limit on the game. The team that is ahead after a certain amount of time is the winner.

2. No dribbling is allowed. This can be done by taking some air out of the ball.

3. Play half-court games. The ball must be brought out to the regulation three-point line when there is a change of possession.

4. Set up a tournament using the **Mix 'n Match** format.

5. Allow six or seven players on a team.

6. Use a different type of ball. A football works well if it is **never** thrown at the basket but shot in the same way as a basketball. It is moved around the floor by passing it.

Floor Diagram: Scoring Zones

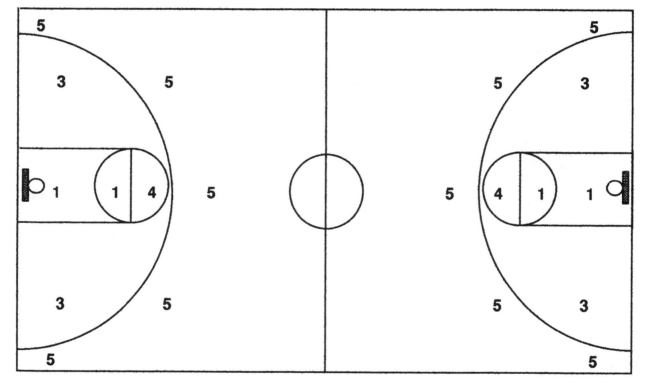

BOWLING TOP GUN

Objective:

◆ To win two or three games in a row at the "top gun" lane.

Essentials:

◆ Bowling alley

◆ Gymnasium

◆ Plastic pins with sand (work best)

◆ Score cards (provided on page 38)

How to Play:

1. Distribute the students over the lanes evenly.

2. Each participant throws two balls, or one frame.

3. Highest score moves to the next lane. If there is a tie, the challenger stays at the same lane.

4. Once at the top lane, attempt to defeat two opponents in a row.

5. Any lose at the "top gun" lane causes that player to start over.

6. Two wins in a row cause that person to start over.

Student Tasks:

1. Become a "top gun."

2. Defeat a past "top gun."

3. Win three consecutive games in a row before getting to the "top gun" lane.

Variations:

1. Make teams and play two frames.

2. Put a time limit on the matches.

3. Use a Frisbee™ instead of a bowling ball.

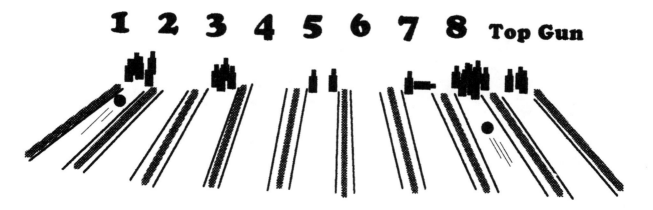

SPARE CHANGE

Objectives:

◆ To outscore the opponents in ten frames.

◆ To develop teamwork by alternating throws each frame with a partner.

Essentials:

◆ Bowling alley

◆ Gymnasium

◆ Plastic pins with sand (work best)

◆ Score cards (provided on page 38)

How to Play:

1. Pair up and challenge another team.

2. The first player on team "A" rolls the first ball. Her/his partner rolls the next one if a strike did not occur. The second partner on team "A" rolls the first ball of the second frame, and so on.

3. Best score at the end of ten frames is declared the winner.

Student Tasks:

1. Pick up two spares with the second ball.

2. Bowl two strikes.

Variations:

1. First shot by player #1 on team "A" must be with the good hand, the second shot from the same player later must be with the off hand.

2. Player #1 bowls only the odd frames and the partner bowls the even frames.

3. Use a Frisbee™ instead of a bowling ball.

STRIKE A MATCH

Objectives:

- ◆ To outscore the opponents in ten frames.
- ◆ To develop teamwork by alternating each frame with a partner.

Essentials:

- ◆ Bowling alley
- ◆ Gymnasium
- ◆ Plastic pins with sand (work best)
- ◆ Score cards (provided on page 38)

How to Play:

1. Pair up and challenge another team.
2. The first player on team "A" rolls the first frame. Her/his partner rolls the second frame. One does the even frames and the other does the odd frames.
3. Best score at the end of ten frames is declared the winner.

Student Tasks:

1. Pick up two spares with the second ball.
2. Bowl two strikes.
3. Come from behind at the fifth or later frame and defeat the opponents.

Variations:

1. First shot by player #1 on team "A" must be off handed, the second shot (if needed) from the same player must be with the good hand.
2. Use a Frisbee™ instead of a bowling ball.

BOWLING SCORE CARDS

Copy and pass out to the students.

Name(s): _____

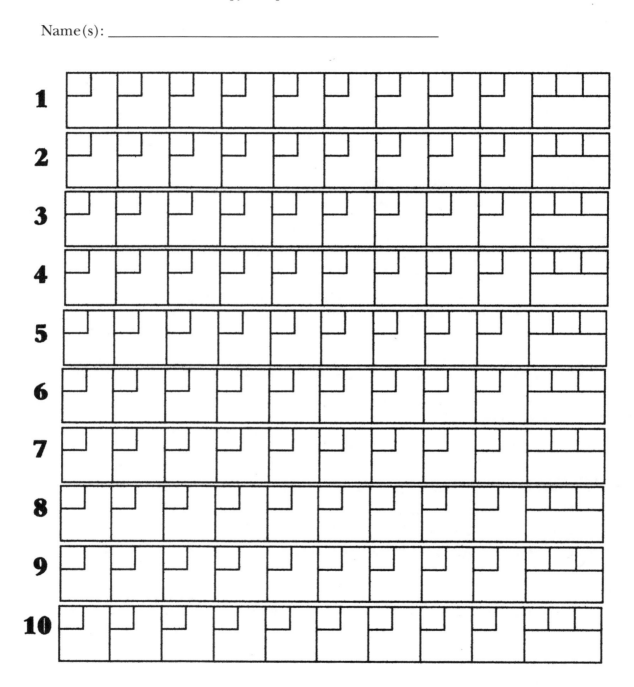

Average _____

Scoring

1. Strike = 10 plus the next two rolls.
2. Spare = 10 plus the next roll.
3. Open = That number of pins knocked down.

ABOUT "CREATE A GAME"

Objectives:

◆ To create one competitive game.

◆ To create one non-competitive (cooperative) game.

◆ To teach one of the new games to the other groups.

Essentials:

◆ Large playing area

◆ 5 to 6 stations with equal types of game equipment (examples: hula hoop, basketball, jump rope, cone, badminton birdie, and/or anything else deemed usable in creating a new game).

How to Play:

1. Show students various books that have games listed in them.

2. Talk about using the mind to create inventions.

3. Present examples of creativity.

4. Make groups of four to six students and send them to an area that has a bag of equipment.

5. Groups are to develop one competitive and one cooperative game.

   a. *Competitive:* Vying with another for gain, an aim, or profit.
   b. *Cooperative:* Working together toward a common goal or purpose.

6. Write, on the form provided, all the essential information, drawings, and guidelines, so that anyone might play this new game.

7. Teach or demonstrate one or two of the best games invented.

Student Tasks:

1. Go home and create a new game involving the entire family.

2. Invent a game without a partner.

Variations:

1. Have the various groups demonstrate one or both of their creations.

2. Draw several of the new games from a hat and have the responsible groups demonstrate the activity.

"CREATE A GAME" WORKSHEET

Date _____

Period _____

Names: _____

_____

Name of game: _____
Our game is: competitive (against) / cooperative (with)

Objective of game:

Safety rules:

Number of players = _____   Number of teams = _____

Equipment needed to play:

Rules and procedures of how to play / diagrams:

(Use another piece of paper if needed.)

CLASS AGAINST CLASS MEET

Objectives:

◆ To complete the course by either running, jogging, walking, or a combination of these.

◆ To obtain a lower total score than the opposition.

Essentials:

◆ Field with designated course

◆ Deck of playing cards with numbers one through ? printed on them (the highest number is equal to the total number of participants)

◆ Stopwatch

◆ 12 to 20 field marking cones to form a funnel

◆ Class against class score sheet

◆ Pencils

How to Play:

1. Challenge other P.E. classes in a cross country meet.

2. Score it like a regular meet where the first place finisher acquires one point, second place receives two points, third place gets three points, and so on.

3. Total each team's place finishes. Lowest combined score wins.

4. *Scoring:* Team "A," for example, gets a 4th, 9th, 11th, 14th, 23rd, 27th, and 30th place finishes. Have them add 4 + 9 + 11 + 14 + 23 + 27 + 30 = **118** total points. Compare this score to the other team scores and the team with the lowest total points is the winner.

5. *Note:* If the smallest team has ten runners, only count the first ten runners' scores from each of the other teams.

6. Be sure to set up the cones so that the runners are funneled into a single line when they are finishing. This allows the cards to be passed out in a sequential order. Put the numbers (1-?) on the playing cards. Playing cards work well since they can be dealt out quickly as the runners finish.

7. The team captain collects all of his/her team cards, adds the numbers, and turns in the roster with this score to the instructor.

Variations:

1. Have the classes run the course in a relay fashion by having one or more batons carried around the course. The baton can go around the course one or more times.

2. Draw a card that says "Add first half of the team's places" or "Add last half of the team's places."

SAMPLE CLASS/CLASS SCORE SHEET

Period: 3   Date: March 25

Team A		Team B		Team C		Team D	
Times	Places	Times	Places	Times	Places	Times	Places
	1		2		3		5
	7		11		4		6
	9		12		8		10
	17		13		15		14
	20		18		19		16
	21		27		25		22
	23		31		26		28
	24		33		34		29
	32		36		38		30
	41		37		39		35
	45		40		42		44
	46		47		43		53
	49		51		48		54
	50		55		52		56
Time Totals	Place Totals	Time Totals	Place Totals	Time Totals	Place Totals	Time Totals	Place Totals
0	*385*	*0*	*413*	*0*	*396*	*0*	*402*
Finished:	**1st**	**Finished:**	**4th**	**Finished:**	**2nd**	**Finished:**	**3rd**

Directions:

1. Fill out the *period* and the *date.*

2. Put the names of the teachers or classes in the *Team* boxes.

3. After the students have run the race, collect the cards that each team has secured and record the number on each card in the *Places* columns. (If the race is run with times instead of places, put these scores in the *Times* columns.)

4. Total the places or times and put this number in the *Place Totals* or *Time Totals* boxes.

5. The team with the **lowest** score is the winner. Place the teams' standings in the *Finished* boxes.

CLASS/CLASS SCORE SHEET

Period:_____   Date: _____

Team A		Team B		Team C		Team D	
Times	Places	Times	Places	Times	Places	Times	Places
Time Totals	Place Totals	Time Totals	Place Totals	Time Totals	Place Totals	Time Totals	Place Totals
Finished:		Finished:		Finished:		Finished:	

FIVE-NUMBER DRAW MEET

Objectives:

- To complete the course by either running, jogging, walking, or a combination of these.
- To collect one number from each station.

Essentials:

- Field with designated course
- 5 stations (cardboard boxes work well):

  #1—white paper with numbers (1 through 100) printed on them

  #2—blue paper with numbers (1 through 100) printed on them

  #3—red paper with numbers (1 through 100) printed on them

  #4—yellow paper with numbers (1 through 100) printed on them

  #5—green paper with numbers (1 through 100) printed on them

- Hat with numbers (5 through 500) printed on paper
- Pencils

How to Play:

(This competition is a take-off based on the old **Poker Run.** Since gambling is illegal, folded pieces of paper with numbers printed on them are used.)

1. Time is not a factor and is not kept for this activity.
2. Runners cover the course and stop at each station. Each runner takes **one** piece of paper out of the box and continues on to the next station.
3. At the finish, each runner should possess five different colored pieces of paper.
4. At the conclusion of the race, draw a number out of a hat (5 through 500).
5. The runner closest to the drawn number, after totaling the five numbers gathered on the run, is the winner.

Variations:

1. Pair up and run in tandem. Only five numbered pieces of paper are collected between the two participants.
2. Use letters instead of numbers. Allow students to be in teams of four. Combine the twenty letters and see which team can create the most words. Paper and pencils will be needed.

STATION NUMBERS

(Cut out and place number at each station.)

1	26	51	76	1	26	51	76
2	27	52	77	2	27	52	77
3	28	53	78	3	28	53	78
4	29	54	79	4	29	54	79
5	30	55	80	5	30	55	80
6	31	56	81	6	31	56	81
7	32	57	82	7	32	57	82
8	33	58	83	8	33	58	83
9	34	59	84	9	34	59	84
10	35	60	85	10	35	60	85
11	36	61	86	11	36	61	86
12	37	62	87	12	37	62	87
13	38	63	88	13	38	63	88
14	39	64	89	14	39	64	89
15	40	65	90	15	40	65	90
16	41	66	91	16	41	66	91
17	42	67	92	17	42	67	92
18	43	68	93	18	43	68	93
19	44	69	94	19	44	69	94
20	45	70	95	20	45	70	95
21	46	71	96	21	46	71	96
22	47	72	97	22	47	72	97
23	48	73	98	23	48	73	98
24	49	74	99	24	49	74	99
25	50	75	100	25	50	75	100

FINAL DRAW NUMBERS

(Cut out and put in a box. Draw one number after all of the runners have finished.)
(The runners total up their five station numbers and the closest to the final drawn number is the win-

1	51	101	151	201	251	301	351	401	451
2	52	102	152	202	252	302	352	402	452
3	53	103	153	203	253	303	353	403	453
4	54	104	154	204	254	304	354	404	454
5	55	105	155	205	255	305	355	405	455
6	56	106	156	206	256	306	356	406	456
7	57	107	157	207	257	307	357	407	457
8	58	108	158	208	258	308	358	408	458
9	59	109	159	209	259	309	359	409	459
10	60	110	160	210	260	310	360	410	460
11	61	111	161	211	261	311	361	411	461
12	62	112	162	212	262	312	362	412	462
13	63	113	163	213	263	313	363	413	463
14	64	114	164	214	264	314	364	414	464
15	65	115	165	215	265	315	365	415	465
16	66	116	166	216	266	316	366	416	466
17	67	117	167	217	267	317	367	417	467
18	68	118	168	218	268	318	368	418	468
19	69	119	169	219	269	319	369	419	469
20	70	120	170	220	270	320	370	420	470
21	71	121	171	221	271	321	371	421	471
22	72	122	172	222	272	322	372	422	472
23	73	123	173	223	273	323	373	423	473
24	74	124	174	224	274	324	374	424	474
25	75	125	175	225	275	325	375	425	475
26	76	126	176	226	276	326	376	426	476
27	77	127	177	227	277	327	377	427	477
28	78	128	178	228	278	328	378	428	478
29	79	129	179	229	279	329	379	429	479
30	80	130	180	230	280	330	380	430	480
31	81	131	181	231	281	331	381	431	481
32	82	132	182	232	282	332	382	432	482
33	83	133	183	233	283	333	383	433	483
34	84	134	184	234	284	334	384	434	484
35	85	135	185	235	285	335	385	435	485
36	86	136	186	236	286	336	386	436	486
37	87	137	187	237	287	337	387	437	487
38	88	138	188	238	288	338	388	438	488
39	89	139	189	239	289	339	389	439	489
40	90	140	190	240	290	340	390	440	490
41	91	141	191	241	291	341	391	441	491
42	92	142	192	242	292	342	392	442	492
43	93	143	193	243	293	343	393	443	493
44	94	144	194	244	294	344	394	444	494
45	95	145	195	245	295	345	395	445	495
46	96	146	196	246	296	346	396	446	496
47	97	147	197	247	297	347	397	447	497
48	98	148	198	248	298	348	398	448	498
49	99	149	199	249	299	349	399	449	499
50	100	150	200	250	300	350	400	450	500

© 1996 Parker Publishing Company

MIX-UP MEET

Objectives:

- ◆ To complete the course by either running, jogging, walking, or a combination of these.
- ◆ To attain a lower total score than the opposition.

Essentials:

- ◆ Field with designated course
- ◆ Deck of playing cards with numbers one through ? printed on them (the highest number is equal to the total number of participants)
- ◆ Stopwatch
- ◆ 12 to 20 field marking cones
- ◆ Cross country roster forms
- ◆ Pencils

How to Play:

1. Divide into teams by using the **Mix 'n Match** format. The maximum number of runners on a team, after combining, is eight.
2. Fill in the rosters.
3. Score the run like it was a real meet.
4. *Scoring:* Team "A" gets a 4th, 9th, 11th, 14th, 23rd, 27th, and 30th place finishes. Have them add 4 + 9 + 11 + 14 + 23 + 27 + 30 = **118** total points. Compare this score to the other team scores and the team with the lowest total points is the winner.
5. Be sure to set up the cones so that the runners are funneled into a single line when they are finishing. This allows the cards to be passed out in a sequential order. Put the numbers (1–52) on the playing cards. Playing cards work well since they can be dealt out quickly as the runners finish.
6. The team captain collects all of her/his team cards, adds the numbers, and turns in the roster with this score to the instructor.

Student Tasks:

1. Finish in the top 50% of the class.
2. Finish in the top ten.
3. As a team, finish in the top three.

Variations:

1. Have the classes run the course in a relay fashion by having one or more batons carried around the course. The baton can go around the course one or more times.

2. Draw a card that says "Add first half of the team's places" or "Add last half of the team's places."

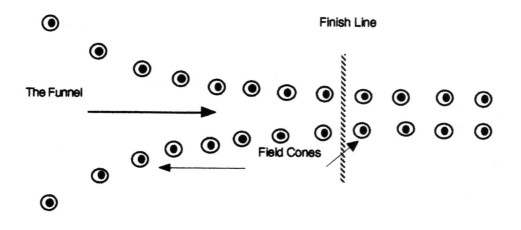

SAMPLE CROSS COUNTRY COURSE

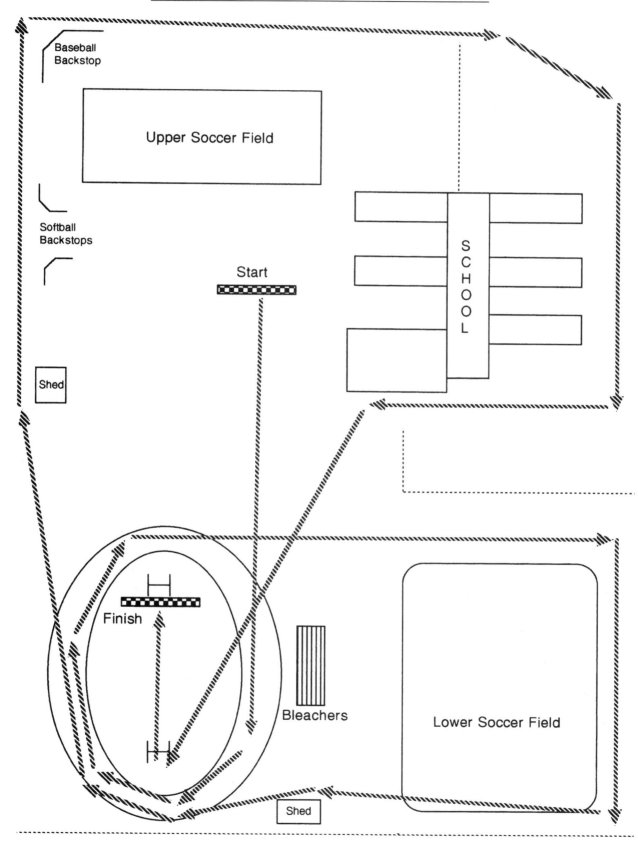

Baseball
Backstop

Upper Soccer Field

Softball
Backstops

Shed

Start

S
C
H
O
O
L

Finish

Bleachers

Lower Soccer Field

Shed

SAMPLE MIX UP ROSTER

(Eight-Runner Limit)

Directions:

1. Fill in the *period* and the *date*.
2. Fill in the *names* of the team members *(optional)*.
3. Run the race and pass out the cards that are sequentially numbered as the runners finish the race.
4. Record their numbers in the *Place* columns.
5. If times are being kept or the race is based on the sum of all of the times, then fill in the *Time* columns.
6. Total the team's placements or times and put the score in the *Totals* boxes.
7. Compare team totals and record the standings in the *Final Standing* boxes.

Period: Third

Date: March 24

© 1996 Parker Publishing Company

Team 1 — Final Standing: 3RD

Team Members	TIME (Optional)	PLACE	FINAL STANDING
John Stark		4	
Billi Wadell		12	
Sue Hoe		9	
Mally Cross		18	
John Spector		8	
Totals		51	

Team 2 — Final Standing: 4TH

Team Members	TIME (Optional)	PLACE	FINAL STANDING
Mirna Smerts		10	
June Colts		13	
Harold Wingle		16	
Bob Nagel		14	
Trish Black		11	
Totals		64	

Team 3 — Final Standing: 1ST

Team Members	TIME (Optional)	PLACE	FINAL STANDING
Ken Cobb		2	
Ellen Downs		20	
Chris Thompson		17	
Jeff Jones		6	
Jill Waton		1	
Totals		46	

Team 4 — Final Standing: 2ND

Team Members	TIME (Optional)	PLACE	FINAL STANDING
Tammi Rush		5	
Mary Cates		19	
Billy Potts		15	
Ken Smit		3	
Joe Delete		7	
Totals		49	

MIX-UP ROSTER

(Eight-Runner Limit)

Period: _____
Date: _____

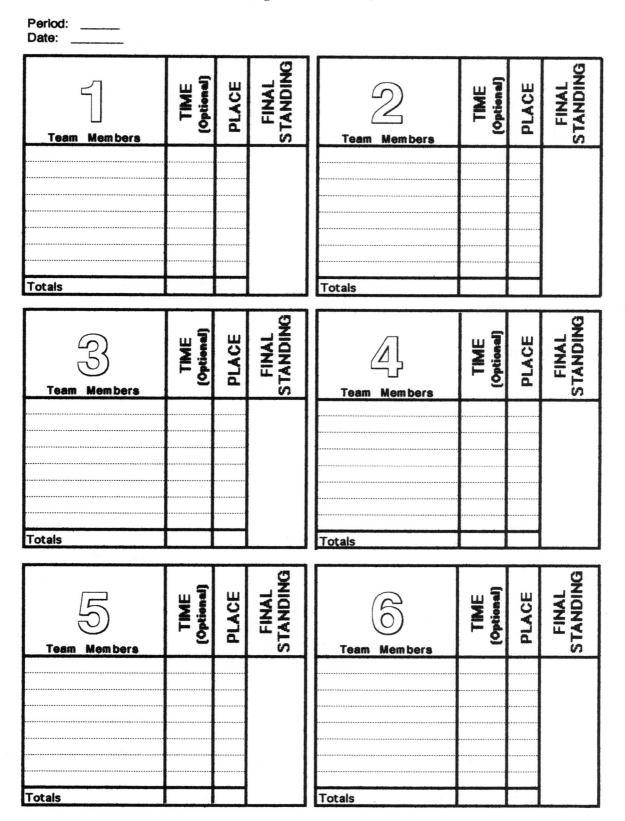

MYSTERY MEET

Objective:

◆ To complete the course by either running, jogging, walking, or a combination of these.

Essentials:

◆ Field with designated course
◆ Stopwatch
◆ Time conversion table (see page 56)
◆ Cross country roster form
◆ Pencils

How to Play:

1. Divide into teams with a maximum of eight runners.

2. Start the runners on the course.

3. As a runner finishes the course, give her/him the time in minutes and seconds.

4. After all of the runners have completed the course, have them go back and line up in the order of finish amongst their own team members.

5. Next, draw four-place counting numbers from a hat. **Example:** Only the second, fourth, fifth, and seventh place times will be added together to determine the lowest timed team. This makes it important for all participants to finish with a fast time.

6. Use the "Time Conversion Chart" and add the times of those four finishers on each team. **Lowest** combined team time wins.

Variations:

1. Draw a card that says "Add first five place times" or "Add last five place times."

2. Draw a card that says "Add 1st, 3rd, 5th, and 7th place times" or "Add 2nd, 4th, 6th, and 8th place times."

REVERSE ORDER MEET

Objective:

◆ To complete the course by either running, jogging, walking, or a combination of these.

Essentials:

◆ Field with designated course
◆ Stopwatch
◆ Reverse course score sheet
◆ Pencils

How to Play:

1. **Do not tell the students you are planning to run this event. If they know, they might have a tendency to run slower times prior to the race.**

2. After each student has run the course (be it one or more times) record their fastest time.

3. Using the "Reverse Course Form," set up a run in which the slowest runner starts first and the fastest runner goes last in accordance with the time delays. See the sample sheet.

4. In theory, all runners should cross the line at the same time.

5. Winners are the first five to finish.

Student Tasks:

1. Finish in the top five.
2. Finish in the top ten.
3. Improve on previous finish standings. An example would be finishing 11th instead of 23rd.

Variation: Run the course in the reverse direction.

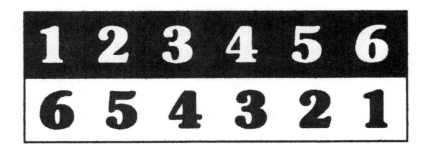

SAMPLE REVERSE COURSE FORM

Directions:

1. Fill in the *period* and *date*.

2. Fill in the *names* with the slowest time at the top.

3. Write in their time in the column *Time of first run*.

4. Use the "Time Conversion Chart" and convert the first run time into seconds. Place this information in the column *Converted 1st run minutes to seconds*.

5. Next, subtract each student's time from the slowest time and record this information in the column *Time delays for 2nd run in seconds*.

6. Convert the time delays in seconds back to minutes in the *Time delays for 2nd run in minutes* column.

7. Record the order of finish in the *Top 10 of the 2nd Run* column.

Period : Second
Date: March 23

Name	Time of first run	Converted 1st run minutes to seconds (Use table provided)	Time delays for 2nd run in seconds	Time delays for 2nd run in minutes		Top 10 of the 2nd Run
Bob Smith	15:55	955	0	Starts Race	1	Terry Porter
Mary Lane	15:26	926	29	0:29	2	Molly Spring
Will Dupree	14:39	879	76	1:16	3	Lee Potts
Jack Jarrall	14:24	864	91	1:31	4	Rita Woods
Molly Spring	14:02	842	113	1:53	5	Tom Franklin
Sue Wilde	13:52	832	123	2:03	6	Sue Wilde
Trish Montoya	13:15	795	160	2:40	7	Sue Montgomery
Fred Perez	12:44	764	191	3:11	8	Mark Trevino
Ken Wallzinski	12:08	728	227	3:47	9	Bob Smith
Terry Porter	11:34	694	261	4:21	10	Iris Miller
Rodger Bing	11:11	671	284	4:44	11	George Brown
Elaine Montgomery	10:55	655	300	5:00	12	Elaine Montgomery
Sue Montgomery	10:27	627	328	5:28	13	Ken Wallzinski
George Brown	10:22	622	333	5:33	14	Fred Perez
Mark Trevino	10:00	600	355	5:55	15	Jack Jarrall
Lee Potts	9:12	552	403	6:43	16	Will Dupree
Iris Miller	8:30	510	445	7:25	17	Rodger Bing
Jim Sportanno	8:00	480	475	7:55	18	Jim Sportanno
Tom Franklin	7:53	473	482	8:02	19	Mary Lane
Rita Woods	7:40	460	495	8:15	20	Trish Montoya
					21	

Slowest ← → Fastest

REVERSE COURSE FORM

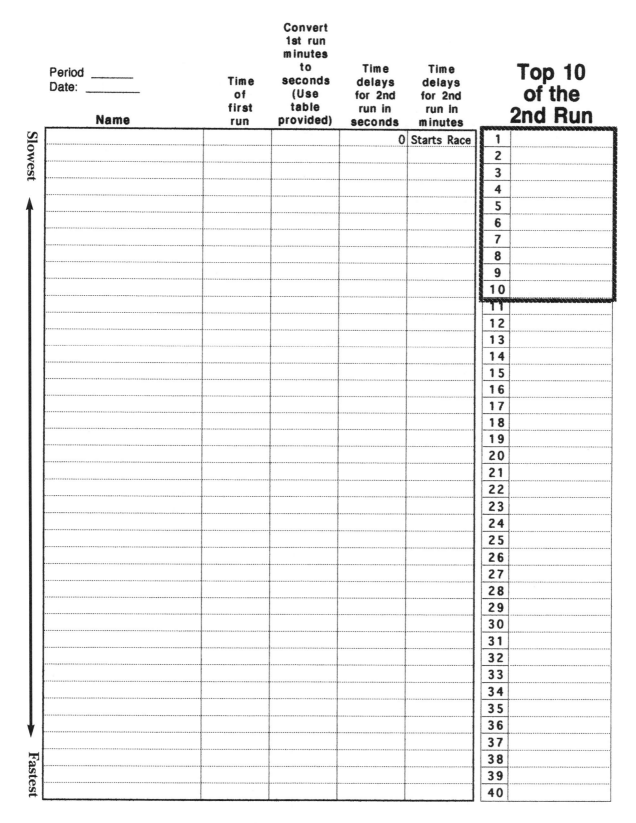

	Name	Time of first run	Convert 1st run minutes to seconds (Use table provided)	Time delays for 2nd run in seconds	Time delays for 2nd run in minutes	Top 10 of the 2nd Run	
Slowest					0	Starts Race	1
							2
							3
							4
							5
							6
							7
							8
							9
							10
							11
							12
							13
							14
							15
							16
							17
							18
							19
							20
							21
							22
							23
							24
							25
							26
							27
							28
							29
							30
							31
							32
							33
							34
							35
							36
							37
							38
							39
Fastest							40

Period _____
Date: _____

TIME CONVERSION TABLE

(Convert Minutes to Seconds or Seconds to Minutes)

MIN	SEC	MIN	SEC	MIN	SEC	MIN	SEC	MIN	SEC
1:00	60	2:00	120	3:00	180	4:00	240	5:00	300
1:05	65	2:05	125	3:05	185	4:05	245	5:05	305
1:10	70	2:10	130	3:10	190	4:10	250	5:10	310
1:15	75	2:15	135	3:15	195	4:15	255	5:15	315
1:20	80	2:20	140	3:20	200	4:20	260	5:20	320
1:25	85	2:25	145	3:25	205	4:25	265	5:25	325
1:30	90	2:30	150	3:30	210	4:30	270	5:30	330
1:35	95	2:35	155	3:35	215	4:35	275	5:35	335
1:40	100	2:40	160	3:40	220	4:40	280	5:40	340
1:45	105	2:45	165	3:45	225	4:45	285	5:45	345
1:50	110	2:50	170	3:50	230	4:50	290	5:50	350
1:55	115	2:55	175	3:55	235	4:55	295	5:55	355
6:00	360	7:00	420	8:00	480	9:00	540	10:00	600
6:05	365	7:05	425	8:05	485	9:05	545	10:05	605
6:10	370	7:10	430	8:10	490	9:10	550	10:10	610
6:15	375	7:15	435	8:15	495	9:15	555	10:15	615
6:20	380	7:20	440	8:20	500	9:20	560	10:20	620
6:25	385	7:25	445	8:25	505	9:25	565	10:25	625
6:30	390	7:30	450	8:30	510	9:30	570	10:30	630
6:35	395	7:35	455	8:35	515	9:35	575	10:35	635
6:40	400	7:40	460	8:40	520	9:40	580	10:40	640
6:45	405	7:45	465	8:45	525	9:45	585	10:45	645
6:50	410	7:50	470	8:50	530	9:50	590	10:50	650
6:55	415	7:55	475	8:55	535	9:55	595	10:55	655
11:00	660	12:00	720	13:00	780	14:00	840	15:00	900
11:05	665	12:05	725	13:05	785	14:05	845	15:05	905
11:10	670	12:10	730	13:10	790	14:10	850	15:10	910
11:15	675	12:15	735	13:15	795	14:15	855	15:15	915
11:20	680	12:20	740	13:20	800	14:20	860	15:20	920
11:25	685	12:25	745	13:25	805	14:25	865	15:25	925
11:30	690	12:30	750	13:30	810	14:30	870	15:30	930
11:35	695	12:35	755	13:35	815	14:35	875	15:35	935
11:40	700	12:40	760	13:40	820	14:40	880	15:40	940
11:45	705	12:45	765	13:45	825	14:45	885	15:45	945
11:50	710	12:50	770	13:50	830	14:50	890	15:50	950
11:55	715	12:55	775	13:55	835	14:55	895	15:55	955
16:00	960	17:00	1020	18:00	1080	19:00	1140	20:00	1200
16:05	965	17:05	1025	18:05	1085	19:05	1145	20:05	1205
16:10	970	17:10	1030	18:10	1090	19:10	1150	20:10	1210
16:15	975	17:15	1035	18:15	1095	19:15	1155	20:15	1215
16:20	980	17:20	1040	18:20	1100	19:20	1160	20:20	1220
16:25	985	17:25	1045	18:25	1105	19:25	1165	20:25	1225
16:30	990	17:30	1050	18:30	1110	19:30	1170	20:30	1230
16:35	995	17:35	1055	18:35	1115	19:35	1175	20:35	1235
16:40	1000	17:40	1060	18:40	1120	19:40	1180	20:40	1240
16:45	1005	17:45	1065	18:45	1125	19:45	1185	20:45	1245
16:50	1010	17:50	1070	18:50	1130	19:50	1190	20:50	1250
16:55	1015	17:55	1075	18:55	1135	19:55	1195	20:55	1255

SPEED WALKING MEET

Objectives:

◆ To complete the course by using the heel-and-toe method of walking.

◆ To attain a lower total score than the opposition.

Essentials:

◆ Field with designated course

◆ Deck of playing cards with numbers one through ? printed on them (the highest number is equal to the total number of participants)

◆ Stopwatch

◆ 12 to 20 field marking cones

◆ Cross country roster forms (see cross country forms)

◆ Pencils

How to Play:

1. Speed Walking is also known as the *"Heel and Toe"* race walk. Do not allow students to run. Both feet must be in contact with the ground at all times, thus the term *"Heel and Toe."*

2. Divide into teams by using the **Mix 'n Match** format. The maximum number of runners on a team, after combining, is eight.

3. Fill in the rosters.

4. Score it like a regular cross country meet.

5. *Scoring:* Team "A" gets a 4th, 9th, 11th, 14th, 23rd, 27th, and 30th place finishes. Have them add $4 + 9 + 11 + 14 + 23 + 27 + 30 = $ **118** total points. Compare this score to the other team scores and the team with the lowest total points is the winner.

Student Tasks:

1. Finish in the top 50% of the class.

2. Finish in the top ten.

3. As a team, finish in the top three.

Variation: Use any of the previous cross country meet formats to create a new type of race.

© 1996 Parker Publishing Company

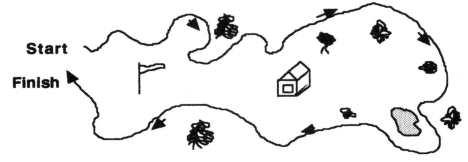

ABOUT "DARTS"

Objective:

◆ To develop hand and eye coordination by hitting selected numbers or objects on a board.

Essentials:

◆ Room or wall
◆ 1 dart board for every 3 to 4 players (carpet or padding around the boards is recommended)
◆ Paper and pencils for scoring
◆ Desks and chairs (optional but helpful)
◆ 4 safety darts (Teflon tipped) per board

How to Play:

1. The grip is light and soft.
2. The toss is done with a wrist-flicking action. It is never brought behind the ear and should have a nice follow-through.
3. Scoring:
   a. Triple-band = three times the number hit.
   b. Double-band = two times the number hit.
   c. Bull's-eye = inner ring is 50 and the outer ring is 25.
4. Rotate the dart to the right when removing it from the board. This keeps the tip tight to the shaft.

Safety:

1. Darts must be tossed and not thrown. The dart is never to go past the ear on the draw back.
2. Only one player is allowed at the toss line. All others must be behind the line.
3. Check darts for defects.
4. After retrieving the darts, hand them to the next person.
5. Remain seated unless scoring or tossing.
6. Toss at the board only.

© 1996 Parker Publishing Company

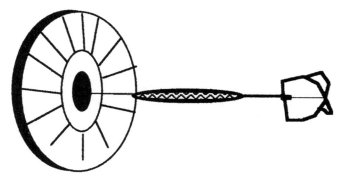

Board Distances

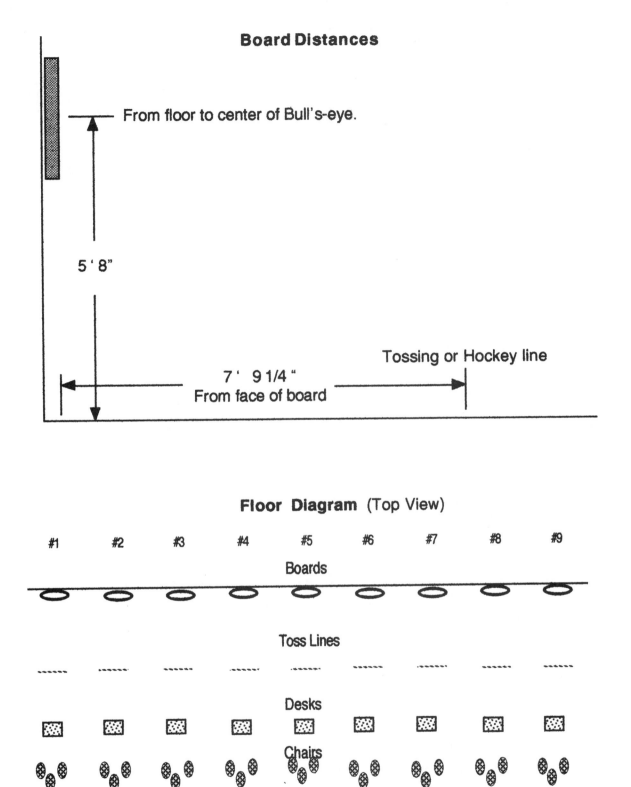

From floor to center of Bull's-eye.

5' 8"

Tossing or Hockey line

7' 9 1/4 "
From face of board

Floor Diagram (Top View)

#1   #2   #3   #4   #5   #6   #7   #8   #9

Boards

Toss Lines

Desks

Chairs

AROUND THE EARTH

Objective:

◆ To be the first player to hit all of the numbers in sequential order starting with number 1 and finishing with number 20.

Essentials:

◆ Room or wall
◆ 1 dart board for every 3 to 4 players (carpet or padding around the boards is recommended)
◆ Paper and pencils for scoring
◆ Desks and chairs (optional but helpful)
◆ 4 safety darts (Teflon tipped) per board

How to Play:

1. Any number of players can participate.
2. Toss two darts in a row.
3. If either dart hits the desired number, then that participant tosses at the next number.
4. If the desired number is missed after two tosses, the next player gets her/his turn.
5. At the start of the second turn, resume throwing at the last number needed.
6. If she/he hits the double band, she/he moves up two numbers; triple band moves up three numbers; bull's-eye moves up five numbers. **Example:** If a player needs to hit the 12 and throws a triple band 12, then she/he throws at the number 15 next.

Student Tasks:

1. Hit a predetermined number of counters in a row.
2. Hit a bull's-eye.
3. Hit two double-band numbers.
4. Hit two triple-band numbers.

Variations:

1. When the last dart thrown counts, then she/he throws two more darts.
2. Make teams of two players.
3. Use the left or off hand.

© 1996 Parker Publishing Company

CRICKET

Objective:

◆ To be the first player to eliminate all of her/his numbers.

Essentials:

◆ Room or wall
◆ 1 dart board for every 3 to 4 players (carpet or padding around the boards is recommended)
◆ Paper and pencils for scoring
◆ Desks and chairs (optional but helpful)
◆ 4 safety darts (Teflon tipped) per board

How to Play:

1. *Number of Players:* 2 to 4.
2. Toss two darts in a row. If a dart hits a number, put a slash mark. If a dart hits that number again or again later, put another slash mark to form an X. If a dart hits that number for the third time, put a circle around the X.
3. When the dart hits only the number, then one hit is recorded. If a player hits one of the double or triple bands, she/he gets to count that toss as two or three hits.
4. A player may eliminate his/her numbers in any order.
5. Winner is the first competitor to eliminate **all** of her/his numbers first.

Bob	#	Mary
X	20	Ⓧ
/	19	
	18	/
	17	X
/	16	
	15	
	Bull's-eye	/

/ = 1 hit
X = 2 hits
Ⓧ = 3 hits and done

Student Tasks:

1. Hit a predetermined number of counters in a row.
2. Hit two bull's-eyes in a row.

Variations:

1. Make teams of two players.
2. Use the left or off hand.
3. Keep going as long as a number has been eliminated on the last toss.

CRICKET SCORECARDS

Cut these out and give them to the players.

Name	Name
Number	
20	
19	
18	
17	
16	
15	
Bull's-eye	
/ = 1 hit X = 2 hits ⊗ = 3 hits	

Name	Name
Number	
20	
19	
18	
17	
16	
15	
Bull's-eye	
/ = 1 hit X = 2 hits ⊗ = 3 hits	

Name	Name
Number	
20	
19	
18	
17	
16	
15	
Bull's-eye	
/ = 1 hit X = 2 hits ⊗ = 3 hits	

Name	Name
Number	
20	
19	
18	
17	
16	
15	
Bull's-eye	
/ = 1 hit X = 2 hits ⊗ = 3 hits	

Name	Name
Number	
20	
19	
18	
17	
16	
15	
Bull's-eye	
/ = 1 hit X = 2 hits ⊗ = 3 hits	

Name	Name
Number	
20	
19	
18	
17	
16	
15	
Bull's-eye	
/ = 1 hit X = 2 hits ⊗ = 3 hits	

Name	Name
Number	
20	
19	
18	
17	
16	
15	
Bull's-eye	
/ = 1 hit X = 2 hits ⊗ = 3 hits	

Name	Name
Number	
20	
19	
18	
17	
16	
15	
Bull's-eye	
/ = 1 hit X = 2 hits ⊗ = 3 hits	

Name	Name
Number	
20	
19	
18	
17	
16	
15	
Bull's-eye	
/ = 1 hit X = 2 hits ⊗ = 3 hits	

Name	Name
Number	
20	
19	
18	
17	
16	
15	
Bull's-eye	
/ = 1 hit X = 2 hits ⊗ = 3 hits	

Name	Name
Number	
20	
19	
18	
17	
16	
15	
Bull's-eye	
/ = 1 hit X = 2 hits ⊗ = 3 hits	

Name	Name
Number	
20	
19	
18	
17	
16	
15	
Bull's-eye	
/ = 1 hit X = 2 hits ⊗ = 3 hits	

CUT THROAT

Objective:

◆ To eliminate the other players first by hitting their numbers.

Essentials:

◆ Room or wall

◆ 1 dart board for every 3 to 4 players (carpet or padding around the boards is recommended)

◆ Score pads for each board

◆ Desks and chairs (optional but helpful)

◆ 4 safety darts (Teflon tipped) per board

◆ Pencils

How to Play:

1. Divide the numbers among the participants:
   a. Two = (1-2-3-4-5-6-7-8-9-10) (11-12-13-14-15-16-17-18-19-20)
   b. Three = (1-2-3-4-5-6) (7-8-9-10-11-12) (13-14-15-16-17-18)
   c. Four = (1-2-3-4-5) (6-7-8-9-10) (11-12-13-14-15) (16-17-18-19-20)

2. As long as a player can eliminate a number, she/he may keep tossing.

3. If a player hits her/his own number, she/he may eliminate that number and continue tossing. She/he may elect not to eliminate her/his own number and pass to the next tosser.

4. If a player hits the bull's-eye, she/he gets a choice of any two numbers to be removed.

5. If a player hits the triple ring, she/he gets a choice of any one number to be removed.

Student Tasks:

1. Hit a predetermined number of counters in a row.
2. Hit a bull's-eye.

Variations:

1. Make teams of two players.
2. Use the left or off hand.

DARTS TOP GUN

Objective:

◆ To get to the top board and win two games in a row.

Essentials:

◆ Room or wall
◆ 1 dart board for every 3 to 4 players (carpet or padding around the boards is recommended)
◆ 4 safety darts (Teflon tipped) per board

How to Play:

1. Number the boards from 1 through ?.
2. Disperse the entire class evenly at all of the boards.
3. Each player gets two tosses. Add the total of the two. Highest score wins.
4. Winners move to the next higher board; losers stay and take on the next challenger.
5. Once at the highest board, the players try to win two or three games in a row. This allows him/her to be the "Top Gun." After winning, she/he returns to the lowest board and starts to work up.
6. Any loss at the highest board will cause that player to return to the lowest board and start over.

Student Tasks:

1. Win at the **Top Gun** board.
2. Win four games in a row at the lower boards.
3. Get to the **Top Gun** board.
4. Defeat any past **Top Gun** champion while playing on a lower board.

Variations:

1. Make teams of two players.
2. Use the left or off hand.
3. A player must win three games in a row at the **Top Gun** board.

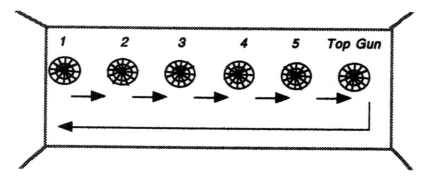

© 1996 Parker Publishing Company

ODD OR EVEN

Objective:

◆ To be the first player to total a predetermined number by hitting only the odd or even numbers.

Essentials:

◆ Room or wall
◆ 1 dart board for every 3 to 4 players (carpet or padding around the boards is recommended)
◆ Score pads for each board
◆ Desks and chairs (optional but helpful)
◆ 4 safety darts (Teflon tipped) per board
◆ Pencils

How to Play:

1. Two players choose or toss for odd or even numbers.
2. Toss two in a row.
3. Only a dart that hits a player's own set of odd or even numbers counts toward a score.
4. First player to reach **exactly** 200 is the winner.
5. A bull's-eye is worth two additional tosses.

Student Tasks:

1. Hit a predetermined number of counters in a row.
2. Hit a bull's-eye.

Variations:

1. Make teams of two players.
2. Use the left or off hand.
3. Choose the white or black numbers.

© 1996 Parker Publishing Company

QUICK DRAW

Objective:

◆ To get a given number of points first.

Essentials:

◆ Room or wall

◆ 1 dart board for every 3 to 4 players (carpet or padding around the boards is recommended)

◆ Paper and colored pens or pencils

◆ Desks and chairs (optional but helpful)

◆ 4 safety darts (Teflon tipped) per board

How to Play:

1. Draw a picture, give it point values, and tape it on the dart board. (See the samples below.)

2. Each player tosses two darts and rotates.

3. First player to get to the predetermined number is the winner.

Student Tasks:

1. Hit a predetermined number of counters in a row.

2. Hit a bull's-eye.

Variations:

1. Make teams of two players.

2. Use the left or off hand.

3. Raise or lower the total points needed to win.

© 1996 Parker Publishing Company

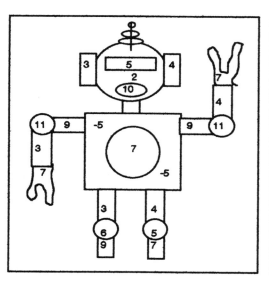
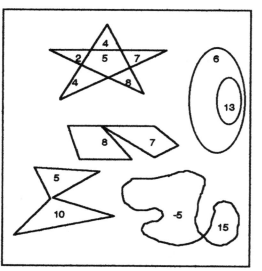

SUM TOTALS

Objective:

◆ To defeat the other players by hitting a predetermined score first.

Essentials:

◆ Room or wall
◆ 1 dart board for every 3 to 4 players (carpet or padding around the boards is recommended)
◆ Score pads for each board
◆ Desks and chairs (optional but helpful)
◆ 4 safety darts (Teflon tipped) per board
◆ Pencils

How to Play:

1. Students only toss two darts so that games move along faster.
2. *501:* Four players, two teams. Start at 501 and subtract scores until students end up **exactly** at zero.
3. *301:* Same as *501.*
4. *99:* Same as *501.*

Student Tasks:

1. Hit a predetermined number of counters in a row.
2. Hit a bull's-eye.
3. Come from behind and win.

Variations:

1. Toss three darts.
2. Use the left or off hand.
3. Alternate hands every other toss.

99 - 12 = 87 - 35 = 52 - 23 = 29 - 24 = 5 - 5 = 0 = WINNER

TEN DARTS

Objective:

◆ To get the most points possible with only ten tosses.

Essentials:

◆ Room or wall
◆ 1 dart board for every 3 to 4 players (carpet or padding around the boards is recommended)
◆ Score pads for each board
◆ Desks and chairs (optional but helpful)
◆ 4 safety darts (Teflon tipped) per board
◆ Pencils

How to Play:

1. Any number of players may be involved.
2. Toss two or five darts in a row and then switch.
3. The player with the highest score possible is the winner.

Student Tasks:

1. Hit two bull's-eyes .
2. Hit two double-band numbers.
3. Hit two triple-band numbers.

Variations:

1. Attempt to get the lowest score possible with the ten tosses.
2. Use the left or off hand.
3. Play a round-robin tournament.

TIC-TAC-TOE

Objective:

◆ To collect three squares in a row.

Essentials:

◆ Room or wall

◆ 1 dart board for every 3 to 4 players (carpet or padding around the boards is recommended)

◆ **Tic-Tac-Toe** score cards for each board

◆ Markers to show which player owns a square

◆ Desks and chairs (optional but helpful)

◆ 4 safety darts (Teflon tipped) per board

◆ Pencils

How to Play:

1. Toss two darts and try to hit a number in any open square.

2. A player gets a second toss if she/he did not want or could not use his/her first toss.

3. Place a colored identification marker (usually cut-up squares of red or blue paper) on the score card if that square has been captured.

Student Tasks:

1. Win by hitting a mark, three consecutive times, when going to the toss line.

2. Defeat two different opponents three out of five games.

Variations:

1. Put a **Tic-Tac-Toe** grid on a piece of paper, then tape the paper to the dart board. Each player gets one or two throws to score. Mark on a blank **Tic-Tac-Toe** grid with an "X" or "O" located on the desk.

2. Use the left or off hand.

3. Change the numbers on the score cards.

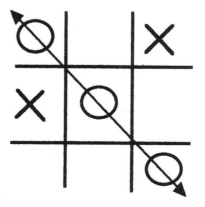

TIC-TAC-TOE SCORECARD

Copy and place one of these on each desk.

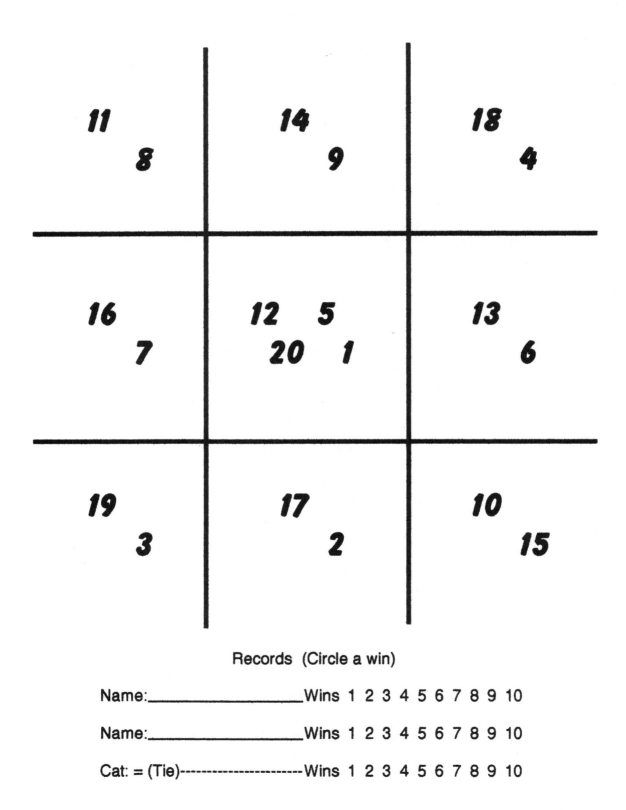

Records (Circle a win)

Name:_____Wins 1 2 3 4 5 6 7 8 9 10

Name:_____Wins 1 2 3 4 5 6 7 8 9 10

Cat: = (Tie)----------------------Wins 1 2 3 4 5 6 7 8 9 10

ABOUT "DODGEBALL"

Dodgeball activities are very popular with the students. These games are great during foul weather conditions, for warming up, for handling a large group of students, or as a filler for a break in the curriculum. Activities can be simple, fitness enhancing, fun, challenging, and quite safe when proper safety precautions are covered and strictly enforced.

Here are a few suggestions to ensure that all students will be successful and safe when these activities are offered:

1. Never force a student to participate in these games. Respect his/her wishes by having him/her keep score, referee, or do some alternative activity such as table tennis. Once students see how much fun and how these games are relatively accident free, they will be willing to participate on a regular basis.

2. Make sure the ball being used is soft enough that it does not sting when it makes contact with the skin. Foam, Nerf™, or Gator Skin® balls are highly recommended.

3. Students should not play with glasses on, unless they are of the safety type. A glasses' strap is also useful.

4. When throwing the ball, a student should use good judgment on the aim and force needed. If a participant does not, then she/he should be removed from the game.

5. Try to allow for the return of any player who has been eliminated.

ALASKAN SOFTBALL

Objective:

◆ To score more runs than the other team by running to one end of the court and back while not being hit by a thrown ball.

Essentials:

◆ Gymnasium
◆ 1 Gator Skin® ball

How to Play Offense:

1. One team lines up behind home plate; the other takes the playing field.
2. Pitch by rolling the ball to your own team as in kickball.
3. The kicker boots the ball and runs to the near or far safe zone. There is no time limit in the safe zone.

4. The runner may not leave a safe zone once the pitcher has possession or before the ball has been kicked by the next person. No leading off is allowed.

5. The runner is out when:

   a. The defense catches a fly ball.

   b. The defense catches a ball that hits the wall, ceiling, or obstruction before it touches the floor.

6. The entire team is out when:

   a. Five runs have been scored.

   b. Three outs have been made.

   c. A runner is hit by the ball and cannot pick it up and hit any defensive player before the **entire** defensive team reaches either safe zone. If a runner can do this, she/he may continue on or return to a safe zone.

7. *The five-run rule:* This rule keeps the game close. A team may score only five runs an inning. If a team is behind by more than five runs, as many runs may be scored as needed to go ahead by one run.

8. A point is scored each time a player can run to the far safe zone and back without getting hit.

How to Play Defense:

1. Players cannot block or interfere with the runners.

2. Players may put out a runner by catching a fly ball, even if it hits something before it touches the floor.

3. Players can put out the entire team by hitting a runner and everyone on defense getting to a safe zone before **any runner** can pick up the ball and hit a defensive person. This will cause the inning to be over, regardless of how many previous outs there were. The defense can pick up the ball, if hit, and hit the runner again. This *hit, hit back, hit,* can go on several times, once the players catch on.

Student Tasks:

1. Make an out.

2. Catch a deflected ball.

3. Kick a home run.

4. Make an assist.

DODGEBALL

Variations:

1. Have a few things in the gym (i.e., backboard) that would equal a home run if they were hit by a fly ball.

2. Give the batter a bat and pitch just like in softball.

3. Allow a ten-run rule.

4. Make four teams and combine two different teams for a best of two out of three. Can a team go undefeated by winning each of the three series?

    a. Series #1 = A + B vs. C + D. Best two out of three.

    b. Series #2 = A + C vs. B + D. Best two out of three.

    c. Series #3 = A + D vs. B + C. Best two out of three.

Safety:

1. Be sure the safe zones are not too close to the walls.

2. Runners should be aware of their own teammates running in the opposite direction.

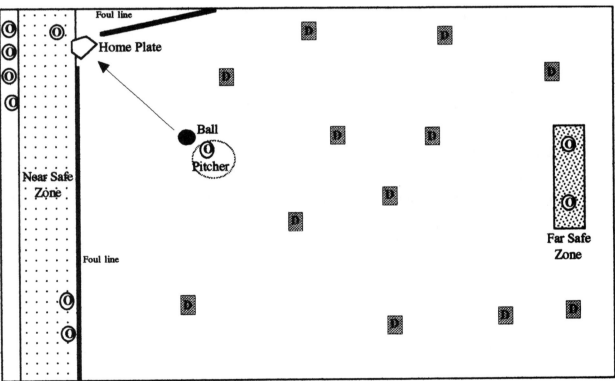

COLONYBALL

Objective:

◆ To score more runs than the other team by running around the bases and not getting hit with the ball.

Essentials:

◆ Gymnasium or large field
◆ 1 Gator Skin® ball

How to Play Offense:

1. Line up behind home plate. Pitch to your own team.

2. Attempt to kick the ball into fair play and run to first base.

3. No bunting is allowed.

4. There is no limit to the number of runners on one base.

5. No leading off is allowed.

6. Must tag up on all caught fly balls.

7. No sliding is allowed.

8. No stealing bases is allowed. If a runner is **not** over half way to the next base when the pitcher has the ball, that runner must go back to the previous base.

9. A runner may return to a base once she/he has left it.

10. The runner is out when:

    a. The defense catches a fly ball.

    b. The defense catches a ball that hits the wall, ceiling, or obstruction before it touches the floor.

    c. Hit in any manner or tagged by the ball below the shoulders before reaching a base. This is true even if the ball hits the wall or floor first.

11. The entire team is out when:

    a. Ten runs are scored.

    b. There are three outs.

12. Any runner left on a base when the third out is made will *go back to that same base* the next time his/her team returns to bat.

13. The ten-run rule: A team may score only ten runs an inning. If a team is behind by more than ten runs, they may score as many runs as needed to go ahead by one run.

How to Play Defense:

1. Players can be anywhere on the field.

2. Players will not block or interfere with the runners.

3. Players may not be in front of the pitcher.

4. Players may put out a runner by:
   a. Catching a fly ball (even if it hits something) before it touches the floor.
   b. Hitting or tagging a runner below the head if she/he is attempting to run.
   c. Forcing an out at first base.

Student Tasks:

1. Be involved in a single or double play.
2. Catch a deflected ball.
3. Kick a home run.
4. Throw a runner out at first base.

Variations:

1. Have a few things in the gym (i.e., backboard) that would equal a home run when hit by a fly ball.
2. Have the players run the bases twice to get one point.
3. Have players pair up and run together.
4. Make four teams, combine two different teams for a best of two out of three. Can a team go undefeated by winning each of the three series?
   a. Series #1 = A + B vs. C + D. Best two out of three.
   b. Series #2 = A + C vs. B + D. Best two out of three.
   c. Series #3 = A + D vs. B + C. Best two out of three.
5. Allow five outs per inning.
6. Use a bat and pitch the ball as in softball.

Safety:

1. Do not put the bases too close to the wall.
2. Runners from second and fifth bases need to watch out for each other.

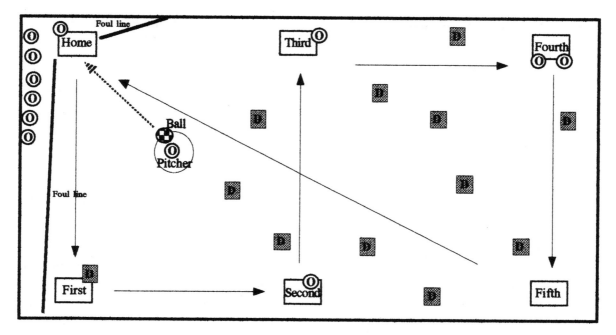

CONEBALL

Objective:

◆ To eliminate the other team by either: (1.) throwing the balls and knocking both cones over, or (2.) putting all of the other teams' players in the return line.

Essentials:

◆ Gym floor
◆ 12 to 15 Gator Skin® balls
◆ 4 cones (bowling pins)

How to Play Offense:

1. Must hit the opponent below the shoulders to put her/him out.
2. May attempt to hit and knock over the cones by throwing balls at them.
3. Must go to the return line if the other team catches a thrown ball.
4. May only possess a ball for five seconds. Bouncing the ball does not give five more seconds.
5. May use a ball to deflect a thrown ball. But if the thrown ball hits the ball out of the hand, then that player is out.
6. If a ball hits player "A" and glances into the air but is caught before it hits the floor by player "B" on the same team, then "A" is out, the thrower is out, and the first person in the return line is back in.
7. Any ball that hits the floor, wall or ceiling first, then hits a player is considered neutral and will not put that player out.

How to Play Defense:

1. May catch a thrown ball that eliminates the thrower and allows the first player on his/her team to reenter the game.
2. When hit below the shoulders, that player must go to the return line.
3. Guarding of the cone:
   a. Only one player may be the guard.
   b. This person must stand.
   c. No player can touch the cone or hold it from going down.
   d. No matter how the cone is knocked over, it must stay down.
   e. If both cones are knocked down before all the players are hit, the game is over.

Return Line:

1. When a player is hit below the shoulders or has a thrown ball caught by the opposing team, she/he is out and must go to the return line and wait.

2. The first player in line may return to the game when a ball is caught by a player on his/her own team.

Student Tasks:

1. Knock over a cone.

2. Catch a ball.

3. Throw and eliminate two defensive players.

Variations:

1. Make four teams and play a round robin.

2. Use the **Mix 'n Match** format.

3. Make four teams and combine two different teams for a best of two out of three. Can a team go undefeated by winning each of the three series?

   a. Series #1 = A + B vs. C + D. Best two out of three.

   b. Series #2 = A + C vs. B + D. Best two out of three.

   c. Series #3 = A + D vs. B + C. Best two out of three.

4. Put a smile face about the size of a dime on one of the balls. If that ball is caught, then **all** team players who are in the return line get to immediately come back onto the court.

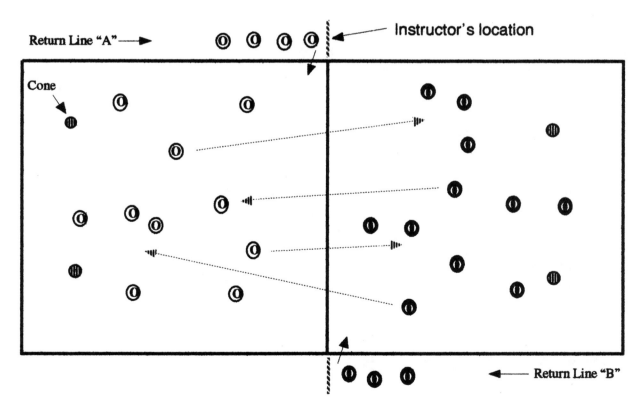

Return Line "A"

Instructor's location

Cone

Return Line "B"

COOL IT

Objectives:

- ◆ To possess the most flags when any player has given up his/her last one.
- ◆ To catch a ball.
- ◆ To accurately throw the ball.
- ◆ To avoid being hit.
- ◆ To run as far away as possible from the thrower.

Essentials:

- ◆ Gymnasium or large open field
- ◆ Make the **Cool It** ball by using a square piece of Nerf™-type foam about the size of a volleyball. Slightly round the corners to allow it to roll a bit. Like a dice, put six numbers on the sides.
- ◆ Take 18 football flags and mark each number on three of them.

How to Play:

1. Each player receives three flags with the same number.
2. A player throws the ball into the air and everyone waits for it to stop rolling.
3. When a player's number is facing up, she/he quickly **grabs** the ball, then **yells** "Cool It."
4. All of the other players are free to run in any direction until they hear "Cool It." They then must immediately stop and remain standing.
5. The person with the ball can take one step in any direction and try to hit any player below the shoulders. If the thrower can do this, she/he collects one flag from that player.
6. If the defense catches the thrown ball or can avoid being hit without moving his/her feet, she/he collects one of the thrower's flags.
7. The game is over when any player has lost all of his/her flags. The winner is the player who has collected the most flags.

Student Tasks:

1. Catch a given number.
2. Throw a certain number of hits.
3. Avoid being hit without moving the feet.
4. Collect a certain number of flags.

Variations:

1. As soon as the ball stops rolling after having been thrown at another player, then that number is it. This is very fast and action packed.
2. Throw at the defense with the odd arm.

3. Allow fewer or more steps toward the defensive players.

4. Make teams of two or three and try to eliminate the whole team.

CROSS-FIRE CONEBALL*

Objectives:

◆ To capture the other territories by knocking all of the players out.

◆ To capture the other territories by knocking over the team pins.

Essentials:

◆ Gymnasium

◆ 12 to 16 Gator Skin® balls

◆ 12 floor cones

◆ 4 team pins (bowling pins work well)

◆ 4 different colored sets of pinnies (one color for each team)

How to Play Offense:

1. Make four equal teams. There can be as many as 25 to 30 on **each** team when this game is played in a large gymnasium.

2. Players cannot cross the boundary line when throwing or retrieving a ball unless that team is out.

3. Players may enter *No Person's Land* at anytime.

4. Must throw and hit an opponent below the shoulders.

5. Can only possess a ball for five seconds and then must get rid of it.

6. May use a ball to block a thrown ball, but is out if she/he drops the held ball.

7. May be in possession of more than one ball.

8. Must go to the return line if a thrown ball is caught—before it touches the floor, wall, or ceiling—by anyone on another team.

9. Will not go to the return line if a thrown ball hits defensive player "A," glances into the air, and is caught by defensive player "B."

10. The last team left is the winner.

11. Rotate one territory to the left and begin a new game. The winning team receives zero balls at the start of the next game.

12. The champions are the team that has accumulated the most wins.

How to Play Defense:

1. Any number of players may stand and surround the team pin in order to protect it, but may not touch it.

Guidelines created by Ken Lumsden and Don McClure, 1980.

2. Alternate between boys and girls as to whom may guard it each new game.

3. Players must go to the return line when hit below the shoulders. Players line up in the order hit.

4. Players in line may reenter if a teammate catches a thrown ball, goes to the front of the return line, and tags the **first** person.

5. No matter how a team pin is knocked over, the entire team **sits down** in the return line area. This is true even if a team accidentally knocks over their own pin.

6. A player is not out if the ball hits the floor, wall, or ceiling first.

Student Tasks:

1. Knock down a tombstone (another team's pin).
2. Catch a ball.

Variations:

1. Combine teams "A" and "D" vs. "B" and "C."
2. All players must throw with the left arm.
3. Use the **Mix 'n Match** format and make a regular unit.
4. Put a smile face about the size of a dime on one of the balls. If that ball is caught, then **all** team players in the return line get to immediately come back onto the court.

Floor Diagram of Game in Progress

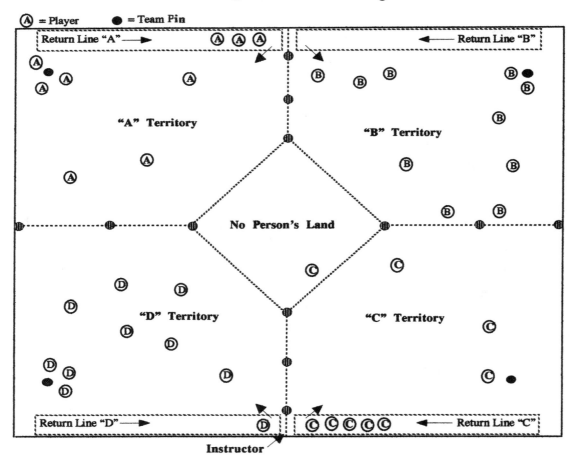

EVERYBODY FOR SELF

Objectives:

- ◆ To eliminate other players by hitting them with the ball.
- ◆ To avoid being hit with the ball.

Essentials:

- ◆ Gym floor
- ◆ 5 Gator Skin® balls

How to Play Offense: *(The instructor will add additional balls as the play moves along.)*

1. Pair up. Teammate may return from the *out zone* if her/his partner catches a thrown ball.
2. The ball is "poison" and can **only** be picked up after it has hit the floor or wall.
3. Must throw the ball at other players. No reaching out and tagging them.
4. Can only be in possession of one ball at a time.
5. Will put another player out if the ball hits him/her below the shoulders.
6. May not have possession of a ball for more than ten seconds.

How to Play Defense:

1. Cannot catch the ball while it is in the air since it is "poison."
2. Not out if hit above the shoulders.
3. A player will go to the *out zone* when hit below the shoulders before the ball touches the floor, wall, or ceiling.
4. Cannot use a held ball to block a shot that is thrown at them.

Student Tasks:

1. Be the last player in the game.
2. Be one of the last five players in the game.
3. Win two games.

Variations:

1. If a thrown ball is caught by a defensive player, then the thrower is out.
2. Play in teams (need pinnies).

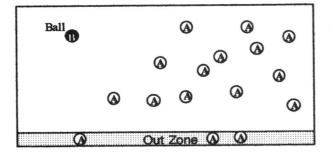

KICKBALL

Objective:

◆ To run around the bases and score a point without getting hit by the ball.

Essentials:

◆ Gymnasium or large field
◆ 1 Gator Skin® ball

How to Play Offense:

1. Line up behind home plate.
2. Pitch by rolling the ball to your own teammates.
3. Attempt to kick the ball and run to first base. (Bases are four by eight feet.)
4. Any number of runners may be on a base at one time.
5. The runner may not leave a base once the pitcher has possession or before the ball has been kicked by the next person. (No leading off.)
6. Must return to and tag that base when fly balls are caught.
7. The runner is out when:
   a. The defense catches a fly ball.
   b. The defense catches a ball that hits the wall, ceiling, or obstruction before it touches the floor.
   c. Hit in any manner or tagged below the shoulders while off base.
8. The entire team is out when:
   a. Five runs have been scored.
   b. There are three outs.
9. The five-run rule: A team may score only five runs an inning. If a team is behind by more than five runs, they may score as many runs as needed to go ahead by one run.

How to Play Defense:

1. Can be anywhere on the field.
2. Cannot block or interfere with the runners.
3. Can have force outs at first base with the first-base person.
4. May put out a runner by:
   a. Catching a fly ball (even if it hits something) before it touches the floor.
   b. Hitting or tagging the runner below the shoulders while that runner is off base.

DODGEBALL

Student Tasks:

1. Put someone out.
2. Be involved in a double play.
3. Catch a deflected ball.
4. Kick a home run.
5. Assist in a play at first base.

Variations:

1. Have a few things in the gym (i.e., backboard) that would equal a home run when hit by a fly ball.
2. Have the players run to 1–2–3–1–2–3 and then to home.
3. Have players pair up and run together.
4. Make four teams and combine two different teams for a best of two out of three. Can a team go undefeated by winning each of the three series?
   a. Series #1 = A + B vs. C + D. Best two out of three.
   b. Series #2 = A + C vs. B + D. Best two out of three.
   c. Series #3 = A + D vs. B + C. Best two out of three.
5. Install a ten-run rule.
6. Use a bat instead of kicking the ball.

Safety: Do not put the bases too close to a wall when playing in a gymnasium.

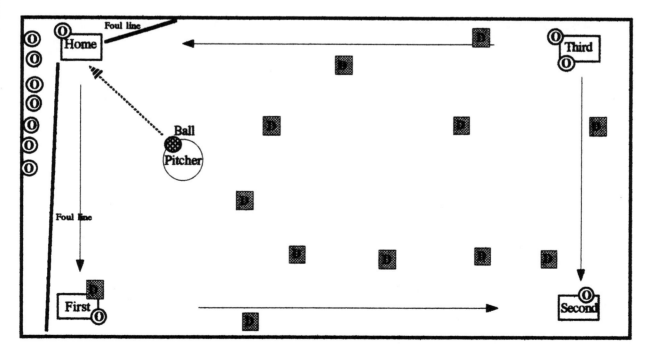

PAY BACK

Objectives:

◆ To eliminate other players by hitting them with the ball.

◆ To avoid being hit with the ball and going to the *Pay Back Shack.*

Essentials:

◆ Gymnasium or large field

◆ 1 Gator Skin® ball

How to Play:

1. Players spread out and the ball is tossed to start play.

2. A player with possession of the ball may **not** take steps. She/he can move closer to other players by bouncing the ball against the wall and fetching it.

3. Any player may intercept the ball after it has touched the wall.

4. Players are to go to the *Pay Back Shack* if:
   a. Hit by the ball before it contacts the wall or floor.
   b. Hit below the shoulders by a thrown ball.
   c. Steps are taken while in possession of the ball.

5. Only five players can be in the *Pay Back Shack*. As new players arrive, the first player returns to play.

6. Do not be in the *Pay Back Shack* when time expires.

Student Tasks:

1. Eliminate a certain number of players in a row.

2. Go to the *Pay Back Shack* the least amount of times.

3. Avoid being hit.

Variations:

1. Use two or more balls.

2. The thrower of a ball that is **caught** goes to the *Pay Back Shack.*

3. Make teams of two or three. Players work together and can pass directly to each other. If one player gets put out, then that entire team is out. Limit the number of teams that can be in the *Pay Back Shack* at one time.

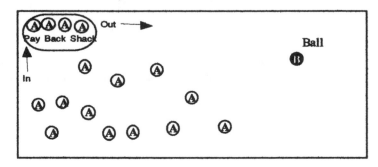

© 1996 Parker Publishing Company

PRISONBALL

Objectives:

- ◆ To put the other entire team into prison.
- ◆ To try not to get hit with the ball.

Essentials:

- ◆ Gymnasium floor
- ◆ 12 to 15 Gator Skin® balls

How to Play Offense:

1. Hit an opponent below the shoulders and send him/her to *prison*.
2. May not go into *prison* to retrieve a ball.
3. May possess a ball for only five seconds.
4. May possess more than one ball at a time.
5. Balls that hit the floor or wall are neutral and will not eliminate anyone.
6. May use a held ball to block a thrown ball. If the held ball is knocked out of the hands, then that player must go to *prison*.
7. Can intentionally throw balls to teammates who are in *prison*.

How to Play Defense:

1. Must dodge or catch a ball that has been thrown.
2. Not allowed to take a ball to *prison* when hit.
3. Must hold hands up and go to *prison* when hit below the shoulders.

Prisoners:

1. Must hit a player to get out.
2. May not take a ball out of *prison* on the return to home.
3. May not pick up a ball that is on the main floor while in *prison*.

Student Tasks:

1. Put out a certain number of players.
2. Avoid getting hit.
3. Catch a certain number of balls.
4. Free the entire team.

Variations:

1. If a thrown ball is caught by the defense, then the thrower must go to *prison*.

2. If a team can make a ball go into the opposite basketball hoop, then **all** of their prisoners are freed from *prison*.

3. Make four teams and combine two different teams for a best of two out of three. Can a team go undefeated by winning each of the three series?
   a. Series #1 = A + B vs. C + D. Best two out of three.
   b. Series #2 = A + C vs. B + D. Best two out of three.
   c. Series #3 = A + D vs. B + C. Best two out of three.

4. Put a smile face about the size of a dime on one of the balls. If that ball is caught, then **all** team players who are in *prison* get to immediately come back onto the court.

Safety:

1. Make two lanes, one on each side of the court, that the prisoners must follow to *prison*. This prevents wasted shots by the offense and a smoother transition from offense to *prison* and back.

2. When a player is going to *prison*, have her/him hold her/his arms up and cross them in front of the face as she/he moves down the prisoner's lane. This helps to prevent a close shot to the face by an individual who does not know this individual is out.

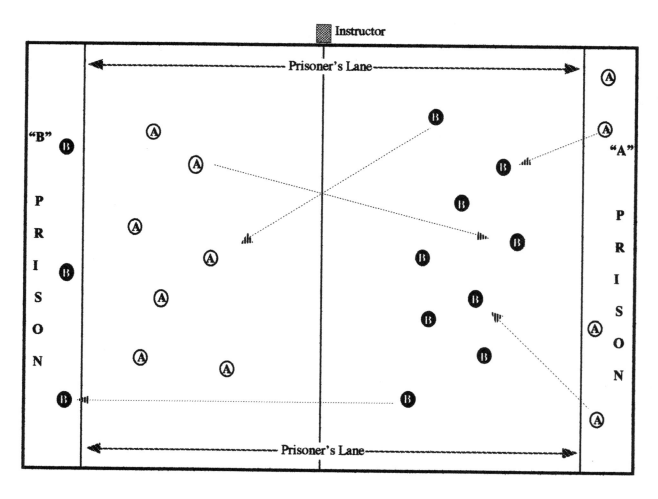

RAT RACE

Objectives:

- ◆ For a team: To carry the food down and back the most times.
- ◆ As a runner (rat): To not get hit by a ball.
- ◆ As a thrower (exterminator): To hit the rats with a ball.

Essentials:

- ◆ Large gymnasium
- ◆ 4 to 6 Gator Skin® balls
- ◆ 2 objects to use as cheese (knee pads work well)

How to Play:

1. Divide into four equal teams.
2. Two teams go to the sides of the court and become the defense.
   a. Each team starts with two or three balls per side.
   b. Exterminators throw the ball at the rats, trying to hit them below the shoulders.
   c. Defensive players may go onto the court to retrieve any stationary balls, but must return to behind the side line in order to throw.
3. Two teams go to one end of the floor, line up in separate lines, and become the runners.
   a. The first person on each of these teams possesses the cheese.
   b. Each team attempts to take the cheese to the safe zone and back. A rat may move in any manner, direction, or speed. One point is awarded for each time this is successfully accomplished. The cheese is then passed to the next runner in line. Bounces and ricochets do not put out a runner.
   c. When a runner is hit with the ball below the shoulders, she/he will immediately sit down on the floor and hold up the cheese. Do not mess with or touch any balls while sitting down.
   d. The next person in line attempts to get to the cheese and either takes it to the other end if it has not yet been there, or brings it directly back to the finish line if it has already been to the safe zone.
   e. Each person in line gets one attempt at carrying the cheese. (This completes an inning.)
   f. Tally the number of times **the cheese went down and back.** Examples would be $1\frac{1}{2}$ times, $3\frac{1}{4}$, or $5\frac{3}{4}$ times.
   g. Rotate the offensive and defensive team positions.
   h. Play a game of three innings; highest score wins.

Student Tasks:

1. Carry the cheese to the safe zone.
2. Bring the cheese over the score line.
3. Hit two different runners.
4. Finish as one of the top two teams.

Variations:

1. Allow the cheese to keep going as long as there are runners to carry it. Rats that have not been hit go to the end of the line and run again when it is their turn. Continue until all of the teams' rats have been eliminated.

2. If the ball hits a rat in any manner such as bouncing off the floor, then that rat is out.

3. Rats sitting on the floor may grab a ball and—from the sitting position—throw it at an exterminator. If the exterminator is hit, she/he must sit down on the side.

4. Put the offensive teams at opposite ends of the floor.

Safety:

1. Do not put the safe zone too close to the wall for fear of rat impact.
2. Runners should be aware of two directions of traffic.

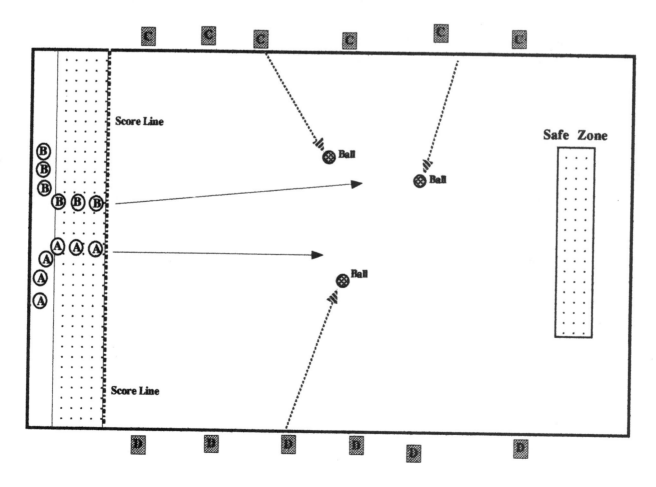

TANDEM TAG

Objectives:

- ◆ To score more runs than the other team.
- ◆ To throw and pass the ball with accuracy.
- ◆ To avoid being hit with the ball.

Essentials:

- ◆ Gymnasium
- ◆ 1 Gator Skin® ball

How to Play Offense:

1. Line up behind home plate.
2. First player in line throws the ball anywhere into the field. The first and second person in line begin to go to the safe zone at the other end of the field. They may travel in any method, speed, or direction desired.
3. A player may only stay in the safe zone for a maximum of ten seconds.
4. If a runner is hit with the ball (below the shoulders) she/he is out and the **next** player in line immediately begins.
5. When a player makes it down and back without being hit, a point is scored and the next person in line begins.
6. There are always **two** runners going at one time.
7. The inning is over when the entire line has attempted to run down and back once.
8. The team with the most runs scored after a set time or number of innings is the winner.

How to Play Defense:

1. Should cover the entire field of play.
2. May not hit a player in the safe zone.
3. May only go into the safe zone to retrieve the ball.
4. **Cannot walk, travel, or run** once the ball has been caught or picked up.
5. May not hit a runner above the shoulders.

Student Tasks:

1. How many ways can you avoid being hit?
2. Make two outs in a row.
3. Get an assist.

Variations:

1. Add another safe zone.

2. Make four teams and combine two different teams for a best of two out of three. Can a team go undefeated by winning each of the three series?

   a. Series #1 = A + B vs. C + D. Best two out of three.

   b. Series #2 = A + C vs. B + D. Best two out of three.

   c. Series #3 = A + D vs. B + C. Best two out of three.

Safety:

1. Do not put the safe zones too close to a wall.

2. Players need to be aware of teammates running in the opposite direction.

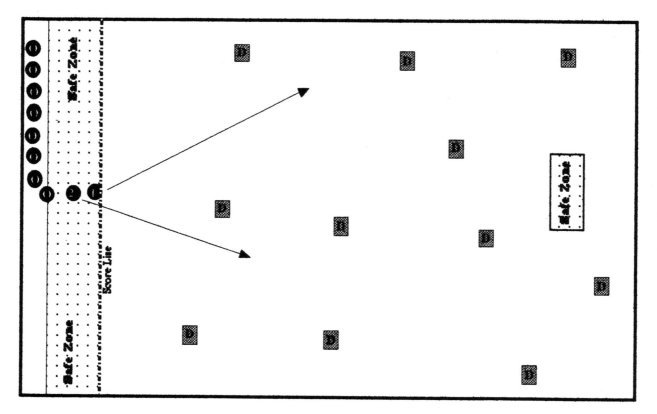

ABOUT "FITNESS TESTING"

Objectives:

◆ To allow a student to evaluate, monitor, and improve her/his own fitness level.

◆ To allow a student to be successful in her/his own fitness development by **not** competing against others.

◆ To allow a student to compare her/his results with the school's best and strive to break a school record if desired.

◆ To get information about student fitness levels and then select the methods for improvement.

Essentials:

◆ Field or gymnasium

◆ See "Stations" below for equipment needed and specific information

◆ Recording forms

Stations:

1. *Height:* Marking device drawn or taped to the wall. Take off shoes.

2. *Weight:* Use a scale. It is **optional** whether a student writes down his/her weight on the score card.

3. *Flexibility:* Measuring stick or box.

   a. Sit on the floor, legs straight, with heels about 12 inches apart.

   b. Three attempts to see how far past the heels the fingers can reach.

4. *Softball Throw:* 12 softballs, cones, or football sideline markers.

   a. Allow three throws.

   b. Record distance in yards.

5. *50-Yard Dash:* Stopwatch, two cones, four erasers. Allow two separate runs with a partner.

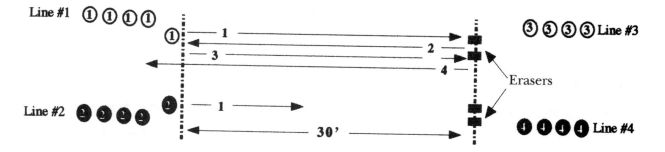

6. *Shuttle Run:* Stopwatch, two cones, four erasers.

   a. Distance between cones is 30 feet, the width of a volleyball court.

   b. Make four lines of runners.

   c. Run down and grab the first eraser, run back to the start line and *set* it down; run back and grab the second eraser, sprint past the start line.

   d. The runners at the other end start next. This saves time by not having to return the erasers. (See the illustration above.)

7. *Standing Long Jump:* Mat with markings drawn on it works best.

   a. Best distance of three jumps.

   b. Mark where the back of the heels land.

8. *Crunches:* Sit-ups that only require the shoulder blades to lift from the mat. Use a stopwatch.

   a. Pair up and have a partner hold the other person's feet.

   b. Count the number done in one minute.

9. *Jump and Reach:* Measuring device.

   a. Only one step is allowed before jumping. Three attempts are given.

   b. Measure the distance between the initial reach and the final touch.

10. *600-Yard Walk/Run:* Stopwatch. Walk, jog or run this distance, then record the time.

11. *Pull-ups:* Suspended bar.

    a. Palms must face away.

    b. Must extend the arms fully.

    c. Chin must go past the bar.

    d. No swinging.

When a student breaks a school record, her/his name goes on the **Wall of Fame.** This record is posted until it is broken or five years has elapsed. This student also receives an achievement card.

SAMPLE FITNESS SCORECARD

Period: 3
Date: Sept. 15
Pretest - ~~Post-test~~
Instructor: Mrs. Green

Roll	Name	AGE	HEIGHT	FLEXIBILITY	SOFTBALL THROW (YDS)	50 YARD DASH	SHUTTLE RUN	STANDING LONG JUMP	CRUNCHES	JUMP REACH	600 YARD RUN / WALK	PULL UPS
1	Anderson, Jane	16	5'-3"	18	43	9.4	7.3	6'-6"	91	24"	2:11	5
2	Black, Will	16	6'-2"	21	67	7.7	6.1	7'-1"	88	29"	1:32	11
3	Dunn, Jim	15	6'	14	46	11.1	9.9	5'-4"	45	16"	3:24	0

Directions:

1. Fill in the class information of period, date, pretest or post test, and the instructor's name.

2. Fill in the student names.

3. Put this sheet on a clipboard and allow each student to fill in her/his own information. It is an honor system since students are only competing against themselves. *If you do not bowl a 300 game, why would you want a trophy that says you did?*

4. Save this sheet and display it on a wall during the post tests. The students need to use this data for a comparison when filling in the *Pre/Post Fitness Scorecards*.

SAMPLE PRE/POST FITNESS SCORES

Name: Anderson, Jane	Height	Flexibility	Softball	50 Dash	Shuttle	L. Jump	Crunches	J. Reach	600 Run	Pull Ups
Pretest 1	5'-3"	18	43	9.4	7.3	6'-6"	91	24	2:11	5
Post Test 2	5'-5"	22	50	9.6	7.4	7'-1"	100	26	2:00	4
Gain or Loss	2	4	7	-0.2	-0.1	7	9	2	-11	-1

Directions:

1. Print and cut into individual strips of paper.

2. After a student has completed the Post Test, she/he can now fill in the data from both tests.

3. Add or subtract as necessary to determine the outcomes.

FITNESS SCORECARD

Period:
Date:
Pretest - Post test
Instructor:

Roll	Name	AGE	HEIGHT	FLEXIBILITY	SOFTBALL THROW (YDS.)	50 YARD DASH	SHUTTLE RUN	STANDING LONG JUMP	CRUNCHES	JUMP REACH	600 YARD RUN / WALK	PULL UPS
1												
2												
3												
4												
5												
6												
7												
8												
9												
10												
11												
12												
13												
14												
15												
16												
17												
18												
19												
20												
21												
22												
23												
24												
25												
26												
27												
28												
29												
30												
31												
32												
33												
34												
35												
36												
37												
38												
39												
40												

PRE/POST FITNESS SCORES

*Cut these out and let the students fill them in with their fitness scores,
then take them home.*

Name:	Height	Flexibility	Softball	50 Dash	Shuttle	L. Jump	Crunches	J. Reach	600 Run	Pull Ups
Pretest 1										
Post Test 2										
Gain or Loss										

Name:	Height	Flexibility	Softball	50 Dash	Shuttle	L. Jump	Crunches	J. Reach	600 Run	Pull Ups
Pretest 1										
Post Test 2										
Gain or Loss										

Name:	Height	Flexibility	Softball	50 Dash	Shuttle	L. Jump	Crunches	J. Reach	600 Run	Pull Ups
Pretest 1										
Post Test 2										
Gain or Loss										

Name:	Height	Flexibility	Softball	50 Dash	Shuttle	L. Jump	Crunches	J. Reach	600 Run	Pull Ups
Pretest 1										
Post Test 2										
Gain or Loss										

Name:	Height	Flexibility	Softball	50 Dash	Shuttle	L. Jump	Crunches	J. Reach	600 Run	Pull Ups
Pretest 1										
Post Test 2										
Gain or Loss										

Name:	Height	Flexibility	Softball	50 Dash	Shuttle	L. Jump	Crunches	J. Reach	600 Run	Pull Ups
Pretest 1										
Post Test 2										
Gain or Loss										

Name:	Height	Flexibility	Softball	50 Dash	Shuttle	L. Jump	Crunches	J. Reach	600 Run	Pull Ups
Pretest 1										
Post Test 2										
Gain or Loss										

Name:	Height	Flexibility	Softball	50 Dash	Shuttle	L. Jump	Crunches	J. Reach	600 Run	Pull Ups
Pretest 1										
Post Test 2										
Gain or Loss										

Name:	Height	Flexibility	Softball	50 Dash	Shuttle	L. Jump	Crunches	J. Reach	600 Run	Pull Ups
Pretest 1										
Post Test 2										
Gain or Loss										

Name:	Height	Flexibility	Softball	50 Dash	Shuttle	L. Jump	Crunches	J. Reach	600 Run	Pull Ups
Pretest 1										
Post Test 2										
Gain or Loss										

FLASH FOOTBALL

Objective:

◆ To run or pass the ball over the goal line and accumulate points.

Essentials:

◆ Large field
◆ Football
◆ 2 different colors of flags
◆ 8 field marking cones

How to Play:

1. Only five to six players on a team.

2. Make the fields short and narrow. Divide a standard football field into four or five smaller fields.

3. Kick Off:

   a. Start from the 25-yard line.

   b. The ball must cross the 50-yard line before it is in play.

   c. If the ball is kicked out-of-bounds, the receiving team may elect to have another kick or take it where it went out-of-bounds.

   d. If it goes over the goal line, it may be run out or taken on the 25-yard line.

   e. There are no fumbles when trying to catch the ball on the kick off.

4. Offense:

   a. Must be on their own side prior to the hike and remain motionless.

   b. Can move across the line of scrimmage when the ball is hiked.

   c. May not huddle.

   d. Has four tries (downs) to score.

   e. May block the defense with the arms folded into the body.

   f. Can spin with the ball while running.

   g. Must have flags available on the hips and cannot flag guard when running. Only one flag needs to be pulled for the runner to be down.

   h. May pitch or pass the ball any number of times or in any direction.

   i. Ball can be hiked in any manner from the ground.

   j. Quarterback must be a new player each down, and may run immediately after receiving the hike.

   k. Teams switch ends after a touchdown.

   l. A player may score only two touchdowns in a row.

5. Defense:

    a. Must be on their own side prior to the offense hiking the ball and can move around freely prior to the hike.

    b. Can only cross the line of scrimmage when the quarterback touches the ball.

    c. Cannot intentionally hit the ball from the hands of a runner.

    d. Will be the referees and make all calls. Their calls are never wrong.

6. General Rules:

    a. The ball goes to the other team on all fumbles and incomplete passes. The other team takes possession where the ball **first** makes contact with the ground.

    b. If the defense deflects the ball to the ground, the offense retains possession but loses a down unless it is fourth down. The offense would get fourth down over in this case.

    c. If a ball hits or is passed incomplete in the end zone, the other team gets possession of it at the 25-yard line.

7. Scoring:

    a. Touchdown = 7 points

    b. Safety = 2 points

Student Tasks:

1. Pull a given number of flags.
2. Complete a given number of passes.
3. Make a given number of interceptions.
4. Pass for a given number of touchdowns.
5. Have each member of a team score a touchdown during the daily games.

Variations:

1. Use the **Mix 'n Match** format.
2. Change the type of ball used.

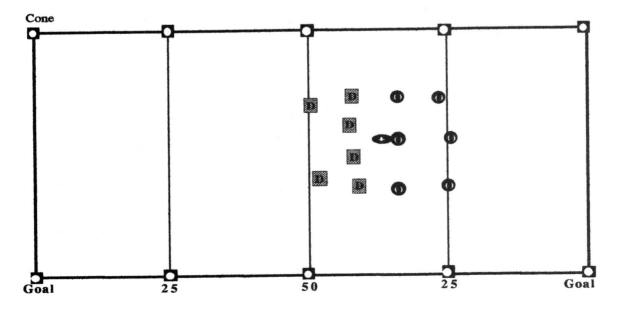

Cone

Goal   2 5   5 0   2 5   Goal

HAWAIIAN FOOTBALL

Objective:

◆ To run or pass the ball over the goal line and accumulate points.

Essentials:

◆ Large field
◆ Football
◆ 2 different colors of flags
◆ 8 field marking cones

How to Play:

1. Only five to six players on a team.
2. Make the fields short and narrow. Divide a standard football field into four or five smaller fields.
3. Kick Off:
   a. Start from the 25-yard line.
   b. The ball must cross the 50-yard line before it is in play.
   c. If the ball is kicked out-of-bounds, the receiving team may elect to have another kick or elect to take it where it went out-of-bounds.
   d. If it goes over the goal line, it may be run out or taken on the 25-yard line.
   e. There are no fumbles when trying to catch the ball on the kick off.
4. Offense:
   a. Must be on their own side prior to the hike and remain motionless.
   b. Can move across the line of scrimmage when the ball is hiked.
   c. May huddle for approximately 30 seconds.
   d. Has four tries (downs) to cross each line to get a first down.
   e. May block the defense with the arms folded into the body.
   f. Can spin with the ball while running.
   g. Must have flags available on the hips and cannot flag guard when running. Only one flag needs to be pulled for the runner to be down.
   h. May only pass the ball forward while behind the line of scrimmage.
   i. Ball must be hiked from the ground and between the legs.
   j. All players number off and rotate one position clockwise after each offensive play. Everyone plays a **different** position each new play.
   k. Teams switch ends after a touchdown and the extra point has been attempted.
   l. A player may score only two touchdowns in a row.

© 1996 Parker Publishing Company

m. Scoring will be 6 points for a touchdown, 1 for an extra point, and 2 points for a safety.

n. The team caught in their own end zone (safety) gets a free kick on the 25-yard line.

5. Defense:

a. Must be on their own side prior to the offense hiking the ball and can move around freely prior to the hike.

b. Can only cross the line of scrimmage when the ball is hiked.

c. Cannot intentionally hit the ball from the hands of a runner.

d. Will be the referees and make all calls. Their calls are never wrong.

Student Tasks:

1. Pull a given number of flags.
2. Complete a given number of passes.
3. Make a given number of interceptions.
4. Pass for a given number of touchdowns.
5. Have each member of a team score a touchdown during the daily games.

Variations:

1. A team will only get a first down if they cross the 50-yard line.
2. Use the **Mix 'n Match** format.

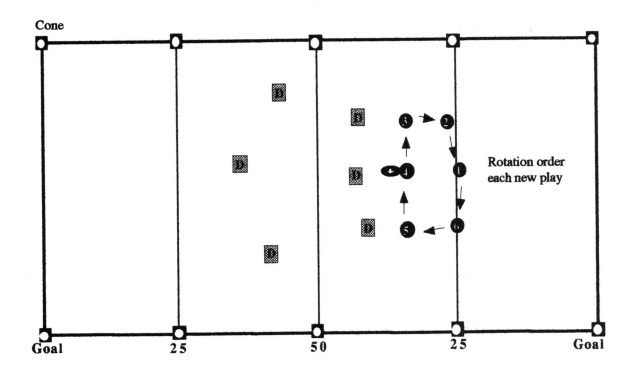

D-I-S-C

Objectives:

◆ To hit a target that other player(s) might miss.

◆ To hit the same target that another player hit first.

Essentials:

◆ Gymnasium or field

◆ 1 disc for each player or pair of players

How to Play:

1. Similar to the game of **HORSE** in basketball.

2. Determine the first thrower, who determines the distance, type of throw, and target. Pick various targets in a gym or on a field.

   a. If the target is hit, the next player must duplicate the distance, throw, and hit.

   b. If the target is missed, then the next player chooses the distance, throw, and target.

3. The last thrower to not spell out D-I-S-C is the winner.

Student Tasks:

1. Cause three letters in a row.

2. Come from behind to win.

Variations:

1. Challenge the last letter of a game by making the person prove her/his shot. If she/he misses the second attempt, then the other player is still in. The first player throws again, though. If she/he makes the same shot twice, then the player who said to prove it is eliminated.

2. Play a game with the off hand.

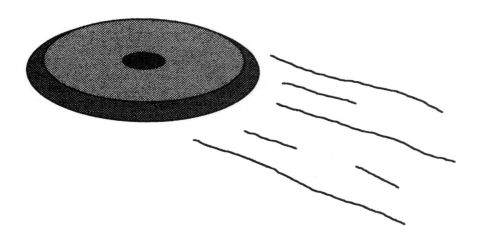

DISC GOLF

Objectives:

- ◆ To cover the course in as few throws as possible.
- ◆ To understand the basic rules and terms of golf.

Essentials:

- ◆ Outdoor fields
- ◆ 1 disc for each student
- ◆ 1 course map and score sheet for each student
- ◆ Pencils

Terms to Know:

1. Bogey — Over Par
2. Par — Average
3. Birdie — One under Par
4. Eagle — Two under Par
5. Hole in One — Made in one throw
6. Fore — Protect your head
7. Pin — Hole or object that is made or hit
8. Away — Player farthest from the hole
9. Lie — Where the disc lands and stops
10. Putt — Any short toss to the pin
11. Mulligan — Free throw that does not cost a stroke

How to Play:

1. Can be played in singles, pairs, or teams.
2. Throw the disc and hit an object.
3. Do not make distracting noises or motions when other players are about to throw.
4. During play, the tee off is determined by the thrower who had the lowest score on the previous hole. The lowest score throws first. If there is a tie, go back one, two, or three holes if necessary.
5. That player who is farthest from the hole during play will always throw first.
6. A player may not step past the lie of the previous throw when attempting her/his next throw.
7. No follow-through steps are allowed within 30 feet of the pin.
8. Any unplayable lie can be relocated with a one-stroke penalty.

FLYING DISC

Student Tasks:

1. Make a hole in one.
2. Make an eagle.
3. Make a certain number of birdies during a round.
4. Hit the pin with a curve shot.
5. Come from behind and win a match.

Variations:

1. Make teams of two or three students. After everyone has thrown, determine the best throw and the team will throw from this point next.
2. Play the course in the reverse manner of 18, 17, 16, etc.
3. Play mixed doubles.
4. Play a handicapped tournament. The handicap is determined by taking a player's average number of throws over a course and subtracting the course par from his/her average. (Example:) Mary averages 92. The course par is 72. Subtract 92 – 72 = 20. Mary has a handicap of 20 and can deduct this from her total throws in the tournament.)
5. Must throw with the left or off hand.
6. Use softballs when the wind starts blowing.
7. Use softballs instead of discs, even if it is not windy.

© 1996 Parker Publishing Company

SAMPLE DISC GOLF SCORECARD

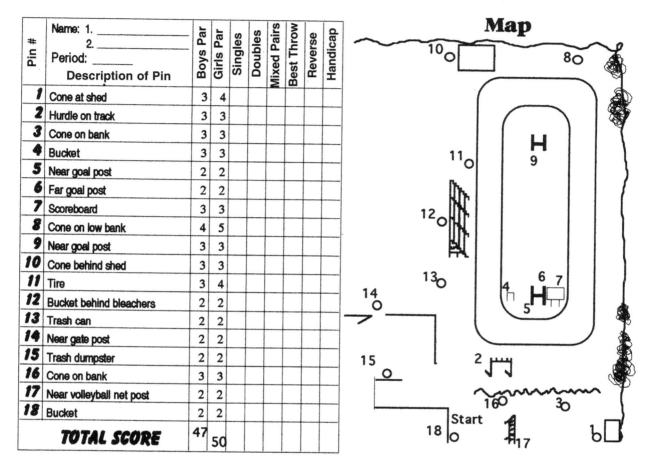

Pin #	Name: 1. _____ 2. _____ Period: _____ Description of Pin	Boys Par	Girls Par	Singles	Doubles	Mixed Pairs	Best Throw	Reverse	Handicap
1	Cone at shed	3	4						
2	Hurdle on track	3	3						
3	Cone on bank	3	3						
4	Bucket	3	3						
5	Near goal post	2	2						
6	Far goal post	2	2						
7	Scoreboard	3	3						
8	Cone on low bank	4	5						
9	Near goal post	3	3						
10	Cone behind shed	3	3						
11	Tire	3	4						
12	Bucket behind bleachers	2	2						
13	Trash can	2	2						
14	Near gate post	2	2						
15	Trash dumpster	2	2						
16	Cone on bank	3	3						
17	Near volleyball net post	2	2						
18	Bucket	2	2						
	TOTAL SCORE	47	50						

Map

Directions:

1. Copy and then cut out the score sheets.

2. Give each student a scorecard.

3. Fill in the *names* and *period* in the spaces provided.

4. Disperse the students to each of the various pins. This allows for **all** of the players to begin and prevents waiting in a line.

5. After a student has finished throwing to the next hole, she/he then marks the corresponding box and records the total number of throws that it took to hit it.

6. Once the course has been finished, total all the scores and put it in the *Total Score* box.

DISC GOLF SCORECARDS

© 1996 Parker Publishing Company

······· Cut Here ·······

Map

Pin #	Name: 1. _____ 2. _____ Period: _____ **Description of Pin**	Boys Par	Girls Par	Singles	Doubles	Mixed Pairs	Best Throw	Reverse	Handicap
1									
2									
3									
4									
5									
6									
7									
8									
9									
10									
11									
12									
13									
14									
15									
16									
17									
18									
	TOTAL SCORE								

······· Cut Here ·······

Map

Pin #	Name: 1. _____ 2. _____ Period: _____ **Description of Pin**	Boys Par	Girls Par	Singles	Doubles	Mixed Pairs	Best Throw	Reverse	Handicap
1									
2									
3									
4									
5									
6									
7									
8									
9									
10									
11									
12									
13									
14									
15									
16									
17									
18									
	TOTAL SCORE								

DISC-ARRAYED

Objective:

◆ To knock down all of the other team's pins first.

Essentials:

◆ Gymnasium or outdoors
◆ 6 to 8 bowling pins for each side
◆ 1 flying disc for every 3 to 4 players
◆ 2 Gator Skin® balls

How to Play:

1. Make two teams.
2. Set up the pins near the free throw line extended across court.
3. Throw **only** at the other team's pins.
4. All discs must be thrown from behind the line.
5. Players may retrieve discs that are on their half of the court, but must return to the throwing line when tossing the disc.

Student Tasks:

1. Knock over a set number of buildings.
2. Knock down a defensive thrown disc from the side.

Variations:

1. Allow two to four players from each team toss Nerf™ balls at the incoming discs from the sidelines.
2. Allow players to place the building anywhere on their side.
3. Form four teams, combining two different teams each game.

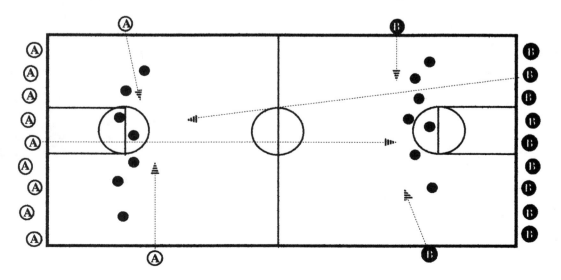

DISCATHON

Objective:

◆ To score and accumulate as many points as possible with the disc.

Essentials:

◆ Gymnasium or field

◆ 2 or 3 discs for each station

◆ Put numbers on the discs for easy identification and accountability

◆ Various objects to place at each lane; items can be anything that will have durability (plastic cups, bowling pins, bleach bottles, yogurt cups, or small boxes are just a few of the items that can be used)

◆ Score cards are optional

How to Play:

1. Make six to eight lanes using the sidelines of the basketball court for the distance to be thrown.

2. All lanes can be the same, or there can be various activities so that students rotate to each one.

3. Each player gets two throws.

4. The participant with the highest total points at the end of the contest is the winner.

Games:

1. Random

2. Ducks

3. Bowling

4. Stacks

5. Turkey Shoot (Use a desk)

6. Bombs Away (Tape a target flat on floor 10′ × 10′)

7. Accuracy (Hang an object from a basketball rim)

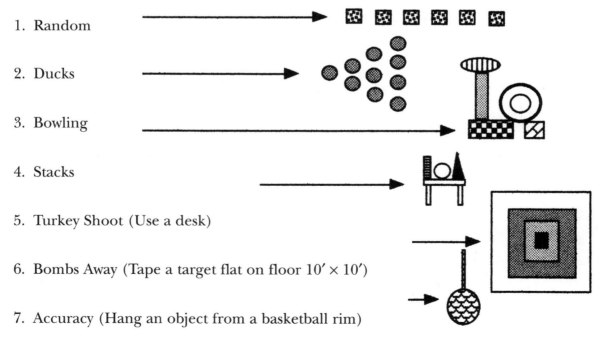

FLYING DISC

Student Tasks:

1. Hit an object with each of the two throws.
2. Hit more than one object with one throw.

Variations:

1. Use the off hand to throw.
2. Pair up with someone.
3. Form teams and compete.

SAMPLE DISCATHON SCORECARD

Date March 12	Points Scored								Event
Events	ONE	TWO	THREE	FOUR	FIVE	SIX	SEVEN	EIGHT	Totals
Random	X	X	X	X					4
Ducks	X	X	X	X	X	X			6
Bowling	X	X	X	X	X	X	X	X	8
Stacks	X	X							2
Turkey Shoot									0
Bombs Away	X	X	X	X	X	X	X		7
Accuracy	X	X	X	X	X				5
Names/s: John Warner							Grand Total		32

Directions

1. Fill out the information for the *date* and *name*.
2. After each throw, mark an X in the boxes.
3. Put the total points accumulated in the *Event Totals* column.
4. Tally the points for all of the activities and place that score in the *Grand Total* box.

DISCATHON SCORECARDS

Cut these out and give them to the students.

Date	Points Scored								Event
Events	ONE	TWO	THREE	FOUR	FIVE	SIX	SEVEN	EIGHT	Totals
Random									
Ducks									
Bowling									
Stacks									
Turkey Shoot									
Bombs Away									
Accuracy									
Names/s:								Grand Total	

Date	Points Scored								Event
Events	ONE	TWO	THREE	FOUR	FIVE	SIX	SEVEN	EIGHT	Totals
Random									
Ducks									
Bowling									
Stacks									
Turkey Shoot									
Bombs Away									
Accuracy									
Names/s:								Grand Total	

Date	Points Scored								Event
Events	ONE	TWO	THREE	FOUR	FIVE	SIX	SEVEN	EIGHT	Totals
Random									
Ducks									
Bowling									
Stacks									
Turkey Shoot									
Bombs Away									
Accuracy									
Names/s:								Grand Total	

Date	Points Scored								Event
Events	ONE	TWO	THREE	FOUR	FIVE	SIX	SEVEN	EIGHT	Totals
Random									
Ducks									
Bowling									
Stacks									
Turkey Shoot									
Bombs Away									
Accuracy									
Names/s:								Grand Total	

ELIMINATION

Objectives:

- ◆ To be the last team or person left.
- ◆ To accurately throw and catch the disc without dropping it.

Essentials:

- ◆ Gymnasium or field
- ◆ 1 disc for each team of 3 to 8 players

How to Play:

1. Team playing area is 15 feet wide by 45 feet long. Use shorter distance for younger players.
2. Each team splits and lines up on opposite ends.
3. After a completed catch and throw, that player steps to the back of his/her own line.
4. If a player misses the disc, she/he is out.
5. The throw and the catch must be made behind the line.
6. All throwers throw at the same time and at about 10-second intervals.

Student Tasks:

1. Put two or more players out.
2. Catch a certain number of throws.

Variations:

1. **Bring 'em Back:** When a team makes three completed catches in a row, they may bring back one player.
2. **Saucer Tossers:** How many successful catches can teams make in one or two minutes. No one is eliminated. All throws must be made from behind the line after retrieving the disc.
3. **Disco–Tech:** Same as **Saucer Tossers** except:
   a. One point for a standard catch.
   b. Two points for a trick catch.
   c. Three points for a jumping trick catch.
4. Add lively music to any of the above activities.

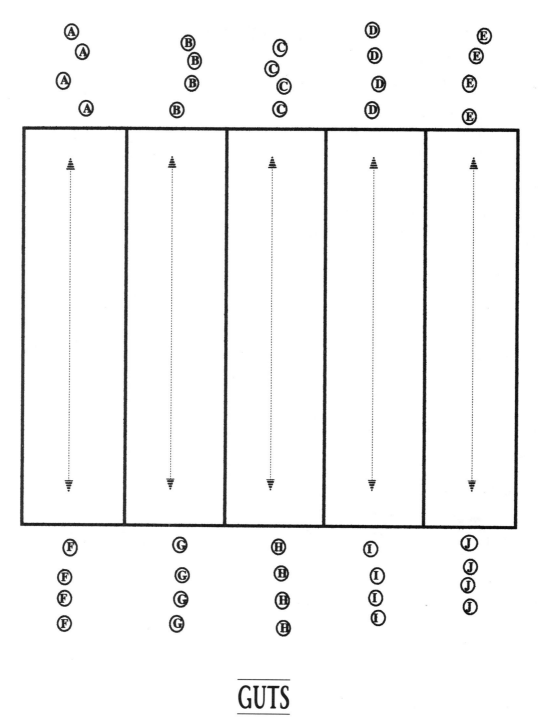

GUTS

Objectives:

- ◆ To make throws within a zone that the opposite team cannot catch.
- ◆ To score 21 points first.

Essentials:

- ◆ Field or gymnasium
- ◆ 1 disc for every game

How to Play Offense:

1. One to five players on a team.
2. Teams line up 15 to 20 yards apart and opposite each other.
3. All throws must not hit the ground or fly above the extended arms of the other team.
4. Throwers may not step across the line before releasing the disc.
5. The disc may not cross the goal in a vertical position (on its side).

How to Play Defense:

1. Must catch the disc.
2. Any number of players may touch the disc while attempting the catch.
3. The last person to touch the disc throws it.
4. If no player touches a scored or missed throw, then anyone may throw it back.
5. All defensive players must remain behind the line until the throw is made.

Scoring Zone:

1. The area is determined by the extended arms of a defensive person, nearest the disc, as it crosses the goal line.
2. If a defensive player jumps and hits the disc, then that throw is considered good.

Student Tasks:

1. Make three catches.
2. Cause two different players to miss.
3. Make three one-handed catches.

Variations:

1. Allow only one-handed catches.
2. Each team throws a disc at the same time.
3. **Disc–Gusted:** Played like above, except teams move to 15 feet apart and throw non-spinning throws.
4. Use the **Mix 'n Match** format.

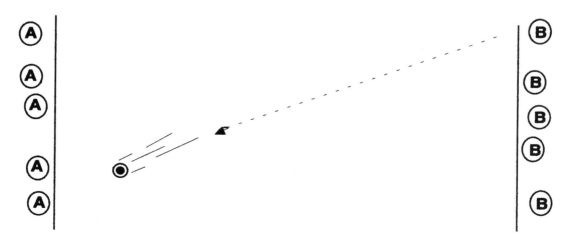

ULTIMATE

Objectives:

◆ To catch the disc inside the end zone.

◆ To throw the disc to a teammate in the end zone.

Essentials:

◆ Field

◆ Pinnies

◆ 1 disc for each game

The Throw-Off:

1. Only five to six players on a team.

2. Make the fields short and narrow. Divide a standard football field into four or five smaller fields.

3. A throw-off will occur after a goal is scored, with both teams switching ends.

4. Starts with six to eight players on their own goal line.

5. No player from team "A" may touch the disc while it is in the air before a player from "B" has.

6. Team "A" throws it to team "B":

   a. If "B" catches it, they may start immediately at that point.

   b. If "B" attempts to catch the disc but drops it, "A" takes it at that point.

   c. If "B" lets it hit the field, they take it at that spot.

   d. If the disc goes out of bounds, "B" can choose to take it at that spot or have "A" throw it again.

   e. If the throw goes into the end zone, "B" takes it on the goal line.

How to Play Offense:

1. Must attempt to throw and **catch** the disc. If the disc is not caught by the offense for whatever reason, the defense takes possession where it first lands.

2. May toss the disc in any manner.

3. The disc may not be handed from one player to another.

4. Players may not take steps once they are in possession. However, momentum must be taken into consideration when a player catches the disc and takes a step or two while trying to stop.

5. A player with possession may use one foot as a pivot.

6. If the disc is dropped, thrown out of bounds, or not caught, the defensive team takes possession at that point.

7. The thrower may not push the defensive person out of the way.

8. The thrower may not catch the disc again after it has been released.

9. The thrower has only 10 to 15 seconds of possession time. If the disc is held longer, the defense gets possession.

10. A point is scored if the disc is caught while both feet are in the end zone.

How to Play Defense:

1. Only one person may guard the player who has possession of the disc.

2. The disc may not be forcefully taken or knocked away from the offense.

3. Play the disc, not the player with the disc.

4. The defense make the calls and is always right.

5. Can count out loud to let the offensive person know the time of possession.

6. If the defense deflects the disc to the ground, they still gain possession.

Student Tasks:

1. Throw a number of completed passes.

2. Deflect a throw.

3. Directly prevent a score.

4. Throw for a score (assist).

Variations:

1. If the disc is dropped or touched by the defense while trying to catch it, the offense maintains possession. If this occurs in the offensive end zone, then the offense takes possession on the one yard line.

2. Use the **Mix 'n Match** format.

3. Make the end zone width smaller.

4. Form four teams, join two different teams each new game, and play a three-game round robin.

5. Do not allow anyone to be within 10 feet of the disc when playing defense.

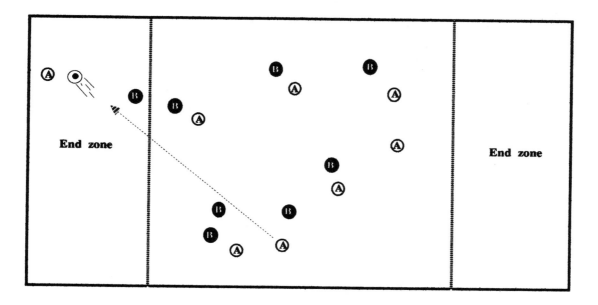

ABOUT "GROUP STUNTS"

Objectives:

- ◆ To work as a team and successfully complete the group stunts.
- ◆ To create new group stunts.
- ◆ To be a spotter.

Essentials:

- ◆ Large room with mats on the floor
- ◆ Group stunt sheets

How to Play:

1. Allow the students to choose their partners.
2. Add an extra person to each group when spotting is necessary.
3. Start with the easy skills and advance to the more difficult ones.
4. Students should rotate positions when possible.
5. Students have a lot of fun when the teacher points to a skill and all groups attempt that skill at the same time. After the two-person stunt sheet has been completed, move to the three-person stunt sheet, and so on.
6. Depending on the time, two different sheets of stunts will take most of the period.

Student Tasks:

1. Complete all stunts.
2. Create a stunt that other groups may find fun and challenging.

Variations:

1. Allow the students to create stunts that are new and challenging.
2. Record and display those created that fit the above descriptions.

Safety:

1. Always put weight over the arms or legs of the support people. Never stand or sit in the middle of their back. (See Illustration below.)

2. The base (lowest people) is **always** the last to disassemble from a group.
3. The lightest people should be near or at the top.
4. Spotters must be used when stunts are risky or people are off the floor.
5. Spotters should hold and support students who are above the floor.

STUNTS FOR TWO

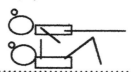

Top person is on back

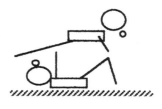

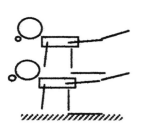

Top person is on back

Top person is on back

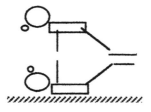

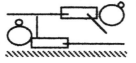

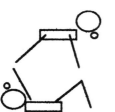

Top person is on back

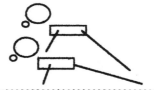

Both on back

Top person is on back

Both on back

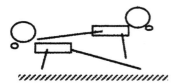

Both on back

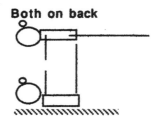

GROUP STUNTS

STUNTS FOR THREE

STUNTS FOR FOUR

STUNTS FOR FIVE

STUNTS FOR SIX

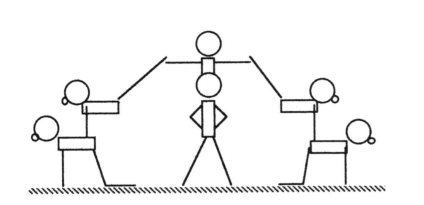

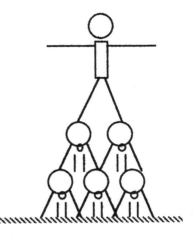

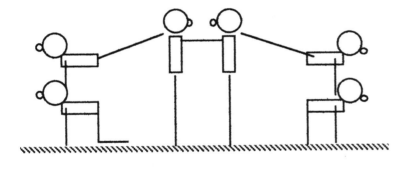

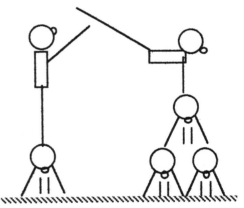

Can you develop various group stunts for 7 - 8 - 9 - 10?

?

ABOUT "GUESS-T-MATE MILE"

Objective:

- ◆ To run, walk, or jog the mile as close to a predicted time as possible.

Essentials:

- ◆ Field or track
- ◆ Stopwatch
- ◆ Recording forms
- ◆ Pencils

How to Play:

1. Each student is instructed to run, jog, walk, or use any combination of the three for a distance of one-quarter mile.
2. Student should try to maintain an even pace, if possible.
3. Upon completion of the quarter mile, she/he uses the prediction chart provided and determines a one-mile time.
4. Record that prediction time on the roster.
5. The next day or so, she/he runs, jogs, or walks a mile and tries to come as close as possible to her/his prediction.
6. A final time that is +6 seconds over the prediction ties with a final time that is –6 seconds under.
7. Watches or timing devices are not to be worn by the participants.
8. As the finishers cross the line, all scores should be announced quietly as to not give an advantage to the remaining participants who are still competing.

Student Tasks:

1. Set a pace the entire distance.
2. Improve your time or prediction on a later run.

Variations:

1. Make teams and have a total plus or minus time.
2. Predict a half mile.
3. Have the students cover the mile with a partner.
4. Do a relay and predict the time.
5. Students **must** jog the curves of the track, but may choose what to do on the straights.

GUESS-T-MATE MILE FORMULAS

One Lap	Mile	One Lap	Mile	One Lap	Mile
1:02	4:08	2:32	10:08	4:02	16:08
1:04	4:16	2:34	10:16	4:04	16:16
1:06	4:24	2:36	10:24	4:06	16:24
1:08	4:32	2:38	10:32	4:08	16:32
1:10	4:40	2:40	10:40	4:10	16:40
1:12	4:48	2:42	10:48	4:12	16:48
1:14	4:56	2:44	10:56	4:14	16:56
1:16	5:04	2:46	11:04	4:16	17:04
1:18	5:12	2:48	11:12	4:18	17:12
1:20	5:20	2:50	11:20	4:20	17:20
1:22	5:28	2:52	11:28	4:22	17:28
1:24	5:36	2:54	11:36	4:24	17:36
1:26	5:44	2:56	11:44	4:26	17:44
1:28	5:52	2:58	11:52	4:28	17:52
1:30	6:00	3:00	12:00	4:30	18:00
1:32	6:08	3:02	12:08	4:32	18:08
1:34	6:16	3:04	12:16	4:34	18:16
1:36	6:24	3:06	12:24	4:36	18:24
1:38	6:32	3:08	12:32	4:38	18:32
1:40	6:40	3:10	12:40	4:40	18:40
1:42	6:48	3:12	12:48	4:42	18:48
1:44	6:56	3:14	12:56	4:44	18:56
1:46	7:04	3:16	13:04	4:46	19:04
1:48	7:12	3:18	13:12	4:48	19:12
1:50	7:20	3:20	13:20	4:50	19:20
1:52	7:28	3:22	13:28	4:52	19:28
1:54	7:36	3:24	13:36	4:54	19:36
1:56	7:44	3:26	13:44	4:56	19:44
1:58	7:52	3:28	13:52	4:58	19:52
2:00	8:00	3:30	14:00	5:00	20:00
2:02	8:08	3:32	14:08	5:02	20:08
2:04	8:16	3:34	14:16	5:04	20:16
2:06	8:24	3:36	14:24	5:06	20:24
2:08	8:32	3:38	14:32	5:08	20:32
2:10	8:40	3:40	14:40	5:10	20:40
2:12	8:48	3:42	14:48	5:12	20:48
2:14	8:56	3:44	14:56	5:14	20:56
2:16	9:04	3:46	15:04	5:16	21:04
2:18	9:12	3:48	15:12	5:18	21:12
2:20	9:20	3:50	15:20	5:20	21:20
2:22	9:28	3:52	15:28	5:22	21:28
2:24	9:36	3:54	15:36	5:24	21:36
2:26	9:44	3:56	15:44	5:26	21:44
2:28	9:52	3:58	15:52	5:28	21:52
2:30	10:00	4:00	16:00	5:30	22:00

SAMPLE GUESS-T-MATE MILE SCORECARD

Period: 2
Date: May 14

	Name	1 Lap Time	Prediction	Actual Time	Plus or Minus
1	Abel, Shirley	1:30	6:15	6:05	-10
2	Brown, Jerry	2:00	8:00	8:30	30

Directions:

1. Fill in the *period* and *date* spaces.

2. Have the students fill in their *names*.

3. After a student finishes one lap, fill in this data in the *1 Lap Time* box.

4. Using the Formula Sheet, have the students write in their predicted time in the *Prediction* box. (In the example above, Shirley put down four times her one lap time **plus** some extra time for possibly being tired.)

5. After a few days, run the mile and have the students put down their time in the *Actual Time* box.

6. Next, add or subtract the predicted time from the actual time and put this data in the *Plus or Minus* box.

7. Closest runners to their predictions, be they under or over, are the winners.

GUESS-T-MATE MILE SCORECARD

Period: _____
Date:_____

No.	Name	1 Lap Time	Prediction	Actual Time	Plus or Minus
1					
2					
3					
4					
5					
6					
7					
8					
9					
10					
11					
12					
13					
14					
15					
16					
17					
18					
19					
20					
21					
22					
23					
24					
25					
26					
27					
28					
29					
30					
31					
32					
33					
34					
35					
36					
37					
38					
39					
40					

FLOOR HOCKEY

Objective:

◆ To hit the puck into the goal net of the opponent.

Essentials:

◆ Full court
◆ 2 half courts
◆ Sticks, pucks, scoreboard
◆ Protective gear (see "Safety")

How to Play:

1. Only five to six players on a team.
2. Goalie:
   a. Must stand while protecting the goal box.
   b. Should wear protective face and chest gear.
   c. Can use only feet and stick to stop or deflect the puck.
   d. Cannot score a goal from his/her own goal box.
3. Players:
   a. May not bring the stick **above the knees** at anytime. This is called high sticks.
   b. Must maintain a spread hand grip on the stick at all times.
   c. There may be only one person from each team at the puck during play.
   d. No hitting or swinging at the puck while it is in the air.
   e. No scoring from beyond the half court line. (This is called icing.)
   f. Defense makes the calls if there are no referees.
   g. Start game with a center bully. (The sticks are tapped three times and then the puck is hit.)
   h. Start play with the puck at center court when a team has scored.
   i. A player may only score two goals in a row.
   j. Players may not intentionally use their feet to control, trap, or stop the puck.
   k. When a puck is stuck in the net, the goalie gets possession.

Student Tasks:

1. Be a goalie.
2. Assist in a score.
3. Do not allow the other team to score.
4. During a series of four or five games for the day, have each member of the team score a goal.

Variations:

1. Use full court with two or more pucks. (Can turn the nets around at the free throw line so that they are facing the wall.)

2. Move the goals out and away from the wall as in ice hockey.

3. Make two half-court games with nets on the side lines of a basketball floor.

4. Remove the nets and use the entire wall as the goal. Utilize several goalies.

5. Have four goals, four teams, and have them all play at once. Use two or more pucks. Each team defends its own net.

6. Use the **Mix 'n Match** eleven-team format and play a tournament with two different games being played at once. One different team sits out each new game.

Safety:

1. Protective face masks should be provided.

2. A chest pad should be worn. (Baseball chest protectors work well.)

3. Shin guards should be worn.

4. Do not allow the goalie to drop to his/her knees.

5. Soft rubber pucks are recommended.

6. **Never** allow players to bring the blade higher than the knees at anytime.

7. Players must keep **both** hands on the stick at all times.

Floor Diagram of Two Games Being Played Simultaneously
A net about 2' tall is strung across floor

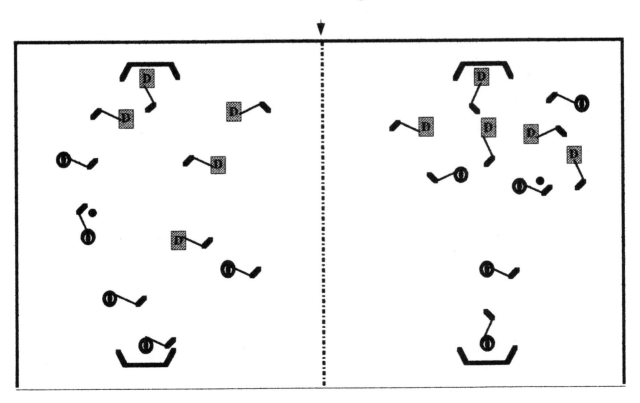

KNEE HOCKEY

Objective:

◆ To hit any one of three different balls into the goal box of the opponent.

Essentials:

◆ Full court
◆ Scoreboard
◆ Small hand-held hockey sticks
◆ 3 softball-sized Gator Skins® balls (either have them differently colored or put a different number on each one)

How to Play:

1. Up to fifteen members on a team with each player having a stick.
2. Using tape, mark a four by eight rectangular-shaped goal on each end wall.
3. The balls will be hit only with the hand-held hockey sticks.
4. The sticks may not be swung above the waist.
5. The balls may not be hit while in the air.
6. The balls are given a different point value of One, Three, and Five. If and when the *three* ball is hit against the wall inside of the goalie box, *three* points are awarded to the team that hit it in.
7. Whenever there is a score, all play is stopped, the balls are collected, and put into play at center court by the team that was scored upon.
8. The game is over when a team has reached a predetermined number of points or time has expired.
9. Goalie may not:
   a. Leave the goalie box to obtain a ball.
   b. Score by hitting the ball at the other goal.
   c. Pass the ball over the half-court line when starting play.
10. Defense:
   a. Must travel around on knees, crab walk, or bear crawl.
   b. Cannot interfere with players who do not have possession of a ball.
   c. Cannot touch a person with the ball but can play defense-like basketball.
   d. Will not interfere with or take a ball away from the goalie.
11. Offense:
   a. Must travel around on knees, crab walk, or bear crawl.
   b. Can advance the ball once they have control.
   c. No holding the arm straight out (stiff arming) to ward off the defense.
   d. A competitor may only score two goals in a row.

© 1996 Parker Publishing Company

HOCKEY

Student Tasks:

1. Be a goalie.
2. Cause a shut out.
3. Assist in a score.
4. Block a shot attempt.

Variations:

1. Use two goalies.
2. Put a different point value on each ball.
3. Make four goals and four teams.

Floor Diagram of Two Teams

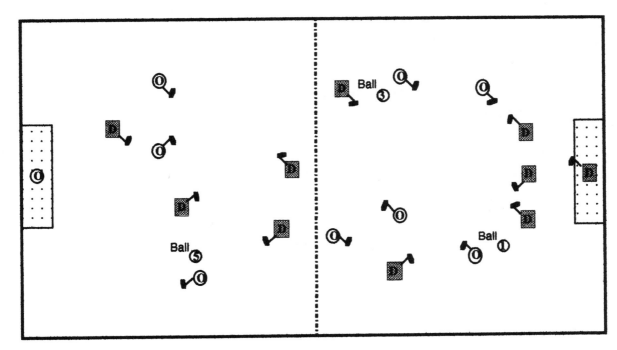

HOOP HORSESHOES*

Objectives:

- ◆ To be the first player or team to score 21 points.
- ◆ To throw the hoop closer than the opponent to the stake.
- ◆ To throw the hoop around the stake *(ringer)*.

Essentials:

- ◆ Gymnasium/smooth floor
- ◆ 4 hula hoops and 2 floor cones make up each pit; cones are placed 30' apart, the width of a volleyball court)

Scoring:

1. Ringer is worth three points.
2. If a hoop is on the cone base or leaning against the cone, this is worth two points.
3. If a hoop is within the width of a hoop from the cone, this is worth one point.

How to Play:

1. One player from each team is at each end. Stand and start even with the cone. One step is allowed.
2. A player tosses his/her first hoop and then the second hoop.
3. Only one team is able to score after all the hoops have been tossed.
4. When tossing a hoop, it must:
   a. Leave the hand in a vertical position. (*Note:* It is important to put a slight back spin on the hoop as it leaves the hand. This aids in control and accuracy and causes the hoop to stop and flop over when it reaches the far cone.)
   b. Remain on the floor as in bowling. (No lofting.)
   c. Be left alone until all hoops have been thrown and scored.
5. Only the closest hoop(s) for a team will score.
6. The closest hoop from Team "A" cancels out all of Team "B" hoops.
7. Ties by opposite hoops cancel out each other, i.e., two ringers, two leaners, or two from the same distance away.
8. A team that scores throws first the next inning.
9. If neither team scores *(Open pit)*, then the team that just threw last gets to start the next inning.

---

* *Created by Ken Lumsden, 1994.*

10. Terms:

    a. Hotel—Two ringers by one person.

    b. Open pit—No score by a team.

    c. Ringer—Any toss that lands around the cone.

11. Game is over when any team reaches 21 points.

Student Tasks:

1. Have both shoes score.

2. Get a ringer.

3. Cancel a ringer that was thrown by the other player.

4. Throw two ringers in a row *(Hotel)*.

Variations:

1. Play a doubles tournament.

2. Play a **Top Gun** tournament. (Winner moves to the next court while the loser stays and takes on a new challenger.)

3. Play a mixed doubles, double elimination tournament.

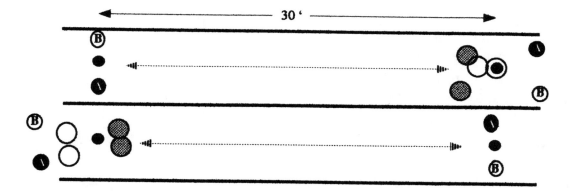

IRON HORSESHOES

Objectives:

- ◆ To be the first player or team to score 21 points.
- ◆ To throw the shoe closer than the opponent to the stake.
- ◆ To throw the shoe around the stake *(ringer)*.

Essentials:

- ◆ Field
- ◆ 6 to 8 courts (40 feet from stake to stake for boys; 30 feet for girls)
- ◆ 4 shoes and 2 stakes for each court
- ◆ The stake should be 12 inches above the ground and lean three inches toward the opposite stake

How to Play:

1. The first contestant pitches both shoes, then the opponent pitches two shoes. This is called an inning.
2. Point winner of each inning pitches first in the following inning. In case of a tie, the player who pitched last in that inning pitches first in the following inning.
3. The pitcher must remain behind the foul line (front edge of the box) until the shoe leaves the hand.
4. No heckling the person who is pitching.
5. No player touches any shoe until the winner and the points of that inning have been agreed upon.
6. No player may go to the other stake or be informed of the position of shoes prior to the end of the inning.
7. Players who are not pitching must remain behind and opposite the thrower.
8. Scoring:
   a. First team to get 21 points wins.
   b. Only one player scores each inning.
   c. A *Ringer* is when a shoe encircles the stake far enough so that both heel calks can be touched with a straight edge, and permit a clearance of the stake.
   d. Closest shoe to the stake scores one point as long as it is within six inches.
   e. Two shoes closer than the opponent's shoes count for two points.
   f. One ringer counts three points; two ringers count six points. (This is called a *Hotel.*)
   g. One ringer and closest shoe of the same player score four points.
   h. If each player has a ringer, the next closest shoe—if within six inches of the stake—scores one.

i. A leaning shoe has no value over one that is touching the stake.

j. All equals count as ties and no points are awarded.

Student Tasks:

1. Have both shoes score.
2. Get a ringer.
3. Cancel a ringer that was thrown by the other player.
4. Throw two ringers in a row *(Hotel)*.

Variations:

1. Play a doubles or mixed doubles tournament.
2. Play a **Top Gun** tournament. (Winner moves to the next court while the loser stays and takes on a new challenger.)
3. Play a double elimination tournament.

Diagram of Horseshoe Pit

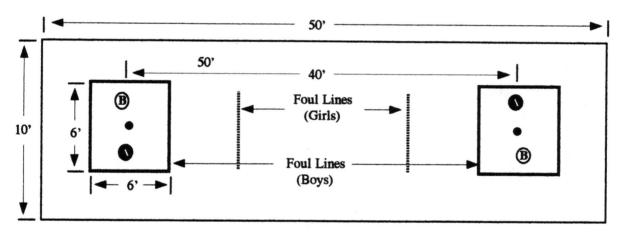

REPETITION JUGGLING

Objective:

◆ To develop hand and eye coordination.

Essentials:

◆ Any large room or area
◆ Beanbags, rings, scarves, clubs, odds and ends

How to Play:

1. See how many times the various objects can be juggled.
2. Tips:
   a. Keep the elbows in at the hips.
   b. Eyes look forward.
   c. Hands make small "U"-shaped movements when throwing and catching.
   d. Concentrate.
3. Copy and post the *Skill Advancement Chart.*

Student Tasks:

1. Juggle three objects without missing:
   a. 10 times.
   b. 25 times.
   c. 50 times.
   d. 100 or more.
2. Teach a friend, family member, or neighbor how to juggle three objects.
3. Move through the progression skill chart.

Variations:

1. Develop a routine.
2. Demonstrate a routine to the class.

SKILL ADVANCEMENT

STEP ONE: TWO BAGS ONLY

1. Clockwise circle with R/L hand.
2. Counterclockwise circle with R/L hand.
3. R/L alternating up and down.
4. Figure eight.
5. Walk as you juggle.
6. Run as you juggle.
7. Can you create something else?

STEP TWO: THREE BAGS ONLY

1. Figure eight.
2. Reverse figure eight.
3. Figure eight off floor.
4. Two in one hand and one in the other.
5. Figure eight off the wall.
6. Can you create something else?

STEP THREE: OTHER ITEMS AND TRICKS

1. Clubs?
2. Rings?
3. Chinese Sticks?
4. Mixing various objects (soccer ball, baseball, golf ball).
5. Fancy starts like beginning with a toss under the leg.
6. Rebounds of different parts (wrist, knee, etc.).
7. Cascade alternating under one leg.
8. Cascade alternating behind the back.
9. Three-bag cascade while in a lying position.
10. Fancy finishing like catching the last object behind the back.
11. Can you create something else?

STEP FOUR: PASSING OBJECTS

1. Pass three bags while standing shoulder to shoulder with a partner.
2. Pass six bags while facing a partner.
3. Pass clubs.
4. Pass rings.

AMERICA'S CUP

Objective:

◆ Try not to be sent to the BRIG.

Essentials: Large area

How to Play:

1. Explain that the students are members of a crew and that the instructor is the "Captain" of the sailing vessel.

2. The crew must always listen to and obey the orders of the "Captain."

3. Rapidly cover all the commands or pass out several sheets and give the crew only a short time to memorize them.

4. Crew members will immediately report to the BRIG if they:

   a. Do not follow or obey an order.

   b. Are one of the last two members to perform a task or get to a place.

   c. Have the wrong amount of players in a group.

5. BRIG: (A designated area where the students will go that is away from the main action.)

   a. Allow only five to eight people in the BRIG at one time.

   b. Until there are the set maximum number of people in the BRIG, no one may leave.

6. Spread the students on the floor.

7. All students must walk around on the deck.

8. No standing around with a partner or in groups.

Student Tasks:

1. Never get sent to the BRIG.

2. Be one of the last five crew members who go to the BRIG.

3. Be in the top 20% that went to the BRIG the fewest times.

Variations:

1. While in the BRIG, students may have to do hard labor (a physical activity such as ten push-ups).

2. When the crew is at **roll call** or **inspection,** play "Captain Says." (Same game as "Simon Says.") If a crew member does something without the instructor first saying "Captain Says," then that crew member goes to the BRIG.

Safety:

1. Students should try to slow down when running to a wall to touch it.

2. This game can cause rapid fatigue if rest-type commands are not used frequently.

"AMERICA'S CUP" ORDERS

> **Bold Text = Name of the order**
> (Parenthesis) = Number of crew members needed
> Plain Text = Description of the order

Port, Starboard, Bow, Stern = (All) — Students run to the corresponding wall and carefully touch it. Last two to get there go to the BRIG.

North, East, South, West = (All) — Students run to that wall and touch it.

Chow time = (3) — Sitting and holding hands to form a table.

Person overboard = (2) — One on hands and knees to form the freeboard, other with their foot on freeboard and scanning the horizon with hand held over the brow.

Abandon ship = (2) — Sit facing each other, hold hands, and row back and forth.

Sharks = (4) — Sit with backs touching, holding hands and arms straight out and splashing the water.

Keel hauling = (3) — One lies down on her/his *back*, the other two grab that person's hands and feet, lift and swing her/him gently about four inches off the floor.

Hit the deck = (All) — Drop and put the belly to the floor while covering the head with the hands.

Clear the deck = (All) — Run to any wall.

Roll call = (All) — Rows of five students. Must be *motionless* while standing at parade rest and looking directly at the back of the head of the sailor in front.

Inspection = (All) — One line, shoulder to shoulder, salute with right arm and remain *motionless* while looking straight ahead.

Up the mast = (2) — Touch the hands over the heads and *alternate* jumps so that both people do not touch the floor at the same time.

Swab the deck = (2) — One in push-up position, other holds partner's feet and gently swings the legs back and forth.

Drop anchor = (3) — Touch backs, *do not* lock arms, squat slightly, and slowly rotate like a capstan.

Mend the sail = (4) — Line up and the last person *zig-zags* through the rest until they get to the front, then the last person begins the weave, and so on.

Iceberg = (All) — Must remain *motionless* no matter what position she/he is in.

Crabs on deck = (3) — Back to back, bend over, reach back between your legs, grab the hands of the other two sailors, and then begin walking around.

Fish net = (All) — Lie down and touch hands to hands, feet to feet, or hands to feet of all the other sailors.

"Captain Says" = (All) — Played just like "Simon Says" when students are in *roll call* or at *inspection*.

FORT KNOX

Objective:

◆ To collect all the gold from the other team.

Essentials:

◆ Field

◆ 20 "Gold Bars" (Frisbees™, towels, football flags, etc.)

◆ Fort Knox boundaries such as cones, chalk, or ropes

◆ Pinnies

How to Play:

1. Divide the class into two equal teams.

2. Safe areas:

   a. A team's own side of the field.

   b. The other team's Fort Knox.

   c. There is no time limit once in a safe zone.

   d. Only one foot needs to be over the line to be safe.

3. Offense:

   a. Try to invade the other team's Fort Knox and capture a bar of gold. A player may only possess one bar at a time. Player returns to their own field and puts the seized gold into his/her own Fort Knox.

   b. Try not to be tagged by the defense. If an offensive player is tagged, she/he must immediately freeze and squat down. She/he may be unfrozen when another player from her/his team leapfrogs over her/him.

   c. If tagged while in possession of a bar of gold, player is frozen and must give up the gold.

4. Defense:

   a. Any defender of Fort Knox must be ten feet away from its boundary.

   b. After tagging any player in possession of a bar of gold, she/he collects the gold and returns it to her/his Fort Knox.

Student Tasks:

1. Retrieve two or more gold bars.

2. Tag a person who is in possession of gold.

3. Defrost a frozen runner.

Variations:

1. Tagged runners must stand, straddle legs. To be unfrozen, she/he must have another player crawl under his/her legs.

2. Form four teams and combine two different teams each game. Play three games in a round-robin match.

3. Make four teams and have four Fort Knox areas. Play for a set time. The winner is the team with the most gold bars.

4. Use the **Mix 'n Match** format.

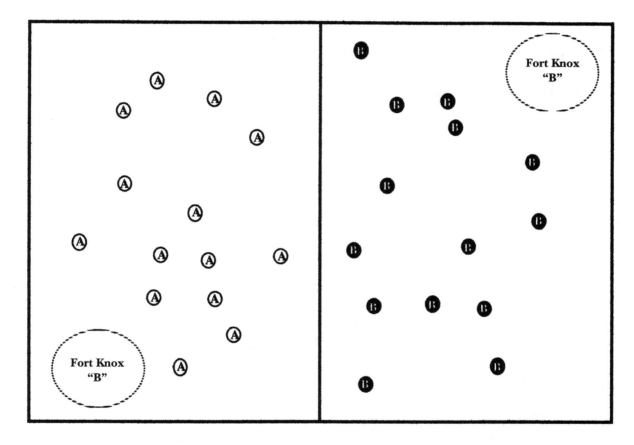

LIVING FOOSBALL*

Objectives:

- ◆ To score more points than the opponents by kicking a ball into the goal.
- ◆ To play in a cooperative manner to achieve success.

Essentials:

- ◆ Gymnasium or large room
- ◆ Indoor soccer or kick ball
- ◆ 6 lengths of heavy duty 3/4″ PVC pipe (these will need to be made from 10-foot sections that screw together)
  - a. Four lengths should be 1/5 shorter than the width of the playing area.
  - b. Two lengths should be 1/3 shorter than the width of the playing area.
- ◆ Pinnies
- ◆ 12 cones

Set Up:

1. Purchase the PVC.
2. Glue a threaded male and female end on each piece. These pieces can then be threaded together to make the desired length needed, yet easily taken apart for storage.
3. Place tape or markings on the lengths of PVC at five-foot intervals so each player knows where to grab and maintain her/his position.
4. Place cones on each side of the court to establish the lanes.

How to Play:

1. Start play by rolling the ball in from the side.
2. If a ball becomes stalled, the instructor or aide will nudge it to get it rolling.
3. Participants must keep at least one hand on the PVC pipe at all times.
4. A player may let go with one hand and pivot around so that she/he may face in the opposite direction. (The pipe is now against her/his back.)
5. Players may only move from left to right and must stay even with the cones that mark the lanes.
6. The ball:
   - a. May not be intentionally kicked into the air. It should stay low and in contact with the floor as much as possible.
   - b. Can only be kicked or touched with the feet.

---

* Guidelines created by Ken Lumsden, 1994.

7. The goalie may only use the feet and legs to deflect a shot.

8. When a ball stops rolling and is between two lanes, the nearest player from each lane have a face-off.

9. Rotate players to a new position after a score or after a set time.

10. To start a new play after a score, roll the ball in from the side, at center court, towards the middle of the playing area.

Student Tasks:

1. Make an assist.

2. Be a goalie.

3. Pass down the line.

4. Complete a set number of successful passes.

Variations:

1. Use two balls.

2. Have partners next to each other but facing the opposite direction.

3. Allow each team to have one or two rovers on each half. The rovers can move about freely.

4. Allow players to move along the PVC pipe freely as long as the pipe does not touch the floor.

5. Add team members along the side of the playing area. They are not allowed to come onto the floor, but can move up and down the side, keeping the ball in play.

6. Use the **Mix 'n Match** format.

Floor Diagram Showing Optional Use of Players Along the Sides

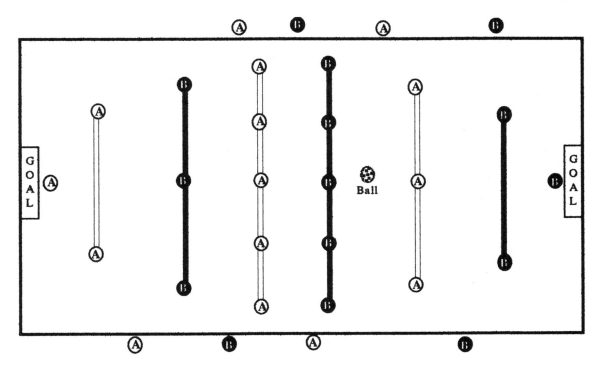

MOVING TARGET

Objectives:

- ◆ To move the target ball over a designated line.
- ◆ To be the team with the fewer points scored against it.

Essentials:

- ◆ Large playing area or gym floor
- ◆ 12 to 16 Nerf™, Gator Skin®, or playground balls for throwing
- ◆ Any different type of ball to use for a target (a soccer or basketball work quite well)

How to Play:

1. Divide into two equal teams.
2. The balls must be **thrown** at the target ball. Players may not hit the target ball by hanging on to a throwing ball.
3. Students may move anywhere along the sideline but may not step over it to throw a ball.
4. Players may not step over the line to retrieve a ball that is not moving and is stationary on the floor of play.
5. The instructor may yell "Clean Sweep," which means that any player may enter the field of play to gather up motionless balls. Do not interfere with the target ball.
6. A point is scored against any team that allows the target ball to cross its goal line.
7. The game is over when any team accumulates five points. The team that has the **lower** points when this happens is the winner.

Student Tasks:

1. Stop a certain number of balls from crossing the line.
2. Hit the target ball that is beyond half way.
3. Be the one who drives the target ball over the sideline.

Variations:

1. Vary the size of the target ball.
2. Vary the type of the target ball.
3. Use more than one target ball.
4. For a smaller room, a balloon works great. Throw plastic practice golf balls at the balloons. (100 to 150 plastic balls work well.)

5. Form four teams and play **Four Way:**
    a. Cannot hold on to the ball and just tap the target ball.
    b. Rotate each team to the right after a point has been scored.
6. Play a tournament using the **Mix 'n Match** format.

Floor Diagram of Two Way

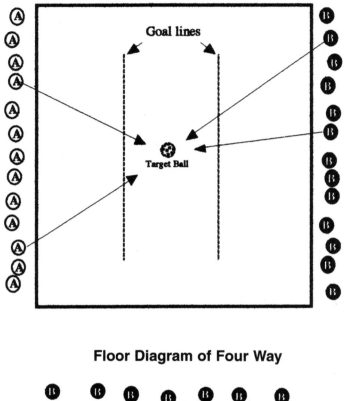

Floor Diagram of Four Way

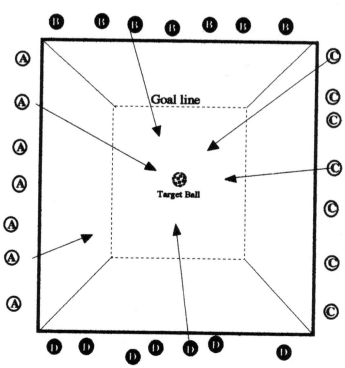

OCTOPUS

Objectives:
- ◆ To run from one end of the playing area to the other.
- ◆ To try to avoid getting tagged by the octopus.
- ◆ To try to avoid getting tagged by the tentacles.

Essentials:
- ◆ Large room or gymnasium
- ◆ Field

How to Play:
1. Select one person to be the octopus. The octopus tries to tag runners.
2. The rest of the class goes to one end of the floor. They try to run to the opposite end as soon as the octopus yells, "Octopus."
3. Any runner who gets tagged will:
   a. Sit down where she/he was tagged and become one of the tentacles. She/he may not move from this spot.
   b. Tentacles should try to reach out and touch runners who then must sit down and do likewise.
4. Runners may avoid being tagged in any manner.
5. The last one, two or three runners are declared winners and become the octopus for the next game.

Student Tasks:
1. Be one of the last five runners.
2. As a tentacle, tag a certain number of runners.
3. Be an octopus.

Variations:
1. Two or three octopus can be used for a larger area or to speed up the game.
2. Pair the runners.
3. Allow the tentacles to stand and pivot with one foot.

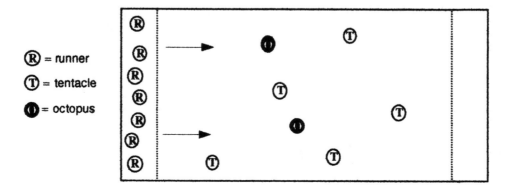

ⓇR = runner
ⓉT = tentacle
●= octopus

PALMBALL

Objective:

◆ To score a goal by hitting a ball against the wall.

Essentials:

◆ Gymnasium
◆ 1 volleyball
◆ Pinnies

How to Play:

1. Divide the class into two teams.

2. Have each of those teams divide again into an offensive (on the floor) and defensive (guard the wall) team.

3. Offensive and defensive teams switch after a set number of points or time.

4. **All** players must use an open flat hand when touching or hitting the ball. The ball may only make contact with the flat palm or back of the hand.

5. All players may dribble the ball as in basketball.

6. A ball that is rolling on the floor may be scooped up with the flat hand.

7. All players may air dribble the ball up as long as it goes above the head each time.

8. No player may kick, catch, throw, or fist the ball.

9. If a violation occurs, the other team acquires the ball at that spot.

10. Scoring:

    a. One point if the ball hits the wall below the extended arms of any defensive player.

    b. Two points if the ball hits an inner goal that has been marked.

11. Any defensive players on the court may block or palm at any offensive player with the ball as long as she/he does not make contact. (Think basketball here.)

12. The defensive players along the wall may not move away from the wall more than one step.

Student Tasks:

1. Block a shot.
2. Steal a ball.
3. Assist in a goal.
4. Cause a loss of possession by the other team.

Variations:

1. Use two balls.

2. Alter the size of the inner goals.

3. Have the students put socks or knee pads over the hands.

4. Form four different teams. Combine two different teams each new game.

5. Allow two points for a ball that is palmed into a basketball goal.

6. Goalies may use the hands and catch the ball.

7. Only the back of the hand is allowed to touch the ball.

8. Use the **Mix 'n Match** format.

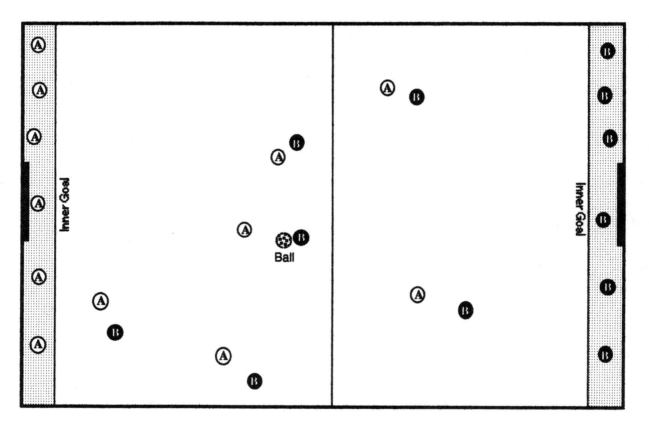

THIEVES

Objective:

◆ To be the first team to retrieve a certain number of beanbags. (This is usually five, six, or seven.)

Essentials:

◆ Field

◆ Gymnasium

◆ 5 hula hoops

◆ 13 to 16 small objects (beanbags work well)

How to Play:

1. Make four equal teams.

2. Put all of the beanbags in the center hoop.

3. On the command "GO," the first person in each line sprints to the middle, retrieves **one** beanbag, returns it to their own hula hoop, sets the bag down (no throwing), and goes to the end of the line.

4. The next in line may leave as soon as the bag has been set down.

5. Only one runner from each team is allowed to be the thief and on the field of play.

6. After the first thieves have taken a bag from the middle hoop, the next runners may go to **any** other team hoop, remove one bag, and return it to her/his own hoop.

7. When a team has collected a predetermined number, they are the winners.

Variations:

1. Decrease the number of bags.

2. Increase the distances to run.

3. Set a time limit and see which team has the most when time expires.

4. Create more teams.

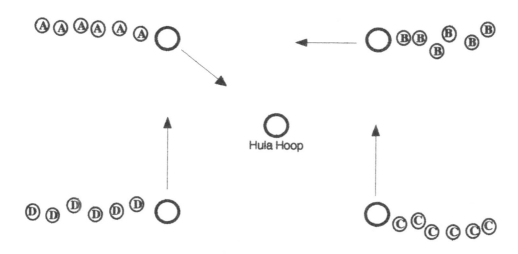

ABOUT "ORIENTEERING"

Objectives:

◆ To finish the course with the correct sum of the various numbers found.

◆ To be able to follow directions, solve riddles, and read a map.

Essentials:

◆ Field

◆ Maps

◆ Instruction sheets

◆ Compasses *(optional)*

◆ Pencils

For the Teacher: (Refer to samples.)

1. Set the course by finding about 15 to 20 different objects throughout the area. Number these objects.

2. Next make a little riddle about each one. This takes a while but is fun.

3. The **KEY** map is made for the instructor. A map without numbers is made for each group of students. Seven to nine maps are made and can be used over and over.

4. Make seven to nine different smaller courses from the master course. These should have about five different sites to find. Print and make copies of each course to hand out to the group.

5. If each individual course takes about 25 to 30 minutes to complete, a teacher will have enough courses to last each group several days.

6. If the courses are short, a group may do several each day.

How to Play:

1. Form groups of three to five students.

2. The group **must always stay together.**

3. Students point the map's arrow at a distant object (if no compasses are used) to determine the direction of travel, read the riddle, and run, jog, or walk to that area and find the station number.

4. They record the number at the first station, then locate their new bearing and move on to the second station.

5. The team's total from the five or six stations should equal that of the key.

6. Students are not allowed to touch or remove numbers at the various stations.

7. Depending on the length of the course, if a group finishes early, they may elect to do another course.

Variations:

1. Time the courses and have a record time that the groups are trying to beat.

2. Challenge a team by switching courses and attempting to beat their time.

ORIENTEERING

SAMPLE "A" COURSE

Period: ___3___

Names:

Mary Wilcott	Sally Small
Joe McDonald	Terry Jacobson
_____	_____

Instructions:

1. Divide into groups of five people and **stay together.**
2. Study the map and follow the indicated directions.
3. Read the riddle to locate the final destination tag and number.
4. Record the tag number once it is found.
5. Continue until finished.
6. Report to the instructor when all tags have been found to verify the score.

DIRECTION TO GO:		**NUMBER**
WNW	It used to stand tall and came from afar, Now it just lies here stopping a car.	7
N	Johnny said this is really neat. Stand here and find a treat to eat.	10
SSE	Sitting here the music sounds great, Also to wood shop you'd never be late.	3
NE	Who is ahead in the Game? If you're not, that's no shame.	15
WNW	People come from there and here, To see and yell and scream a cheer.	11
	Total	46

BONUS:	If you have time.	
SSE	Three hits maximum is the rule, Especially if you attend our school.	5
	Grand Total	51

COURSE FORM

Student Handout

Period: _____

Names:

_____   _____

_____   _____

_____   _____

Instructions:

1. Divide into groups of five people and **stay together.**
2. Study the map and follow the indicated directions.
3. Read the riddle to locate the final destination tag and number.
4. Record the tag number once it is found.
5. Continue until finished.
6. Report to the instructor when all tags have been found to verify the score.

DIRECTION TO GO: **NUMBER**

_____

_____

_____

_____

_____

                                                Total _____

BONUS: If you have time.

                                    Grand Total _____

ORIENTEERING

COURSE POINT TOTALS

(Instructor's Key)

A.		B.		C.		D.	
7		1		12		9	
10		6		8		13	
3		9		2		6	
15		13		14		1	
11		7		1		15	
46		36		37		44	TOTAL
5		4		3		7	BONUS
51		40		40		51	GRAND TOTAL

E.		F.		G.	
10		8		4	
15		12		11	
8		6		5	
4		9		8	
12		5		14	
49		40		42	TOTAL
2		11		3	BONUS
51		51		45	GRAND TOTAL

SAMPLE ORIENTEERING MAP

Instructor's Key
Note: *Student maps do not have numbers printed on them.*

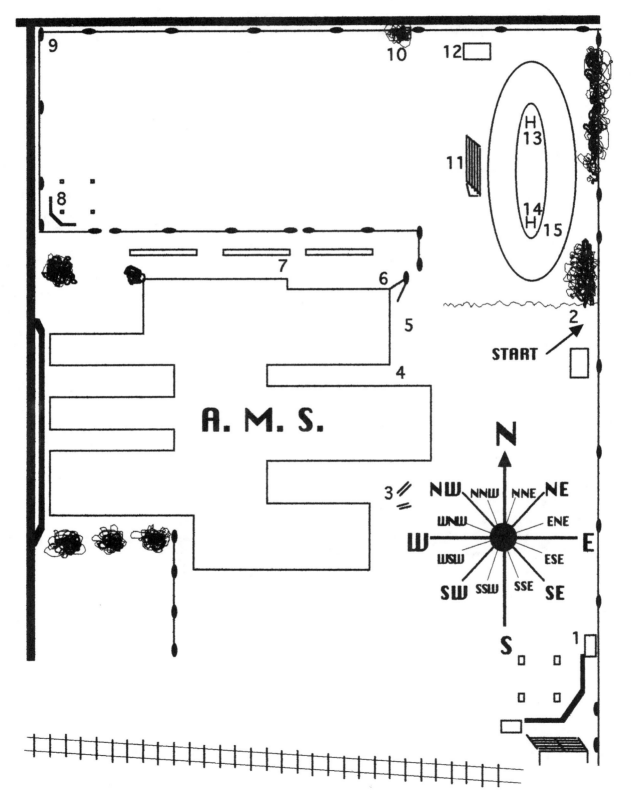

SAMPLE RIDDLE ANSWERS

** It used to stand tall and came from afar,
Now it just lies here stopping a car. **LOG IN PARKING LOT**

** Johnny said this is really neat.
Stand here and find a treat to eat. **APPLE TREE**

** Sitting here the music sounds great,
Also to wood shop you'd never be late. **BENCHES**

** Who is ahead in the Game?
If you're not, that's no shame. **SCORE BOARD**

** People come from there and here,
To see and yell and scream a cheer. **BLEACHERS**

** Three hits maximum is the rule,
Especially if you attend our school. **VOLLEYBALL COURTS**

** Your team is at bat so remain seated.
United you'll win, divided you'll be defeated. **DUGOUT**

** It receives your rubbish but don't be a fool,
Remember to recycle, that is a wiser rule. **RECYCLE BIN**

** This forms a 90-degree angle here,
STOP and look since you are very near. **STOP SIGN**

** One point or three, that would be good,
If kicked too far, it might hit a car's hood. **NORTH FOOTBALL GOAL**

** Games, games, games and more,
Here Michael Jordan would surely soar. **OUTDOOR HOOPS**

** Once in here you could not see,
Windows with glass were not meant to be. **TRACK SHED**

** This place is wide and tall,
Can't stop the wind, but sure can a ball. **BACK STOP**

** Ruffles have ridges and that's no goof,
This place also has a two toned roof. **PUMP SHED**

** I'm closest to the school and look like a letter,
But the numbers 1 and 3 represent me better. **SOUTH FOOTBALL GOAL**

ABOUT "PENTATHLON"

Objective:

◆ To obtain as high a score as possible by participating in five events and relating the times and distances to a set of point values.

Essentials:

◆ Track
◆ High jump equipment
◆ Shot put
◆ Discus
◆ Starting blocks
◆ Ten hurdles
◆ Measuring tapes
◆ Stop watches
◆ Rake
◆ Student score sheets
◆ Score conversion tables

How to Play:

1. Set up the track, demonstrate the various activities, cover the skills, and allow the students to practice. (This unit should last a week or two depending on the amount of time allotted for each period.)

2. Each participant must select **one** event from each pair below, and **both** events must be selected in one of the pairs. This gives her/him the five events to compete in.

| 400 meters
1500 meters | High jump
Long jump | Shot Put
Discus | 100 meter dash
70 meter hurdles |

3. Each participant fills in her/his own pentathlon scores.

4. Post the *Score Conversion Tables* so students may look up the points. **Note:** A blank set of *Score Conversion Tables* is provided. Grade levels can be adjusted from the school's best track and field records to equal 1000 points. Also, a different set can be posted that is created from the girls' best records.

5. After all of the events have been held, the participants tally the five scores and record them on the *Score Sheet*.

6. Post the top 20% of each event.

7. Post the top 20% total place finishers.

PENTATHLON

Student Tasks:

1. Finish in the top 20% in any event.
2. Finish in the top 20% of the class.
3. Improve in distance or height in three consecutive attempts.

Variations:

1. Allow a student to toss out her/his worst event score in the final tally.
2. Have students compete in more than five events.
3. Have students compete in less than five events.
4. Make teams and allow a tally of the total points gained by each member.
5. Substitute a softball throw instead of the discus.
6. Substitute sandbags in place of the shot put.
7. Substitute the standing long jump in place of the running long jump.
8. Add two more events and do the decathlon.
9. Change the length of the various running events.
10. Combine several classes and allow students to rotate freely at the events.

Example: After covering the skill and practicing, begin the events.

Competition 1

a. 70-Meter low hurdles	Teacher 1
b. Shot Put (Girls)	Teacher 2
c. Discus (Boys)	Teacher 3
d. Long Jump	Teacher 4
e. 400 M Run (last 15 min.)	Teacher 1

Competition 2

a. 100 Meters	Teacher 1
b. Shot Put (Boys)	Teacher 2
c. Discus (Girls)	Teacher 3
d. Long Jump	Teacher 4
e. 1500 Meters (last 15 min.)	Teacher 1

Competition 3

a. High Jump	Teacher 1
b. Make-ups	Teacher 2
c. Activity for those done	Teachers 3 and 4

Competition 4–5

a. Make-ups	Teachers 1 and 2
b. Activity for those done	Teachers 3 and 4

Safety:

1. Properly stretch before competing.
2. Be alert when throwing or returning the shot or discuss.

SAMPLE PENTATHLON SCORECARD

Period: 3

Date: April 22

Refer to *Score Conversion Tables* and put those points in the columns.

	Name	1500 M	400 M	100 M	70 M	L. Jump	H. Jump	Shot	Discus	Total
1	Abel, Shirley	600	700	745	880	750	860	300	540	5375
2	McGlothlin, Jim	280	400	370	235	370	400	720	680	3455
3										

Directions:

1. Fill in the *period, date,* and *name.*

2. Record the total points scored for each event using the *Score Conversion Tables.*

3. Add all the scores from each event and record that data in the *Total* column.

PENTATHLON SCORECARD

Period:
Date:

Refer to Score Conversion Tables and put those points in the columns.

	Name	1500 M	400 M	100 M	70 M	L. Jump	H. Jump	Shot	Discus	Total
1										
2										
3										
4										
5										
6										
7										
8										
9										
10										
11										
12										
13										
14										
15										
16										
17										
18										
19										
20										
21										
22										
23										
24										
25										
26										
27										
28										
29										
30										
31										
32										
33										
34										
35										
36										
37										
38										
39										
40										

SAMPLE PENTATHLON SCORE TABLES

Each Second = 3 pts.

1500 M		400 M		Shot Put		Discus		
Time	Pts.	Time	Pts.	Feet	Pts.	Feet	Yds.	Pts.
6:30	1000	55	1000	50	1000	153	51	1000
6:37	980	56	980	49	980	150	50	980
6:44	960	57	960	48	960	147	49	960
6:51	940	58	940	47	940	144	48	940
6:58	920	59	920	46	920	141	47	920
7:05	900	1:00	900	45	900	138	46	900
7:12	880	1:01	880	44	880	135	45	880
7:19	860	1:02	860	43	860	132	44	860
7:26	840	1:03	840	42	840	129	43	840
7:33	820	1:04	820	41	820	126	42	820
7:40	800	1:05	800	40	800	123	41	800
7:47	780	1:06	780	39	780	120	40	780
7:54	760	1:07	760	38	760	117	39	760
8:01	740	1:08	740	37	740	114	38	740
8:08	720	1:09	720	36	720	111	37	720
8:15	700	1:10	700	35	700	108	36	700
8:22	680	1:11	680	34	680	105	35	680
8:29	660	1:12	660	33	660	102	34	660
8:36	640	1:13	640	32	640	99	33	640
8:43	620	1:14	620	31	620	96	32	620
8:50	600	1:15	600	30	600	93	31	600
8:57	580	1:16	580	29	580	90	30	580
9:04	560	1:17	560	28	560	87	29	560
9:11	540	1:18	540	27	540	84	28	540
9:18	520	1:19	520	26	520	81	27	520
9:25	500	1:20	500	25	500	78	26	500
9:32	480	1:21	480	24	480	75	25	480
9:39	460	1:22	460	23	460	72	24	460
9:46	440	1:23	440	22	440	69	23	440
9:53	420	1:24	420	21	420	66	22	420
10:00	400	1:25	400	20	400	63	21	400
10:07	380	1:26	380	19	380	60	20	380
10:14	360	1:27	360	18	360	57	19	360
10:21	340	1:28	340	17	340	54	18	340
10:28	320	1:29	320	16	320	51	17	320
10:35	300	1:30	300	15	300	48	16	300
10:42	280	1:31	280	14	280	45	15	280
10:49	260	1:32	260	13	260	42	14	260
10:56	240	1:33	240	12	240	39	13	240
11:03	220	1:34	220	11	220	36	12	220
11:10	200	1:35	200	10	200	33	11	200
11:17	180	1:36	180	9	180	30	10	180
11:24	160	1:37	160	8	160	27	9	160
11:31	140	1:38	140	7	140	24	8	140
11:38	120	1:39	120	6	120	21	7	120
11:45	100	1:40	100	5	100	18	6	100
11:52	80	1:41	80	4	80	15	5	80
11:59	60	1:42	60	3	60	12	4	60
12:06	40	1:43	40	2	40	9	3	40
12:13	20	1:44	20	1	20	6	2	20
12:20	0	1:45	0	0	0	3	1	0

SAMPLE PENTATHLON SCORE TABLES

100 M Dash

Time	Pts.	Time	Pts.
11.5	1000	16.6	235
11.6	985	16.7	220
11.7	970	16.8	205
11.8	955	16.9	190
11.9	940	17	175
12	925	17.1	160
12.1	910	17.2	145
12.2	895	17.3	130
12.3	880	17.4	115
12.4	865	17.5	100
12.5	850	17.6	85
12.6	835	17.7	70
12.7	820	17.8	55
12.8	805	17.9	40
12.9	790	18	25
13	775	18.1	10
13.1	760		
13.2	745		
13.3	730		
13.4	715		
13.5	700		
13.6	685		
13.7	670		
13.8	655		
13.9	640		
14	625		
14.1	610		
14.2	595		
14.3	580		
14.4	565		
14.5	550		
14.6	535		
14.7	520		
14.8	505		
14.9	490		
15	475		
15.1	460		
15.2	445		
15.3	430		
15.4	415		
15.5	400		
15.6	385		
15.7	370		
15.8	355		
15.9	340		
16	325		
16.1	310		
16.2	295		
16.3	280		
16.4	265		
16.5	250		

70 M Hurdles

Time	Pts.	Time	Pts.
9	1000	14.1	235
9.1	985	14.2	220
9.2	970	14.3	205
9.3	955	14.4	190
9.4	940	14.5	175
9.5	925	14.6	160
9.6	910	14.7	145
9.7	895	14.8	130
9.8	880	14.9	115
9.9	865	15	100
10	850	15.1	85
10.1	835	15.2	70
10.2	820	15.3	55
10.3	805	15.4	40
10.4	790	15.5	25
10.5	775	15.6	10
10.6	760		
10.7	745		
10.8	730		
10.9	715		
11	700		
11.1	685		
11.2	670		
11.3	655		
11.4	640		
11.5	625		
11.6	610		
11.7	595		
11.8	580		
11.9	565		
12	550		
12.1	535		
12.2	520		
12.3	505		
12.4	490		
12.5	475		
12.6	460		
12.7	445		
12.8	430		
12.9	415		
13	400		
13.1	385		
13.2	370		
13.3	355		
13.4	340		
13.5	325		
13.6	310		
13.7	295		
13.8	280		
13.9	265		
14	250		

SAMPLE PENTATHLON SCORE TABLES

High Jump

Ht.	Pts.
6-2	1000
6-1	980
6-0	960
5-11	940
5-10	920
5-9	900
5-8	880
5-7	860
5-6	840
5-5	820
5-4	800
5-3	780
5-2	760
5-1	740
5-0	720
4-11	700
4-10	680
4-9	660
4-8	640
4-7	620
4-6	600
4-5	580
4-4	560
4-3	540
4-2	520
4-1	500
4-0	480
3-11	460
3-10	440
3-9	420
3-8	400
3-7	380
3-6	360
3-5	340
3-4	320
3-3	300
3-2	280
3-1	260
3-0	240
2-11	220
2-10	200
2-9	180
2-8	160
2-7	140
2-6	120
2-5	100
2-4	80
2-3	60
2-2	40
2-1	20
2-0	0

Long Jump

Ht.	Pts.	Ht.	Pts.
21-0	1000	12-6	490
20-10	990	12-4	480
20-8	980	12-2	470
20-6	970	12-0	460
20-4	960	11-10	450
20-2	950	11-8	440
20-0	940	11-6	430
19-10	930	11-4	420
19-8	920	11-2	410
19-6	910	11-0	400
19-4	900	10-10	390
19-2	890	10-8	380
19-0	880	10-6	370
18-10	870	10-4	360
18-8	860	10-2	350
18-6	850	10-0	340
18-4	840	9-10	330
18-2	830	9-8	320
18-0	820	9-6	310
17-10	810	9-4	300
17-8	800	9-2	290
17-6	790	9-0	280
17-4	780	8-10	270
17-2	770	8-8	260
17-0	760	8-6	250
16-10	750	8-4	240
16-8	740	8-2	230
16-6	730	8-0	220
16-4	720	7-10	210
16-2	710	7-8	200
16-0	700	7-6	190
15-10	690	7-4	180
15-8	680	7-2	170
15-6	670	7-0	160
15-4	660	6-10	150
15-2	650	6-8	140
15-0	640	6-6	130
14-10	630	6-4	120
14-8	620	6-2	110
14-6	610	6-0	100
14-4	600	5-10	90
14-2	590	5-8	80
14-0	580	5-6	70
13-10	570	5-5	60
13-8	560	5-4	50
13-6	550	5-3	40
13-4	540	5-2	30
13-2	530	5-1	20
13-0	520	5-0	10
12-10	510	4-10	0
12-8	500		

PENTATHLON SCORE TABLES

Each Second = 3 pts.

1500 M		400 M		Shot Put		Discus		
Time	Pts.	Time	Pts.	Feet	Pts.	Feet	Yds.	Pts.
	----1000		----1000		----1000			----1000
	----980		----980		----980			----980
	----960		----960		----960			----960
	----940		----940		----940			----940
	----920		----920		----920			----920
	----900		----900		----900			----900
	----880		----880		----880			----880
	----860		----860		----860			----860
	----840		----840		----840			----840
	----820		----820		----820			----820
	----800		----800		----800			----800
	----780		----780		----780			----780
	----760		----760		----760			----760
	----740		----740		----740			----740
	----720		----720		----720			----720
	----700		----700		----700			----700
	----680		----680		----680			----680
	----660		----660		----660			----660
	----640		----640		----640			----640
	----620		----620		----620			----620
	----600		----600		----600			----600
	----580		----580		----580			----580
	----560		----560		----560			----560
	----540		----540		----540			----540
	----520		----520		----520			----520
	----500		----500		----500			----500
	----480		----480		----480			----480
	----460		----460		----460			----460
	----440		----440		----440			----440
	----420		----420		----420			----420
	----400		----400		----400			----400
	----380		----380		----380			----380
	----360		----360		----360			----360
	----340		----340		----340			----340
	----320		----320		----320			----320
	----300		----300		----300			----300
	----280		----280		----280			----280
	----260		----260		----260			----260
	----240		----240		----240			----240
	----220		----220		----220			----220
	----200		----200		----200			----200
	----180		----180		----180			----180
	----160		----160		----160			----160
	----140		----140		----140			----140
	----120		----120		----120			----120
	----100		----100		----100			----100
	----80		----80		----80			----80
	----60		----60		----60			----60
	----40		----40		----40			----40
	----20		----20		----20			----20
	----0		----0		----0			----0

PENTATHLON SCORE TABLES

100 M Dash

Time	Pts.	Time	Pts.
----------	1000	----------	235
----------	985	----------	220
----------	970	----------	205
----------	955	----------	190
----------	940	----------	175
----------	925	----------	160
----------	910	----------	145
----------	895	----------	130
----------	880	----------	115
----------	865	----------	100
----------	850	----------	85
----------	835	----------	70
----------	820	----------	55
----------	805	----------	40
----------	790	----------	25
----------	775	----------	10
----------	760		
----------	745		
----------	730		
----------	715		
----------	700		
----------	685		
----------	670		
----------	655		
----------	640		
----------	625		
----------	610		
----------	595		
----------	580		
----------	565		
----------	550		
----------	535		
----------	520		
----------	505		
----------	490		
----------	475		
----------	460		
----------	445		
----------	430		
----------	415		
----------	400		
----------	385		
----------	370		
----------	355		
----------	340		
----------	325		
----------	310		
----------	295		
----------	280		
----------	265		
----------	250		

70 M Hurdles

Time	Pts.	Time	Pts.
----------	1000	----------	235
----------	985	----------	220
----------	970	----------	205
----------	955	----------	190
----------	940	----------	175
----------	925	----------	160
----------	910	----------	145
----------	895	----------	130
----------	880	----------	115
----------	865	----------	100
----------	850	----------	85
----------	835	----------	70
----------	820	----------	55
----------	805	----------	40
----------	790	----------	25
----------	775	----------	10
----------	760		
----------	745		
----------	730		
----------	715		
----------	700		
----------	685		
----------	670		
----------	655		
----------	640		
----------	625		
----------	610		
----------	595		
----------	580		
----------	565		
----------	550		
----------	535		
----------	520		
----------	505		
----------	490		
----------	475		
----------	460		
----------	445		
----------	430		
----------	415		
----------	400		
----------	385		
----------	370		
----------	355		
----------	340		
----------	325		
----------	310		
----------	295		
----------	280		
----------	265		
----------	250		

PENTATHLON SCORE TABLES

High Jump			Long Jump		
Ht.	Pts.		Ht.	Pts.	Ht.	Pts.
----------	1000		----------	1000	----------	490
----------	980		----------	990	----------	480
----------	960		----------	980	----------	470
----------	940		----------	970	----------	460
----------	920		----------	960	----------	450
----------	900		----------	950	----------	440
----------	880		----------	940	----------	430
----------	860		----------	930	----------	420
----------	840		----------	920	----------	410
----------	820		----------	910	----------	400
----------	800		----------	900	----------	390
----------	780		----------	890	----------	380
----------	760		----------	880	----------	370
----------	740		----------	870	----------	360
----------	720		----------	860	----------	350
----------	700		----------	850	----------	340
----------	680		----------	840	----------	330
----------	660		----------	830	----------	320
----------	640		----------	820	----------	310
----------	620		----------	810	----------	300
----------	600		----------	800	----------	290
----------	580		----------	790	----------	280
----------	560		----------	780	----------	270
----------	540		----------	770	----------	260
----------	520		----------	760	----------	250
----------	500		----------	750	----------	240
----------	480		----------	740	----------	230
----------	460		----------	730	----------	220
----------	440		----------	720	----------	210
----------	420		----------	710	----------	200
----------	400		----------	700	----------	190
----------	380		----------	690	----------	180
----------	360		----------	680	----------	170
----------	340		----------	670	----------	160
----------	320		----------	660	----------	150
----------	300		----------	650	----------	140
----------	280		----------	640	----------	130
----------	260		----------	630	----------	120
----------	240		----------	620	----------	110
----------	220		----------	610	----------	100
----------	200		----------	600	----------	90
----------	180		----------	590	----------	80
----------	160		----------	580	----------	70
----------	140		----------	570	----------	60
----------	120		----------	560	----------	50
----------	100		----------	550	----------	40
----------	80		----------	540	----------	30
----------	60		----------	530	----------	20
----------	40		----------	520	----------	10
----------	20		----------	510	----------	0
----------	0		----------	500	----------	

TOP 20% FINAL STANDINGS

Duplicate several copies and write the name of each event in the top vertical columns.
Add names and total points for the top twenty percent of the students in the columns for each event.

Event		Event		Event		Event		Event	
Name	Pts.	Name	Pts.	Name	Pts.	Name	Pts.	Name	Pts.

PERSONAL DEFENSE CIRCUIT

Objectives:

- ◆ To develop an awareness of personal safety through anticipation and prevention.
- ◆ To understand that the best defense is to avoid the need to defend yourself.
- ◆ To know that time and distance are extremely important in self defense.
- ◆ To develop the basic skills needed to defend against a possible physical threat.

Essentials:

- ◆ Gymnasium or large room
- ◆ 6 football hand-held blocking pads
- ◆ 6 tall football blocking pads

How to Play:

1. Cover the skills and safety guidelines with demonstrations and/or with an outside resource person(s). These could be a martial arts instructor or a police officer.
2. **After** all the skills have been covered and practiced, post the (20-25) skillcards around the room.
3. Allow the students to rotate around the circuit in pairs. Each station lasts two minutes.
4. Each station covers a different skill or task. (See Sample Skill Cards.)

Student Tasks:

1. To properly demonstrate the skills.
2. To safely demonstrate the skills.

Variations:

1. Assign a number to each skill station. Allow each student to draw two or more numbers from a hat. They then have to properly demonstrate that skill in front of the class.
2. Allow students to demonstrate, after review, skills that they might have learned from other sources.

WHERE THE HIT AND RUN IS **NOT** A FELONY

SAMPLE CIRCUIT STATIONS

Card No. Name of Station	Information
1—*Arm Swing.*	Partner grabs your upper arm, you make a circle in either direction.
2—*Avoid a Kick*	Step back and push the leg on by, or catch the leg and direct kick to the knee.
3—*Bear Hugs*	How many different methods can you demonstrate so that you could get free?
4—*Choke Hold*	Try: a. finger bend; b. wedge through; c. arm over top and down.
5—*Combinations Strikes.*	Hit the hand bag. Use the spear, chop, heel, elbow, knee.
6—*Deflections*	Partner uses hand bag. (Same as *Wax On* in the movie "Karate Kid".) Step back while reaching up and out.
7—*Elbow Lock.*	Push their elbow toward your hand, then side direct kick to their knee.
8—*Use the Elbow*	Use the hand bag. Swing the arm both coming, going, front, or back side.
9—*Forearm Choke*	Partner is behind. Grab their arm at your neck and do a pull down. Kick back.
10—*Full Nelson*	Try one of these: a. push forehead back; b. finger lift; c. drop through.
11—*Hair Pulling*	How do you get out of long and/or short hair pulls?
12—*Hammer Lock.*	Reach back and push down on wrist, kick back to their knee.
13—*Knee Kicks.*	Turn your body sideways, then start the motorcycle, that being their knee.
14—*Perry.*	Partner uses hand bag. (Same as *Wax Off* in the movie "Karate Kid".) Step back and push or slap the bag on by.
15—*Pushing.*	Step forward and contact both of their front upper shoulders. Push, turn, and run.
16—*Reflex Speed*	Play hot hands or quick draw.
17—*Round House Kick*	Use the floor bag. Kick the bag 10 times with your shoe laces. Point the toe.
18—*Shin Kick.*	Use the floor bag. Use the right and left legs to shin kick, shin drag.
19—*Wrist Grab.*	Always kick first. Either make a circle or do a finger lift.
20—*Wrist Lock*	Push against the back of your hand and then kick to their knee.

Station Number

Sample Circuit Station Card

4

WRIST LOCK

**PUSH AGAINST THE BACK OF YOUR HAND.
**KICK TO THE KNEE

HOT HANDS

Objectives:

- ◆ To develop hand and eye coordination.
- ◆ To avoid getting the back of the hand(s) hit by improving reflex awareness.

PERSONAL DEFENSE

Essentials:

◆ Large room

How to Play:

1. Have two students face each other with their arms bent at the elbows.
2. The defensive participant rests his/her palms facing down on the offensive player's palms, which are facing up.
3. The offense tries to quickly hit the back side of either one or both hands of the defensive opponent.
4. There is no faking.
5. A miss causes players to change positions.
6. If the first offensive person gets five hits in a row, the defensive person switches to offense and must make five hits in a row or becomes the vanquished.
7. First player to accumulate five hits is declared the winner.
8. Take on a new challenger after a match is over.

Student Tasks:

1. Defeat three different opponents.
2. Make five hits in a row without a miss.
3. Defeat a previously unbeaten player.

Variations:

1. Use only the right hand.
2. Use only the left hand.
3. Both players must close their eyes after the palms touch.
4. Allow the offensive player to fake a maximum of three times.

Stance Diagram

Defense   Offense

QUICK DRAW

Objectives:

- ◆ To develop hand and eye coordination.
- ◆ To avoid getting the back of the hand(s) hit by improving reflex awareness.

Essentials:

- ◆ Large room

How to Play:

1. Have two students face each other.
2. The offense has a hand on each hip and tries to quickly hit the back side of one or both hands of the defensive opponent. The action is that of a Western gunfighter drawing a pistol from the holster.
3. The defensive participant has his/her arms extended out in front, bent at the elbow and hands together with the palms touching. Slide the hands apart in any fashion or manner possible when the offense makes a move.
4. There is no faking.
5. A miss causes players to change positions.
6. If the first offensive person gets five hits in a row, the defensive person switches to offense and must make five hits in a row or becomes the vanquished.
7. First player to accumulate five hits is declared the winner.
8. Take on a new challenger after a match is over.

Student Tasks:

1. Defeat three different opponents.
2. Make five hits in a row without a miss.
3. Defeat a previously unbeaten player.

Variations:

1. Use only the right hand.
2. Use only the left hand.
3. Allow the offensive player to fake a maximum of three times.

Stance Diagram

ABOUT "PICKLE-BALL"

Objective:

◆ To be the first player to score eleven points.

Essentials:

◆ Doubles badminton court

◆ Wood paddles

◆ Plastic perforated balls

◆ Badminton standards with the nets set 3 feet above the floor.

How to Play: *(Rules are like badminton.)*

1. Serving:

    a. Can only score when serving.

    b. Must serve underhanded and contact the ball below the waist while it is in the air. No bounces.

    c. Must serve from the right side of the court on all even-numbered scores.

    d. Serve must be diagonal to the receiver, while clearing the 7-ft. non-volley zone.

    e. If the ball contacts the net and still goes over the 7-ft. zone, it is called a "let" and is hit again.

2. Receiving:

    a. The ball must bounce once on each side, past the 7-ft. zone, before it can be volleyed in a rally.

    b. If a player sees that the ball is going to land in the no-volley zone, she/he can move into the zone before it bounces, but must let it bounce before returning it.

3. Loss of possession:

    a. Hitting the ball out of bounds. The line is good.

    b. Hitting the net while the ball is in play.

    c. Stepping into the non-volley zone and volleying the ball in a rally before it has bounced once on each side of the net.

    d. While serving, the ball does not go over the net.

    e. When playing doubles, the server has a double "let."

4. Doubles:

    a. At the beginning of each game, the team serving first is allowed only one fault before returning the ball over the net.

    b. Throughout the rest of the game, both team members serve, alternating court sides until the receiving team has won two faults.

    c. When the serve is won by the receiving team, the player positioned on the right side of the court always starts serving first.

d. The serving team is usually back at the base line due to the double-bounce rule.

e. The receiving team can play one up at the edge of the 7-ft. zone and one back at the base line.

f. The serving team cannot charge the net because the opponent's return must bounce first on his/her own side of the court.

Student Tasks:

1. Serve a certain number in a row.

2. Win a game after it was tied at eleven.

3. Come from behind to win.

Variations:

1. Allow the ball to be hit without bouncing.

2. Allow more players on a team.

3. Serve and score as in:
   a. Volleyball.
   b. Table tennis.
   c. Tennis.

4. See **TableTennis** and **Tennis** for a list of the many different games that can be adapted for play.

5. Use a volleyball court and play the game just like volleyball, using six or more players on a side. *Note:* Be aware of paddle space when swinging.

Floor Diagram for Doubles Play

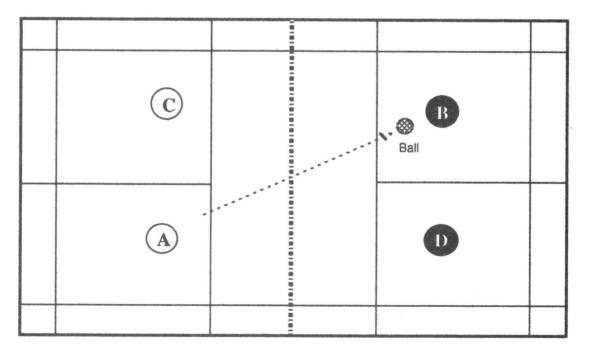

ABOUT "PILLOW POLO"

Objective:

◆ To score more points than the opponent by hitting the ball through the goal.

Essentials:

◆ Field
◆ Pinnies
◆ Polo sticks
◆ Medium-size playground ball

How to Play:

1. Only five to six players on a team.

2. Make the fields short and narrow. Divide a standard football field into four or five smaller fields.

3. May not bring the polo stick above the waist, prior to or after an attempted shot. (High Sticking)

4. Violations result in an indirect ball placement from where the infraction occurred.

5. There may be only one person from each team **at** the ball during play.

6. No hitting the ball out of the air. Players may not bunt the ball out of the air.

7. The goalie may use only her/his feet or the stick to stop the ball.

8. The defense makes the calls if there are no referees.

9. Start game with a center bully. (The sticks are tapped three times and then the puck is hit.)

10. Start play with the ball at the center of the field. The team scored upon puts the ball into play by hitting it to a team member. The defense must be ten feet away from the ball on the initial hit.

11. There is no offsides. Participants may go anywhere at anytime.

12. A student may only score two goals in a row.

13. A player may not intentionally use his/her foot to control, trap, or stop the ball.

14. The ball is placed on the sideline and hit with the stick when putting it back into play.

PILLOW POLO

Student Tasks:

1. Be a goalie.

2. Get an assist.

3. Do not allow the other team to score.

4. Dribble a certain distance.

5. During a series of four or five games for the day, have each member of the team score a goal.

Variations:

1. Have more than one goalie.

2. Use two balls in one game.

3. Using a square field, make four teams and have four goals. Use two or more balls.

4. Use the **Mix 'n Match** format and play several short-timed games of only five to six minutes each.

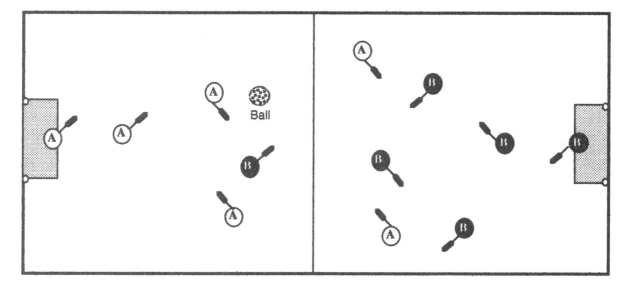

ABOUT "RESEARCH PAPER"

Objectives:

- ◆ To research two different topics of interest that are related directly or indirectly to the field of physical education.
- ◆ To write a paper with proper form and content.
- ◆ To gain knowledge in the interest areas.

Essentials:

- ◆ Library or reference room
- ◆ Student handouts

How to Do:

1. *Note:* Check with the librarians to find out how much information is obtainable so that a class at the end of the day will have materials available. This class might be taught at different weekly intervals because of a lack of data.
2. Pass out the *Research Paper Handout.*
3. All students go to the library to secure reference materials.
4. Each student has one week to finish the project.

Student Tasks:

1. Create an illustrated cover.
2. Place personal drawings of importance within the research paper.

Variations:

1. Allow students to work in pairs.
2. Assign this paper as extra credit. A student would have to do research on his/her own time.

TOPICS FOR RESEARCH

Student Handout

The Origin, History, and Facts of:

Badminton
Baseball
Basketball
Bicycling
Bowling
Dance
Boxing
Field Hockey
Fishing
Flag Football
Fly Fishing
Football
Golf
Gymnastics
Horseshoes

Hunting
Jogging/Running
Mountain Climbing
Olympics
Sailing
Shuffleboard
Soccer
Softball
Swimming/Diving
Table Tennis
Team Handball
Tennis
Volleyball
Wrestling
Y.M.C.A. / Y.W.C.A.

Life of a Famous Athlete

Careers Related to Healthy Active Living:

Agent for Athletes
Announcer/Broadcaster
Athletic Trainer
Beautician
Coach
Dancer/Aerobics Instructor
Dietitian
Doctor
E.M.T./Paramedic
Health Teacher

Model
Nurse
Outdoor Recreation Specialist
Physical Education Teacher
Physical Therapist
Professional Athlete
Referee/Official
Sports Journalist/Photographer
Sportswear Designer
Y.M.C.A./Y.W.C.A. Director

Special Topics:

Drugs in athletics.
Drug testing for athletes.
The facts about steroids.
The importance of diet in life.
What is somatotyping?
Benefits of a healthy living.
Choice!

RESEARCH PAPER FORMAT

Student Handout

This paper will be:

1. Double spaced.
2. Correct in punctuation and spelling.
3. Neatly printed in ink or typed.
4. Written on one side of the paper only.
5. Be completed by the designated date(s): _____
6. Have a proper bibliography.
7. Be graded in two parts:
   a. Content (thicker and heavier is no guarantee of an "A.")
   b. Structure
8. Extra credit can be earned by having personalized hand-drawn illustrations on the cover or of items within the context of the paper.

BIBLIOGRAPHIC CITATIONS

Student Handout

1. **For a book with one author:**

   Author. <u>Title.</u> Publisher, copyright, number of pages.

   Example:

   Sperry, Armstrong. <u>All about the Arctic and the Antarctic.</u> Random House, 1994, 146 pp.

2. **For a book with two authors:**

   Author (last name, first name) and second author (first name, last name). <u>Title.</u> Publisher, copyright, number of pages.

   Example:

   Murphy, Barbara and Norman Baker. <u>Thor Heyerdahl and the Reed Boat.</u> Lippincott, 1988, 64 pp.

3. **For an encyclopedia article:**

   "Article," <u>Encyclopedia name,</u> volume number, last copyright, pages.

   Example:

   "Ethiopia," <u>The New Book of Knowledge,</u> vol. 5, 1991, pp. 296-301.

4. **For a magazine article:**

   Author (if known). "Article," <u>Magazine.</u> date, page.

   Example:

   Cumming, Joseph B. Jr. "Terrible Twists of Fate," <u>National Wildlife.</u> June/July 1990, p. 29

FIELD SOCCER

Objective:

◆ To kick a ball into the goal.

Essentials:

◆ Field or large gym
◆ Cones
◆ Soccer balls
◆ Pinnies

How to Play:

1. Only five to six players on a team.
2. Make the fields short and narrow. Divide a standard football field into four or five smaller fields.
3. Goalie:
   a. Ten-yard boundary for picking up the ball.
   b. A goal is scored if the ball goes between the cones and is below the extended hands.
   c. Must have a new goalie each game.
4. Players:
   a. Can go anywhere on the field at anytime. There are no offside calls.
   b. Only one player from each team may be at the ball.
   c. No wild kicks or blasting of the ball. It is only passed or dribbled.
   d. The entire ball must go over a line before it is out of play or a goal.
   e. No heading for safety reasons.
   f. May use hands to protect face, chest, or groin.
   g. No slide tackling.
   h. May only score two goals in a row.
   i. Violations outside of the goalie area will result in an indirect kick. If a violation occurs in the goalie box, then there will be a direct kick at the goalie.
   j. There is no scoring from beyond the half-field markers.

Student Tasks:

1. Be a goalie.
2. Block three shots on goal during the same game.
3. Create a shutout.
4. Assist a score.

5. Be a referee.

6. During a series of four or five games for the day, have each member of the team score a goal.

Variations:

1. Combine any number of teams and use two or more balls at once.

2. Allow two or more goalies.

3. Move the goals away from the end lines.

4. Use two balls in a regular game.

5. Play with four goals, four teams, and two or more balls.

6. Use the **Mix 'n Match** format and play several short-timed games of only five to six minutes each.

7. Play in a large gym (eight on a team) and use a Gator Skin® foam ball. Play the ball off anything since there is no out of bounds.

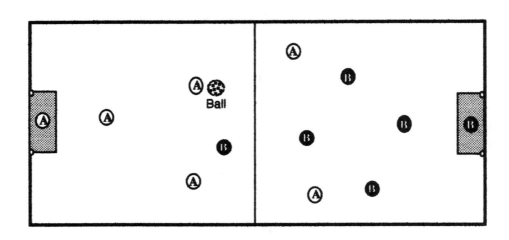

INDOOR SOCCER

Objective:

- ◆ To kick a ball into the goal.

Essentials:

- ◆ Large gym
- ◆ 2 goals
- ◆ 2 Gator Skin® or Nerf™ balls
- ◆ Pinnies

How to Play:

1. Up to 15 players on a team.
2. There are no boundaries since the ball is played off of anything.
3. Goalie:
   a. May not pick up the ball outside the marked goalie box.
   b. Must have a new goalie each game.
   c. The entire ball must go over a line before it is scored a goal.
4. Players:
   a. When a goal is scored, both balls are returned to the goalies.
   b. Can go anywhere on the floor at anytime. There are no offside calls.
   c. Only one player from each team may be at the ball.
   d. Will not touch a ball that is in the goalie box.
   e. No wild kicks or blasting of the ball. It is only passed or dribbled.
   f. May use hands to protect face, chest, or groin.
   g. No slide tackling.
   h. May only score two goals in a row.
   i. A ball cannot be trapped for more than five seconds.
   j. Violations will result in that player going to a penalty box for 30 seconds.

Student Tasks:

1. Be a goalie.
2. Block three shots on goal during the same game.
3. Create a shutout.
4. Assist a score.
5. Be a referee.
6. During a series of four or five games for the day, have each member of the team score a goal.

Variations:

1. Combine any number of teams.
2. Allow two or more goalies.
3. Move the goals away from the middle.
4. Play with four goals, four teams, and two or more balls.
5. Allow only a certain ball to be scored in a given goal box.
6. Use the **Mix 'n Match** format and play several short timed games of only five to six minutes each.

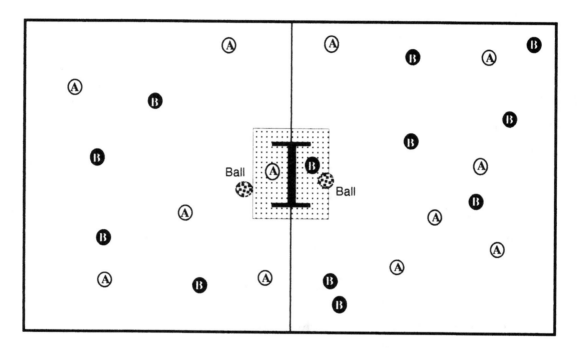

MAT SOCCER

Objective:

◆ To score points by throwing the ball into a goal.

Essentials:

◆ Large area covered with mats
◆ Knee pads for students
◆ 1 Gator Skin® ball
◆ Goal box 4 feet high by 8 feet wide and located on the wall (use wide masking tape)
◆ Pinnies

Soccer

How to Play:

1. Using tape, mark a four-by-eight rectangular-shaped goal on each end wall.
2. Goalie may not:
   a. Leave the goalie box with the ball.
   b. Score by throwing the ball at the other goal.
   c. Pass the ball over the half-court line when starting play.
3. Defense:
   a. Must travel around on knees, crab walk, or bear crawl.
   b. Cannot interfere with players who do not have possession of the ball.
   c. Cannot touch the person with the ball but can play defense-like basketball.
   d. Will not interfere with or take a ball away from the goalie.
4. Offense:
   a. Must travel around on knees, crab walk, or bear crawl.
   b. **Cannot** move around once they have control or possess the ball.
   c. No holding the arm straight out (stiff arming) to ward off the defense.
   d. May possess a ball for no longer than five seconds.
   e. A competitor may only score two goals in a row.

Student Tasks:

1. Be a goalie.
2. Cause a shut out.
3. Assist in a score.
4. Block a shot attempt.
5. During a series of four or five games for the day, have each member of the team score a goal.

Variations:

1. Use two goalies.
2. Use two balls at once.
3. Put a different point value on each ball.
4. Use four goals, four teams, and two balls.

SOCKEY*

Objective:

◆ To score points through the goal from either direction.

Essentials:

◆ Large field

◆ Goals (field cones) placed 10 yards in from the end lines and about 5 yards apart

◆ Pillow polo sticks can be substituted for hockey sticks

◆ Field marking cones for goals and sidelines

◆ Gator Skin® balls work best

◆ Pinnies

How to Play:

1. Only five to six players on a team.

2. Make the fields short and narrow. Divide a standard football field into four or five smaller fields.

3. Goals (field cones) are placed ten yards in from the end lines and are about five yards apart.

4. Goalie:

   a. Is not allowed to throw or kick the ball over the half-field line.

   b. May use arms, body, or feet to deflect, trap, kick, or stop an attempted goal.

   c. Can throw or kick the ball into play.

   d. May only go one step beyond the goal line or cone.

   e. Can step through the goal line once she/he has possession of the ball.

   f. May not score while in the goal box.

   g. Only the goalie is allowed in the goal box.

5. Players:

   a. Start the game with the ball in the center or after a score.

   b. Only one player from each team is allowed at the ball during play.

   c. No high sticking (bringing the stick higher than the waist) if students are near.

   d. Can only swing at the ball if it is on the ground.

   e. May use the stick to bunt the ball to the ground if it is in the air or bouncing.

   f. Players may not intentionally kick the ball to gain control.

   g. When a ball goes out of play, it is placed on the line and hit back into play.

   h. Defense calls all violations and is always right.

   i. Intentional throwing, hitting, or jousting with the sticks is not allowed.

---

*Created by Ken Lumsden and John Lefler, 1993.

© 1996 Parker Publishing Company

j. Ball must go between the cones and below the top of the goalie's head.

k. A goal can be scored from either direction.

Student Tasks:

1. Be a goalie.

2. Block shots on goal.

3. Create a shutout.

4. Assist a score.

5. Be a referee.

6. During a series of four or five games for the day, have each member of the team score a goal.

Variations:

1. Turn the goal area 90 degrees or parallel to the sides of the field.

2. Combine any number of teams and use two or more balls at once.

3. Allow two or more goalies.

4. Use two balls in a regular game.

5. Use a square field and play with four goals, four teams, and two or more balls.

6. Use the **Mix 'n Match** format and play several short-timed games of only five to six minutes each.

(Goal area is equal to one step away by a goalie)

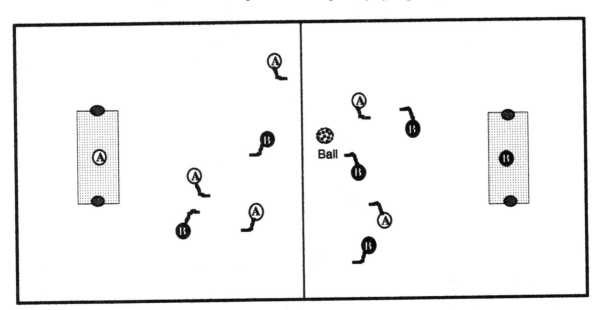

SPEEDBALL

Objectives:

◆ To combine the elements of soccer and flag football into a game.

◆ To score more points than the opponents by: (a) passing the ball into the end zone, and (b) kicking the ball into a goal.

Essentials:

◆ Large field

◆ 1 soccer ball per field

◆ Football flags for each player

◆ Field marking cones for the goals and lines

How to Play:

1. From five to eight players on a team.

2. Make the fields short and narrow. Divide a standard football field into four or five smaller fields.

3. Terms:

   a. **Aerial ball**—Any ball raised in the air directly from kicks, punts, kick-ups, drop kicks, thrown balls, or monkey jumps (ball brought up to hands from between the feet).

   b. **Ground ball**—When the ball has touched the ground by rolling, bouncing, or is stationary.

   c. **Pivot**—Moving the body around in a circle or part of a circle, while one foot remains in contact with the ground.

4. Players may advance the ball by the feet by:

   a. Dribbling as in soccer.

   b. Drop-kicking.

   c. Punting.

   d. Place-kicking.

5. Players may advance the ball by the hands by:

   a. Passing.

   b. Throwing.

   c. **Juggle-catching**—Throwing the ball from one hand to the other. This can be done only once per possession.

6. Players may stop the ball by blocking it as in soccer. Trapping is securing the ball under a foot or between both legs. No one may kick the ball from under the foot at this time.

7. Once the ball is trapped, the player has five seconds to decide a next move.

8. The removable flags are used to stop a player who is running with the ball.

9. If a player has her/his flag pulled while in possession of the ball, the other team receives it on the ground at that point.

10. Only one person is allowed to guard the player with the ball.

11. The ball is put on the midline to begin a game and after every score with a "lift-up" to another player. That player has five seconds before she/he can have a flag pulled. This person can:

   a. Run with the ball.

   b. Throw the ball.

   c. Kick the ball.

   d. Put the ball on the ground and kick it as in soccer.

12. The rules of soccer apply to the goalie on any out-of-bounds ball or fouls.

13. Scoring:

   a. **2 points**—Soccer goal between cones and no higher than the raised hands of the goalie.

   b. **1 point**—Passing the ball to a player behind the end zone but not between the cones.

Student Tasks:

1. Be a goalie.
2. Make a certain number of complete passes.
3. Pull a flag.
4. Intercept a throw.
5. Assist in a score.

Variations:

1. Use two or more balls.
2. Make four teams, use four goals, and two balls.
3. Use the **Mix 'n Match** format.

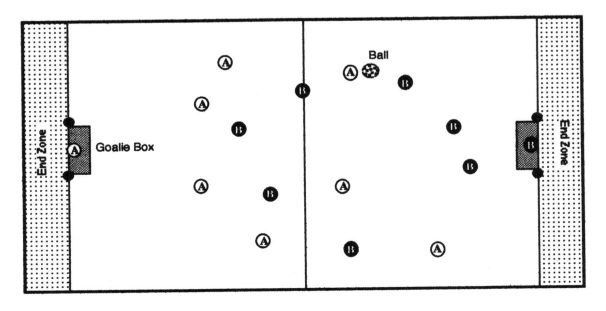

CRAZYBALL

Objective:

◆ To score more runs than the opposition by hitting the ball and running around the bases safely.

Essentials:

◆ Field
◆ 4 bases, 2 bats, 1 super soft softball for each field
◆ Safety cones to mark the next batter box if no back stops are available
◆ Face mask and chest protector for each catcher

How to Play:

1. All of the same rules of softball apply to this game.
2. After the ball has been hit, the runners must run the ball in the **opposite** direction. This takes the advantage away from the right-handed batters.

Student Tasks:

1. Get a single, double, triple, or home run.
2. Assist in an out.
3. Catch a fly ball.
4. Be involved in a double play.
5. Tag a runner.
6. Be a pitcher.
7. Have everyone on the team score a run during the game(s).
8. Trap a runner between two bases and then tag him/her out.

Variations:

1. All throws must be with the off arm.
2. Batters must hit the ball from the weaker side.
3. Divide each team into two small teams. These two teams must switch from infield to outfield each time out.

Safety:

1. If there are no back stops, future batters are to be no less than 25 feet from home plate.
2. Face masks and chest protectors should be worn by the catcher.
3. The super soft softball is great to use for all levels since:
   a. It will not sting the hands.
   b. It has less potential for injuries to the body.
   c. It makes gloves and mitts unnecessary to play the game.

JUGBALL

Objective:

◆ To score more runs than the opposition by getting people to hit the ball and run around the bases safely.

Essentials:

◆ Field
◆ 4 bases
◆ Face mask and chest protector
◆ 1 jug bat (see diagram)
◆ 1 medium-sized Gator Skin® foam ball

How to Play:

1. All of the same rules of softball apply to this game.
2. The bases are only 45 feet apart.

Student Tasks:

1. Get a single, double, triple, or home run.
2. Assist in an out.
3. Catch a fly ball.
4. Be involved in a double play.
5. Tag a runner.
6. Be a pitcher.
7. Have everyone on the team score a run during the game(s).

Variations:

1. Have the batters run the bases in the opposite direction to score.
2. Partner must run for the batter and then switch roles the next time.
3. Divide each team into two small teams. These two teams must switch from infield to outfield each time out.

How to Build Jug Bat:

1. Items Needed:
   a. One large plastic water bottle (commercial type).
   b. One $1^1/_2$-inch diameter by 33-inch long round dowel.
   c. One $1^1/_2$-inch long wood screw and washer.
   d. Duct or athletic tape.

2. Directions:

   a. Insert the dowel through the opening of the jug.

   b. Fasten the screw and washer through the end of the jug into the wood dowel.

   c. Put tape around the jug, the neck, and the handle to help prevent cracking, the handle from moving, and slipping out of the hands when batting the ball.

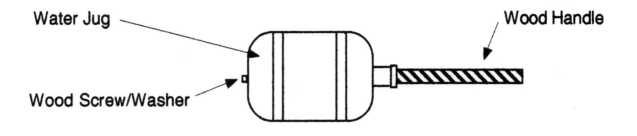

Note: Remember to wrap tape around the jug and down the handle for extra support.

LIGHTNINGBALL

Objective:

◆ To score more runs than the opposition by getting people to hit the ball and run around the bases safely.

Essentials:

◆ Field

◆ 4 bases, 2 bats, 1 super soft softball for each field

◆ Safety cones to mark the next batter box if no back stops are available

◆ Face mask and chest protector for each catcher

How to Play:

1. All of the rules of softball apply to this game.

2. **Three** teams, with four players each, are at one field.

   a. One team is at bat.

   b. The second team plays the infield.

   c. The third team plays the outfield.

3. After three outs or the five-run rule, the teams rotate playing areas.

Student Tasks:

1. Get a single, double, triple, or home run.
2. Assist in an out.
3. Catch a fly ball.
4. Be involved in a double play.
5. Tag a runner.
6. Be a pitcher.
7. Have everyone on the team score a run during the game(s).

Variations:

1. Have the batters run the bases in the opposite direction to score.
2. Partner must run for the batter and then switch roles the next time.
3. Use the **Mix 'n Match** format.

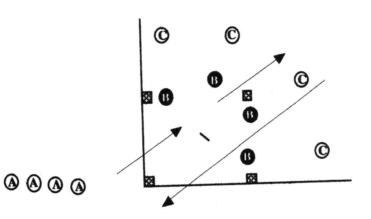

MUSHBALL

Objective:

◆ To score more runs than the opposition by getting people to hit the ball and run around the bases safely.

Essentials:

◆ Field
◆ 4 bases, 2 bats, 1 14″ to 16″ mushball for each field
◆ Safety cones to mark the next batter box if no back stops are available
◆ Face mask and chest protector for each catcher

How to Play:

1. All of the rules of softball apply to this game.
2. The bases are only 45 feet apart instead of 60.

Student Tasks:

1. Get a single, double, triple, or home run.
2. Assist in an out.
3. Catch a fly ball.
4. Be involved in a double play.
5. Tag a runner.
6. Be a pitcher.
7. Have everyone on the team score a run during the game(s).

Variations:

1. Have the batters run the bases in the opposite direction to score.
2. Partner must run for the batter and then switch roles the next time.
3. Divide each team into two small teams. These two teams must switch from infield to outfield each time out.
4. Use the **Mix 'n Match** format.

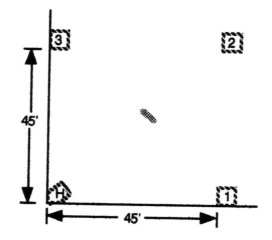

SLOW-PITCH SOFTBALL

Objective:

◆ To score more runs than the opposition by hitting the ball and running around the bases safely.

Essentials:

◆ Field

◆ 4 bases, 2 bats, 1 super soft softball for each field

◆ Safety cones to mark the next batter box if no back stops are available

◆ Face mask and chest protector for each catcher

How to Play Offense:

1. The batter:
   a. Must grip the bat with both hands.
   b. No bunting.
   c. The batter is out if any player is within 25 feet of the swing.
   d. The next batter must stay behind the 25-foot cone or back stop.
   e. Batter is out if the bat is thrown more than four bat lengths from the home base.
   f. If the batter hits his/her own pitcher with a ball, then the batter is out because of interference.
   g. Will get only three pitches in which to hit a fair ball.
   h. May get one extra pitch on a fouled third pitch *(optional)*.

2. The runner:
   a. Is not allowed to slide for safety reasons to self and others.
   b. Cannot lead off before the ball is hit.
   c. Must touch each bag when running the bases.
   d. Cannot run past second or third base.
   e. Cannot run out of the baseline to avoid a tag.
   f. Must tag the base again on all caught fly balls.
   g. Is out if hit by a batted ball while off base or while running.
   h. Gets one base on any thrown ball that goes out of play.

3. The team:
   a. Provides a pitcher for its own team.
   b. The pitcher must not intentionally interfere with a hit ball. If this happens, the runner is out. If it is unintentional, replay the same pitch.
   c. Goes to the field after three outs.

d. Is out after scoring five runs. A team may score only five runs per inning, unless they are behind by more than five runs. In that case they can score as many runs as needed to go ahead by one run. This prevents blow outs and keeps the game much more interesting and fun.

How to Play Defense:

1. Cannot stand on top of any base on a force out.
2. Cannot block a base runner or stand in the baseline when not possessing the ball.
3. Must tag the runner on all unforced plays.
4. Makes all the calls and are never wrong.

Student Tasks:

1. Get a single, double, triple, or home run.
2. Assist in an out.
3. Catch a fly ball.
4. Be involved in a double play.
5. Tag a runner.
6. Be a pitcher.
7. Trap a runner between two bases and then tag him/her out. *(Pickle)*

Variations:

1. Partner must run for the batter and then switch roles the next time.
2. Divide each team into two small teams. These two teams must switch from infield to outfield each time they go out to play defense.
3. Use the **Mix 'n Match** format.

Safety:

1. If there are no back stops, future batters are to be no less than 25 feet from home plate.
2. Face masks and chest protectors should be worn by the catcher.
3. The super soft softball is great to use for all levels since:
    a. It will not sting the hands.
    b. It has less potential for injuries to the body.
    c. It makes gloves and mitts unnecessary to play the game.

WORK UP

Objectives:

◆ To stay at bat as long as possible by safely running around the bases.

◆ To work up to the batter's position.

◆ To allow all players to play every position.

Essentials:

◆ Field

◆ 4 bases, 2 bats, 1 super soft softball

◆ Face mask and chest protector for each catcher

How to Play:

1. Allow three or four batting positions.

2. Allow ten to thirteen defensive positions.

3. All of the basic rules of softball apply.

4. A player may continue to bat until she/he has been put out by the defense.

5. Batters are only allowed two pitches.

6. The batter is out, even if the second swing is a foul ball. (This speeds up the game.)

7. If the pitch is ruled a bad one, then an extra pitch is allowed.

8. When a runner is thrown or tagged out, she/he goes to the last position in the field of play. All other players move up one position.

9. If any player catches a fly ball, she/he will immediately go to the batting line. The batter is out and takes the last position in the field. Only those positions behind the person who caught the fly ball rotate up one position.

Student Tasks:

1. Get a single, double, triple, or home run.

2. Assist in an out.

3. Catch a fly ball and trade with the batter.

4. Be involved in a double play.

5. Tag a runner.

6. Be a pitcher and strike a batter out.

7. Bat four times in a row without going out.

8. Bat six times in a row without going out.

Variations:

1. Have the batters run the bases in the opposite direction to score.
2. Shorten the distance between bases from the original 60 feet.
3. Pitcher must put a 15- to 20-foot arc on the ball as in **Slow-Pitch Softball.**
4. Allow three or four pitches.
5. When the ball is caught, that person and the batter change positions.

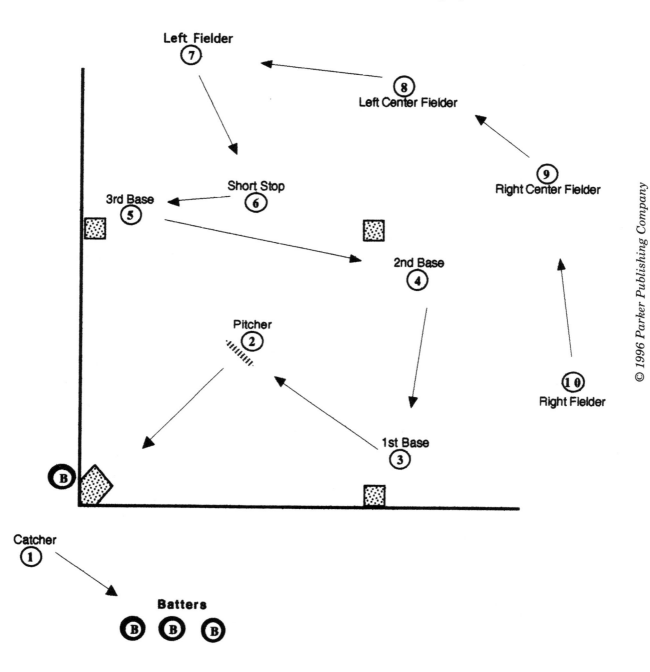

ABOUT "TABLE TENNIS"

Objective:

◆ To score 21 points first.

Essentials:

◆ Gymnasium or large room
◆ 6 to 10 tables
◆ Paddles for each student
◆ 1 ball per table

Server:

1. Toss the ball vertically from a flat open palm without putting spin on it.
2. Ball must be hit from behind the server's end line.
3. Ball must hit the server's court first.
4. Serve until five points are scored in any combination.
5. "Let" serve occurs when the ball:
   a. Touches the net and passes over.
   b. Is delivered and the receiver is not ready.
   c. Cannot be returned because of interference.
6. When serving in singles play, the ball may be served anywhere.
7. When serving in doubles play:
   a. Service is made to diagonal court from the right side of the table.
   b. All serves must touch the receiver's right half court. Liners are good.
   c. The team serving the ball first decides which partner is to serve and the opponents decide which is to receive.
   d. At the end of each five points, the one who has been receiving becomes the server and the partner of the previous server becomes the receiver.
   e. Partners must alternate hitting the ball until a point is awarded.

Scoring:

1. A game consists of 21 points and must be won by two.
2. A point is awarded each serve.
3. A player loses a point if she/he:
   a. Fails to make a good serve except in the case of a "let."
   b. Touches the table with the free hand during play.
   c. Moves the playing surface.
   d. Hits the ball before it touches his/her side.
   e. Hits the ball twice consecutively.
   f. Fails to hit the ball to the other side.

Student Tasks:

1. Forehand drive
2. Backhand drive
3. Forehand chop
4. Backhand chop
5. Right or left spin shot, left curve
6. Slap shot

Variations:

1. Doubles (mixed-same)
2. Three on a team
3. Continuous Volley Charts (50-99, 100-149, 150-199, 200-249, 250-299, 300+ Club). These charts are posted and students try to make it to the top without a miss. (See volley charts provided.)

SAMPLE VOLLEY CHART

How many volleys can you do in a row without a miss?
Put your name in the column each time you move up.

50-99	100-149	150-199	200-249	250-299	300+Club
Nancy Lee	*Nancy Lee*	*Nancy Lee*			
Tom Brown					
Fred Jones					

Directions:

1. Print one of these for each period.
2. Fill in the *Period* line.
3. Post this form on the wall and have the students fill in their names as they reach each higher numbered plateau. These are for consecutive volleys without a miss. Students must start over if they make an error.

VOLLEY CHART

How many volleys can you do in a row without a miss?
Put your name in the column each time you move up.

Period _____

50-99	100-149	150-199	200-249	250-299	300+Club

HIT AND GET

Objective:

◆ To be the last person at a table.

Essentials:

◆ Gymnasium or large room
◆ 6 to 10 tables
◆ Paddles for each student
◆ 1 ball per table

How to Play:

1. Any number of students can play.
2. When a player goes out, she/he should go to another table and practice.
3. Play several games so that 8 to 10 of the previous winners can have a tournament.
4. All regular rules to table tennis apply.
5. Split the group and send them to form a line at each end of the table.
6. Server hits the ball and immediately goes to the back of the other line. This is called **Hit and Get!**
7. The receiver hits the ball back and immediately goes to the back of the other line. This continues until there is a miss and that person is eliminated.
8. When there are only three players left, make sure the **serving** end of the table has two players present.
9. When there are only two players left, each person stays at her/his own end and must spin a 360-degree circle after hitting the ball.

Student Tasks:

1. Finish in the top five.
2. Eliminate a past champion.
3. Get invited to the tournament.

Variations:

1. Use the left or off hand only.
2. Have a partner.

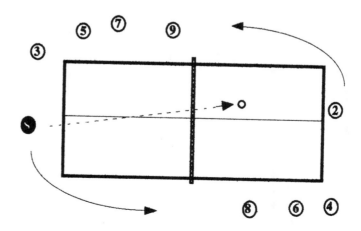

© 1996 Parker Publishing Company

ORGANIZED CHAOS

Objective:

◆ To be the first team to score 21 points.

Essentials:

◆ Large room or gymnasium

◆ Put 2 tables together

◆ May have to make a common center net holder (see **Square "NOT"** for information)

◆ Paddles for all and 2 balls for each table (*Note:* Eight or more players can be at this table)

How to Play:

1. Same rules as in **Table Tennis.**

2. Form eight sides with one or more players on each.

3. Four different games are played simultaneously (only against the team that is directly opposite).
   a. Team A vs. Team F
   b. Team B vs. Team E
   c. Team C vs. Team H
   d. Team D vs. Team G

4. All four teams (A, B, C, and D) will serve at **exactly** the same time. "Ready, serve" is called out by one of the players to insure that this occurs.

5. When an error happens during any of the rallies, the other games continue playing. When the final game rally is over, all balls are put into play simultaneously for the second serve.

6. A team will error on a:
   a. Missed shot.
   b. Missed serve.
   c. Ball that hits the wrong table.
   d. Ball that touches any part of the center net post, even if it goes over.

7. If a ball collides with another ball during play, **no** points are awarded to either team.

8. When a team reaches 21, they win the game. All other placements (two through eight) are determined by the team's total points.

---

*Created by Ken Lumsden, 1994.

Student Tasks:

1. Finish in the top two places.
2. Win the match twice.
3. Finish higher than a past champion during another match.

Variations:

1. Reduce the score to 11 or 15 with a team only serving three serves in a row.
2. Use the **Mix 'n Match** format and play a tournament.

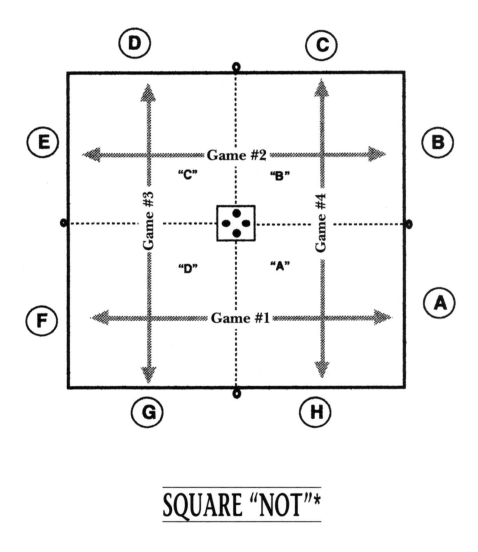

SQUARE "NOT"*

Objective:

◆ To stay in the "A" court as long as possible by not committing any hitting errors.

Created by Ken Lumsden and John Lefler, 1994.

TABLE TENNIS

Essentials:

♦ Large room or gymnasium

♦ Put 2 tables together

♦ May have to make a common center net holder (see diagram below and directions)

♦ Paddles for all and 1 ball for each table (*Note:* Eight or more players can be at this table)

How to Play:

1. Same rules as in schoolyard four-square.

2. Players may hit the ball into any square.

3. A player goes to the end of the line if she/he:
   a. Misses a shot.
   b. Misses a serve.
   c. Hits the ball and it touches the center net post, even if it goes over.

4. All other rules are the same as in regulation table tennis.

Student Tasks:

1. Stay at the top spot a certain number of times.

2. Get to the top spot a certain number of times.

3. Eliminate a past champion.

Variations:

1. Switch places with a player if your shot was an ace to his/her court (not touched).

2. Allow two or more errors before a player must go to the end of the line.

Common Net Holder:

1. **Base:** 6 to 8 inches wide × 1 to $1^1/_2$ inches thick. (A piece of a 2 × 8 works well.)

2. **Net Supports:** 4 nails or dowels 6 to 8 inches tall, set into the base about 1 inch apart to form a square.

Side View Of Base

Top View Of Base

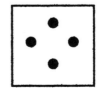

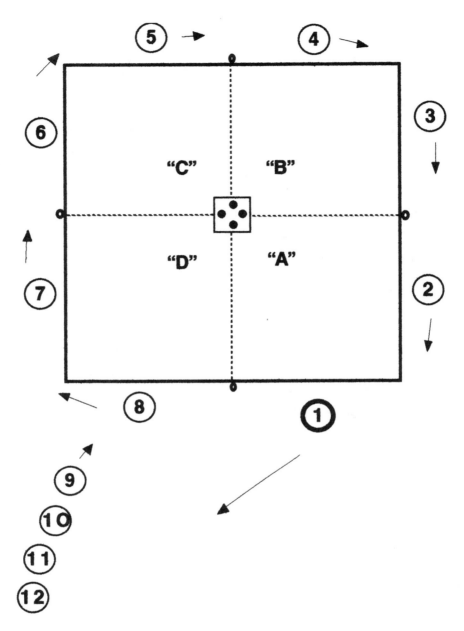

TABLE TENNIS TOP GUN

Objective:

◆ To make it to the "Top Gun" table and win two games in a row.

Essentials:

◆ Gymnasium or large room
◆ 6 to 10 tables

◆ Paddles for each student

◆ 1 ball per table

How to Play:

1. One player is at the end of each table.
2. The game is over when either player scores two points.
3. Alternate serves after each score.
4. Challengers (new person at the end of the table) serves second.
5. The victor of the game moves to the next higher table.
6. Vanquished players stay at the same table and serve first to the challenger.
7. The dominant table:
   a. Must win two games in a row to be a "Top Gun."
   b. After a player has won back-to-back games, both she/he and the defeated player restart at the lowest table.
   c. If a player is defeated at the highest table, she/he must return to the lowest table and play toward the highest table.

Student Tasks:

1. Win one game at the best table.
2. Win four games in a row at the lower tables.
3. Get to the premier table.
4. Defeat any past "Top Gun" while playing on a lower table.

Variations:

1. Play games that last a specific amount of time.
2. Make doubles teams.
3. A player or team must win three or more at the foremost table.
4. A player or team must win three or more points at any table to advance.

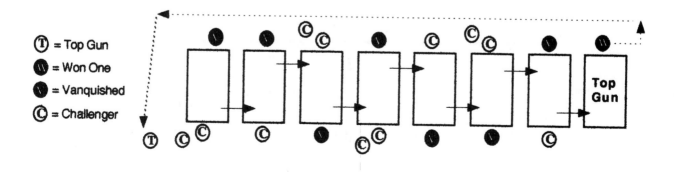

Ⓣ = Top Gun
Ⓦ = Won One
Ⓥ = Vanquished
Ⓒ = Challenger

TERMINATOR

Objective:

◆ To eliminate the other team first by making the least amount of mistakes when returning the ball.

Essentials:

◆ Gymnasium or large room

◆ 4 to 6 tables

◆ Paddles for each student

◆ 1 ball per table

How to Play:

1. Teams can be any size and/or number.

2. Teams are opposite each other and in a straight line.

3. All table tennis rules apply.

4. When a player hits the ball, she/he must return immediately to the end of his/her own team line.

5. When an error is made, that player is eliminated.

6. The team that lost a player begins serve for the next round.

Student Tasks:

1. Eliminate two opponents.

2. Bring back a player on your team.

Variations:

1. Play two lines at each end as in doubles.

2. A team may elect to bring back a player instead of having the other team lose a player.

3. Make four teams that each defend a section of a **Square "NOT"** table.

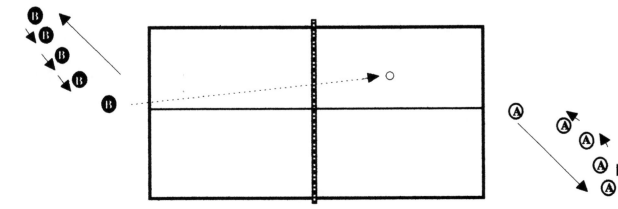

"X" MARKS THE SPOT*

Objective:

◆ To be the first team to score 21 points.

Essentials:

◆ Large room or gymnasium
◆ Put 2 tables together
◆ May have to make a common center net holder (see **Square "NOT"** for information)
◆ Paddles for all and 2 balls for each table (*Note:* Eight or more players can be at this table)

How to Play:

1. Same rules as in table tennis.
2. Form four teams with two players on each.
3. Two different games will be played simultaneously (diagonally).
   a. Team A vs. Team C
   b. Team B vs. Team D
4. The two serving teams, A and B, serve at **exactly** the same time. "Ready, serve" is called out by one of the players to ensure that this occurs.
5. When an error happens during one of the rallies, the other game continues playing. When the second game rally is over, both balls are put into play simultaneously for the second serve.
6. A team will error on a:
   a. Missed shot.
   b. Missed serve.
   c. Ball that hits the wrong table.
   d. Ball that touches any part of the center net post, even if it goes over.
7. If a ball collides with another ball during play, **no** points are awarded to either team.
8. The entire game is over when one team reaches 21. They are deemed the winners. The second, third, and last places are determined by their present score.

Student Tasks:

1. Come from behind and win a game.
2. Win two games in a row.
3. Defeat a past winner.
4. Finish in the top two at the end of a game.

Created by Ken Lumsden, 1994.

Variations:

1. Reduce the score to 11 or 15 with a team only serving three serves in a row.
2. Use the **Mix 'n Match** format and play a tournament.

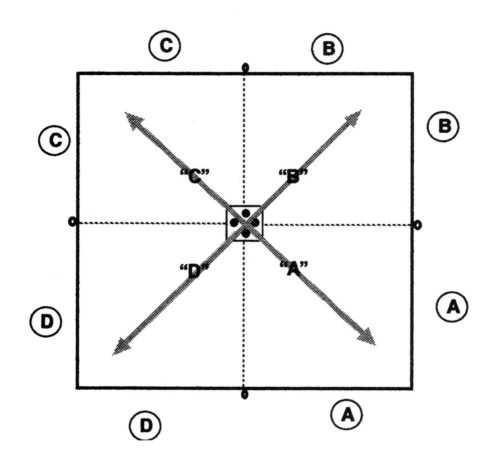

ABOUT "TEAM HANDBALL"

Objective:

◆ To throw the ball past a goalie for a score.

Essentials:

◆ Gymnasium
◆ Team handball, volleyball or the white volleyball sized Gator Skin® ball
◆ Pinnies
◆ Goals

How to Play:

1. Make teams of five or six players each.
2. Begin play with a jump ball like in basketball.
3. A goal is scored when the ball goes into the goal of the opponent.
4. Any part of the body, except the shins or feet, may be used to play the ball while it is on the playing floor.
5. A participant may hold the ball (stationary) for a maximum of five seconds.
6. All offensive and defensive players follow the same rules of basketball when dribbling, passing, fouling, or guarding the ball.
7. An offensive player may leap over the goalie area line and attempt a shot as long as she/he releases the ball before touching the goalie's floor.
8. It is prohibited to:
   a. Intentionally throw the ball back to the team's own goalie.
   b. Dive for the ball that is lying or rolling on the floor. (Except the goalie.)
   c. Obstruct an opponent who does not have the ball.
   d. Push or force an opponent into the goal area.
   e. Intentionally throw the ball at or through a defensive player.
   f. Fake a shot at the goalie.
9. The goalie/goal area:
   a. The goalie area is that area **inside** the three-point line in basketball.
   b. Only the goal keeper is allowed to enter or be in the goal area. The penalty for entering the goal with the purpose of defense is a penalty shot.
   c. No penalty is called if accidental entry into the goal area occurs or if the entry does not interfere with the shot.
   d. Once the ball is inside the goal area, it belongs to the goalie. The ball is considered inside the goal area once it touches the goal line or is rolling on the floor.
   e. The goalie may use any part of his/her body to block a shot.
   f. The goalie may move about with the ball **without** any restrictions regarding steps or time.

g. The goalie may leave the goal area **without** the ball. Once on the playing court, she/he must abide by all of the floor rules.

h. The goalie may not leave the goal area to retrieve the ball. She/he cannot reach out of the goal area to grab the ball.

i. The goalie may not score while in his/her own goal area.

j. After a score the goalie throws the ball to a teammate who is **not** past half court.

10. Types of throws:

a. **Side-out**—Made when the ball crosses the side line. It is thrown in the same way as in soccer, over the head, both feet on the floor.

b. **Corner**—Used when the goalie deflects the ball over the base line. It is thrown into play using the same method as the side-out.

c. **Indirect**—Is executed from the place where an infraction occurred. The ball may be thrown in any manner but cannot be thrown directly at the goal for a score. The defense must be at least 10 feet away.

d. **Direct**—This is awarded for serious infractions of the rules. It is a single throw at the goal, from the top of the goalie area, in a do-or-die fashion.

Student Tasks:

1. Be a goalie.
2. Block three shots on goal in one game.
3. Create a shutout.
4. Assist a score.
5. During a series of four or five games for the day, have each member of the team score a goal.

Variations:

1. Remove the nets and use the entire wall as the goal. Utilize several goalies.
2. Use the **Mix 'n Match** eleven-team format. Play two-half court games with the nets on the side line of a basketball floor.
3. Do not allow any dribbling.
4. Allow two points for a shot that goes into the basketball hoop located over the goalie area.

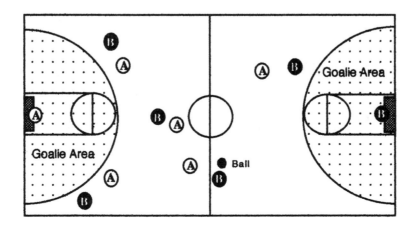

ABOUT "TENNIS"

Objective:

◆ To learn the basics of tennis as a life-long activity.

Essentials:

◆ Large gymnasium or courts
◆ Rackets
◆ Low compression balls or foam balls
◆ Reference: *USTA Schools Program Tennis Curriculum* (one of the best for ideas). Write to: Publications Department, United States Tennis Association, 707 Alexander Road, Princeton, New Jersey 08540-6399 (1991)

How to Play: (Simplified rules that create success.)

1. The line is good.
2. Can score as in table tennis with a change after five serves. Game is 11, 15, or 21 points.
3. Can let the ball double bounce. *(optional)*
4. Can shrink the court size to 20' by 40'.
5. Any number of players can be in the various activities and games (singles, doubles, or team).
6. May serve underhand, in front of the baseline, as long as it goes to the opposite diagonal court.
7. Players get two attempts at the serve.
8. The serve must bounce before a defensive person may hit it.

Areas for Instruction:

1. Safety:
   a. No street shoes.
   b. Never jump over the nets.
   c. Be careful when swinging the racket while others are near.
2. Sportsmanship, courtesy, and ethics prevail when on the court.
3. Scoring:
   a. Regulation
   b. As in table tennis
4. Hitting Skills:
   a. Grips
   b. Forehand
   c. Backhand

    d. Racket control

    e. Ground strokes

    f. Volley

    g. Lob

    h. Overhead smash

5. Serving:

    a. Regulation

    b. Underhand if in front of the service line

6. Play Strategy:

    a. Singles

    b. Doubles

Student Tasks:

1. Racket bounces.

2. A certain number of volleys in a row.

3. Serve an ace.

4. Lob in a game for a point.

5. Forever rally.

COURT-MARTIAL

Objective:

◆ To get an entire team on the court first.

Essentials:

◆ Large gymnasium or courts

◆ Rackets

◆ Low compression balls or foam balls

How to Play:

1. Form two teams with four or five players on each.

2. The teams next go to opposite sides of the court and line up at the baselines.

3. The first player from each team is on the court.

4. If a player makes a mistake, she/he goes to the end of his/her team line and the other team gets to add a player.

5. Serves are underhand only.

6. Smash shots are not allowed.

7. When a team gets their last player on the court, that team must win the next point in order to be victorious.

8. If only one player is on the court, the other team must hit to the singles court.

Student Tasks:

1. Put a certain number of players out.
2. Never go out.
3. Serve an ace.

Variations:

1. Players must use off hand.
2. Forehand or backhand shots only.
3. No player may receive the ball two times in a row unless she/he is the only one on the court.
4. Have a round robin tournament with several teams.

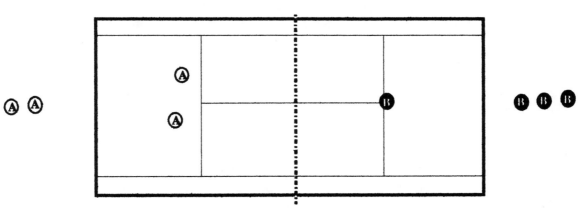

TENNIS ACTIVITIES

Objective:

◆ To play a variety of tennis games.

Essentials:

◆ Large gymnasium or courts

◆ Rackets

◆ Low compression balls or foam balls

Activities (Practice Games):

1. **Ups**—How many times can you bounce the ball off the racket in 30 seconds? This can be made into a relay race.

2. **Downs**—Same as the above but bounce the ball to the court. This can be made into a relay race. (Walking the dog.)

3. **Flip Flops**—How many times can the ball be bounced in the air while alternating the face of the racket?

4. **Inch Worm Relays**—Form groups of four or five players. Ball starts with the last person and is passed to the next person in line by using the rackets only. The last person then goes to the front of the line and waits for the ball to work its way up. Set a certain distance the team must travel to win.

5. **Drop-Hit-Catch**—Pair up and try to catch the ball the most times in a set period of time or the highest number without a miss. Alternate after every three hits. Keep the distance about 15 feet.

6. **Alley-Rally**—Pair up and get two rackets and three balls. (See the diagram.) Place a ball at each player's feet, about four to five feet apart. The doubles alley works well. Next, each player takes one step back and to the side of his/her own ball. Start with a drop shot and try to hit his/her partner's ball. Keep the rally going if possible, always trying to hit the opposite ball. Two hits is a win.

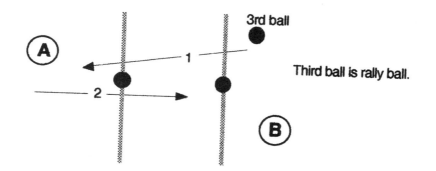

7. **Bombs Away**—Teams on opposite side of a court. Each player gets one ball. Be the first team to hit a target, basket or designated area a certain amount of times. After the first player in line hits a lob she/he must get an incoming ball and return to the end of his/her own team line.

8. **Regular Tennis**—Play games with two, three, or four players on a side.

TENNIS TOP GUN

Objective:

◆ To make it to the "Top Gun" court and win two games in a row.

Essentials:

◆ Large gymnasium or courts
◆ Rackets
◆ Low compression balls or foam balls

How to Play:

1. One player is at the end of each court.
2. The game is over when either player scores two points.
3. Alternate serves after each score.
4. Challengers (new person at the end of the court) serves second.
5. The victor of the game moves to the next higher court.
6. Vanquished players stay at the same court and serve first to the challenger.
7. The dominant court:
   a. Must win two games in a row to be a "Top Gun."
   b. After a player has won back-to-back games, both she/he and the defeated player restart at the lowest court.
   c. If a player is defeated at the highest court, she/he must return to the lowest court and play toward the top.

Student Tasks:

1. Win at the highest court.
2. Win four games in a row at the lower courts.
3. Get to the premier court.
4. Defeat any past "Top Gun" while playing on a lower court.

Variations:

1. Make doubles teams.
2. A player or team must win three or more at the best court.
3. A player or team must win three or more points at any court to advance.
4. Play games based on a time limit.

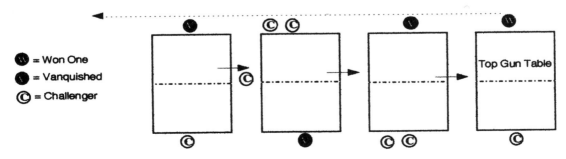

ABOUT "TRACK AND FIELD"

Objectives:

- ◆ To allow the students to compete as a team and as individuals in the various events.
- ◆ To allow students to experience the various events.

Essentials:

- ◆ Field
- ◆ Each event lists the items needed or options available
- ◆ Track and field forms

Activities:

1. **Shot Put:** Softballs work very well and are safe; tape or lines drawn to mark distance
2. **Discus:** Flying discs can be substituted; tape or cones on the field to mark distance
3. **Hurdles:** 12; stopwatch
4. **Long Jump:** Rake; tape measure
5. **40 to 60 Meter Dash:** 6 starting blocks; stopwatch
6. **High Jump:** Chinese jump ropes that are hooked together or an elastic band make a great cross bar
7. **600 Meter Run:** Stopwatch
8. **400 Meter Relay:** Batons, balls, hoops, or various other objects make good hand-off items; stopwatch

How to Play:

1. Form teams of equal ability with four to five members each.
2. Go over the activities for a certain duration so the students can learn and practice the skills.
3. Give each team a sign-up form. A student can be in only two events plus the relay.
4. Allow practice time.
5. Relays can have any number of runners as long as each team has the same amount.

© 1996 Parker Publishing Company

The Meet:

1. This can last two or more days.

2. Have students who are not participating at given times help with timing, retrieving throws, and picking place finishers.

3. Run preliminary heats if there are not enough lanes.

4. Time or record distances.

5. Students get only two jumps or throws in the field events.

6. Give awards (Achievement Cards) to the first-place team.

Scoring:

First   =   6 points
Second =   5 points
Third   =   4 points
Fourth =   3 points
Fifth   =   2 points
Sixth   =   1 point

Variations:

1. Have everyone on a team do each event. Combine the times or distances.
   Example: In the 100-yard dash the runners on team #1 ran:

   12.4
   13.7
   14.5
   15.3

   Total Team Time Combined = 55.9

2. Have everyone on a team do each event. Average the times or distances. Using the example above, the total team time average = 13.975.

3. Have everyone do each event. Put six numbered cards in a hat. Pull out only three of the cards after each event and count those placers only.
   Example: Numbers 1, 4, and 6 were pulled from the hat. Those places for the long jump on every team are the only ones that can be combined to give the team a total distance.

SAMPLE TEAM ROSTER

Use this form for student sign-ups.

Period: 5
Date: May 10

1 Team Members	EVENTS: (PICK TWO)							(Entire Team) 400 RELAY
	Discus	Shot Put	High Jump	Long Jump	Hurdles	Short Dash	600 Run	
Smith, Sue	X	X						

5 Team Members	EVENTS: (PICK TWO)							(Entire Team) 400 RELAY
	Discus	Shot Put	High Jump	Long Jump	Hurdles	Short Dash	600 Run	

Directions:

1. This form is used by the students so that they must choose **two** events in which to participate.
2. Fill in the *Period* and *Date* slots.
3. Have the students fill in their name in the *Team Members* box.
4. Next have them put an "X" in the box of the two *Events* they elect.
5. Take this information and transfer it to the *Event Results* form.

TEAM ROSTER

Use this form for student sign-ups.

Period: _____
Date: _____

1

Team Members

EVENTS: (PICK TWO)

Discus	Shot Put	High Jump	Long Jump	Hurdles	Short Dash	600 Run	(Entire Team) 400 RELAY

2

Team Members

EVENTS: (PICK TWO)

Discus	Shot Put	High Jump	Long Jump	Hurdles	Short Dash	600 Run	(Entire Team) 400 RELAY

3

Team Members

EVENTS: (PICK TWO)

Discus	Shot Put	High Jump	Long Jump	Hurdles	Short Dash	600 Run	(Entire Team) 400 RELAY

4

Team Members

EVENTS: (PICK TWO)

Discus	Shot Put	High Jump	Long Jump	Hurdles	Short Dash	600 Run	(Entire Team) 400 RELAY

5

Team Members

EVENTS: (PICK TWO)

Discus	Shot Put	High Jump	Long Jump	Hurdles	Short Dash	600 Run	(Entire Team) 400 RELAY

6

Team Members

EVENTS: (PICK TWO)

Discus	Shot Put	High Jump	Long Jump	Hurdles	Short Dash	600 Run	(Entire Team) 400 RELAY

7

Team Members

EVENTS: (PICK TWO)

Discus	Shot Put	High Jump	Long Jump	Hurdles	Short Dash	600 Run	(Entire Team) 400 RELAY

8

Team Members

EVENTS: (PICK TWO)

Discus	Shot Put	High Jump	Long Jump	Hurdles	Short Dash	600 Run	(Entire Team) 400 RELAY

SAMPLE EVENT RESULTS

Period: _3_
Date: _May 14_

Scoring:
First............= 6
Second ......= 5
Third ....= 4
Fourth........= 3
Fifth...........= 2
Sixth...........= 1

Discus

Name	Team Number	Results	Place	Place Points	Total Team Pts
Smith, Sue	1	66			
	1				
Williams, Bill	2	82	4	3	3
	2				
Chaney, Ken	3	78	5	2	2
	3				
Minner, Fred	4	59			
	4				
Gert, Sally	5	62			5
	5				
Jacobs, Peter	6	92	1	6	6
	6				
Holton, Craig	7	84	3	4	4
	7				
Miller, Jon	8	73	6	1	6
Larkinski, Phil	8	88	2	5	

Directions:

1. Use this form to place student names in the events that they chose.

2. See the *Team Roster* form for their selections.

3. Fill in the *Period* and *Date* blanks.

4. Using the roster, place the *Name* to the appropriate team number.

5. These can now be cut out and used at the events on competition day.

6. After the completion of the events, fill in the *Results* box with the distance.

7. Compare the results and put in the *Place* box the results' placements.

8. Assign point values to the placements in the *Place Points* box. Use the box in the top right-hand corner to determine these scores.

9. Add the score as in the case of team #8 since they had two entries in the discus. Put these scores in the *Total Team Points* box.

EVENT RESULTS

Period: _____
Date: _____

Discus

Scoring:
First...........= 6
Second ......= 5
Third ....= 4
Fourth........= 3
Fifth ....= 2
Sixth...........= 1

Name	Team Number	Results	Place	Place Points	Total Team Pts
	1				
	1				
	2				
	2				
	3				
	3				
	4				
	4				
	5				
	5				
	6				
	6				
	7				
	7				
	8				
	8				

Shot Put

Scoring:
First...........= 6
Second ......= 5
Third ....= 4
Fourth........= 3
Fifth ....= 2
Sixth...........= 1

Name	Team Number	Results	Place	Place Points	Total Team Pts
	1				
	1				
	2				
	2				
	3				
	3				
	4				
	4				
	5				
	5				
	6				
	6				
	7				
	7				
	8				
	8				

EVENT RESULTS

Period: _____
Date: _____

Scoring:
First..........= 6
Second ......= 5
Third ....= 4
Fourth..........= 3
Fifth............= 2
Sixth...........= 1

Distance

Name	Team Number	Results	Place	Place Points	Total Team Pts
	1				
	1				
	2				
	2				
	3				
	3				
	4				
	4				
	5				
	5				
	6				
	6				
	7				
	7				
	8				
	8				

Scoring:
First..........= 6
Second ......= 5
Third ....= 4
Fourth..........= 3
Fifth............= 2
Sixth...........= 1

Relay

Name	Team Number	Results	Place	Place Points	Total Team Pts
	1				
	2				
	3				
	4				
	5				
	6				
	7				
	8				

EVENT RESULTS

Period: _____
Date: _____

Scoring:
First...........= 6
Second ......= 5
Third ....= 4
Fourth.......= 3
Fifth...........= 2
Sixth..........= 1

High Jump

Name	Team Number	Results	Place	Place Points	Total Team Pts
	1				
	1				
	2				
	2				
	3				
	3				
	4				
	4				
	5				
	5				
	6				
	6				
	7				
	7				
	8				
	8				

Scoring:
First...........= 6
Second ......= 5
Third ....= 4
Fourth.......= 3
Fifth...........= 2
Sixth..........= 1

Long Jump

Name	Team Number	Results	Place	Place Points	Total Team Pts
	1				
	1				
	2				
	2				
	3				
	3				
	4				
	4				
	5				
	5				
	6				
	6				
	7				
	7				
	8				
	8				

TRACK AND FIELD

EVENT RESULTS

Period: _____
Date: _____

Hurdles

Name	Team Number	Results	Place	Place Points	Total Team Pts
	1				
	1				
	2				
	2				
	3				
	3				
	4				
	4				
	5				
	5				
	6				
	6				
	7				
	7				
	8				
	8				

Dash

Name	Team Number	Results	Place	Place Points	Total Team Pts
	1				
	1				
	2				
	2				
	3				
	3				
	4				
	4				
	5				
	5				
	6				
	6				
	7				
	7				
	8				
	8				

TRACK AND FIELD

SAMPLE MEET RESULTS

Track and Field
Period: 5
Date: May 18

	Team 1 Pts	Total	Team 2 Pts	Total	Team 3 Pts	Total	Team 4 Pts	Total	Team 5 Pts	Total	Team 6 Pts	Total	Team 7 Pts	Total	Team 8 Pts	Total
Discus	2	2	1	1	3	3		0	5	5		0	6	6	4	4
		2		1		3		0		5		0		6		4
Shot Put	5	+ 5	4	+ 7		+ 0		+ 0	2	+ 2		+ 0	6 = 10	+	1	+ 1
		7	+ 3	8		3		0		7		0	+ 4	16		5
High Jump	2 = 8	+		+ 0		+ 0	1	+ 1	5	+ 5	4	+ 4		+ 0	3	+ 3
	+ 6	15		8		3		1		12		4		16		8
Long Jump																
Hurdles																
Dash																
600 Run																
Relay																
Totals		15		8		3		1		12		4		16		8

Directions:

1. Use this form to calculate and tally the meet results and the final standings.
2. Fill in the *Period* and *Date* slots.
3. Take the information from the *Event Results* sheet and put that information in each of the events for each team.
4. Fill in the *Totals* box.
5. Fill in the *Team No.* boxes to show the meet standings.
6. *Note:* Example shows calculations after three events. Notice that Teams 2 and 7 had two people place in the shot put. Also Team 1 had two people place in the high jump.

TRACK AND FIELD

MEET RESULTS

Track and Field
Period:_____
Date:_____

	Team 1		Team 2		Team 3		Team 4		Team 5		Team 6		Team 7		Team 8	
	Pts	Total	Pts	Total	Pts	Total	Pts	Total	Pts	Total	Pts	Total	Pts	Total	Pts	Total
Discus																
Shot Put																
High Jump																
Long Jump																
Hurdles																
Dash																
600 Run																
Relay																
Totals		15		8		3		1		12		4		16		8

Standings

Place   Team Number
First.............No._____
Second.............No._____
Third.............No._____
Fourth.............No._____
Fifth.............No._____
Sixth.............No._____
Seventh.............No._____
Eight.............No._____

ABOUT "TUMBLING"

Objectives:

◆ To allow students to be successful regardless of size or skill factor.

◆ To provide movement alternatives.

◆ To allow self-testing situations.

◆ To allow students to be creative by designing their own unique routine.

Essentials:

◆ Large area with mats or pads

◆ Post the *Can You Do This?* lists

◆ Copy and cut the routine sheets

How to Play:

1. All students spread out and face the same direction towards the instructor.

2. After warming up and stretching, students follow the commands of the teacher on the *Can You Do This?* list. This takes several days to complete.

3. Allow time to practice the movement skills. Post several lists around the room so students may better utilize all of the various stunts.

4. Students combine movements to form a routine using the *Tumbling Routine* slips that are copied and passed out in class.

5. Students can demonstrate their routine to the class for extra credit.

Student Tasks:

1. Put together a routine of a set number of movements.

2. Spot others properly.

Variations:

1. Work in pairs to do a routine.

2. Work in groups to do a routine.

Safety:

1. Allow plenty of stretching and warm-up time.

2. Cover spotting when doing head and hand stands.

3. Make sure all movement is going in the same direction to help prevent or minimize collisions.

CAN YOU DO THIS?

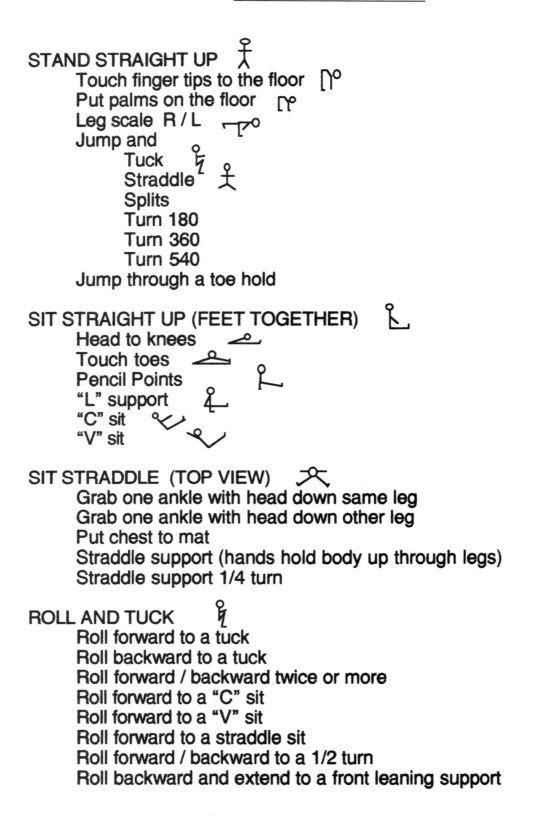

STAND STRAIGHT UP

       Touch finger tips to the floor

       Put palms on the floor

       Leg scale R / L

       Jump and

              Tuck

              Straddle

              Splits

              Turn 180

              Turn 360

              Turn 540

       Jump through a toe hold

SIT STRAIGHT UP (FEET TOGETHER)

       Head to knees

       Touch toes

       Pencil Points

       "L" support

       "C" sit

       "V" sit

SIT STRADDLE (TOP VIEW)

       Grab one ankle with head down same leg

       Grab one ankle with head down other leg

       Put chest to mat

       Straddle support (hands hold body up through legs)

       Straddle support 1/4 turn

ROLL AND TUCK

       Roll forward to a tuck

       Roll backward to a tuck

       Roll forward / backward twice or more

       Roll forward to a "C" sit

       Roll forward to a "V" sit

       Roll forward to a straddle sit

       Roll forward / backward to a 1/2 turn

       Roll backward and extend to a front leaning support

CAN YOU DO THIS?

(Continued)

Can You Do This? (continued)

FRONT LEANING SUPPORT
    Turn to a rear leaning support
    Turn back to a front leaning support
    R / L leg up
    Hands and knees only touch
    Straddle
    Walk through to a rear leaning support
    Squat through vault
    R / L side flank vault
    Drag toes to a pike
    Pike to a forward roll
    Pike to a head stand
    Pike to a hand stand

LIE FLAT ON Back
    Log roll
    R / L leg up
    Both legs up
    Tuck
    Egg roll
    Bicycle
    Crab stand
        R / L leg up
        Walk forward / backward / circle
        Kick over
    Roll and kip to a crab stand
    Stand and drop backwards to a crab stand
    Standing backward walk over / front walk over
    Kip to feet
    Kip from the floor to a standing position

STRADDLE STAND
    Back bend
    Forward / backward roll to a straddle stand
    Wider, wider, wider to the splits

INVERTED
    Bipod
    Tripod
    Forearm balance
    Headstand

CAN YOU DO THIS?

(Continued)

INVERTED HEADSTANDS
    Straddle
    Splits
    Circles

    Handstand
        To a crab stand
        Walk
        Walk and turn around

FLOOR STUNTS
    Swedish drop
        From the knees
        Standing
    Body lever
    Cartwheel
        R / L
        One hand
        Round off

ROUTINE
    Combine any seven to ten of the above moves and make a routine
        One person
        Two or more people

TUMBLING ROUTINE

Cut these out and give them to the students to record their routine on.

Period _____
Names: 1. _____ 2. _____ 3. _____
My routine is made up of these movements:

1. _____ 2. _____ 3. _____ 4. _____ 5._____

6._____ 7. _____ 8. _____ 9. _____ 10._____

Optional: (Worth 1 bonus point each) 11. _____ 12. _____

Period _____
Names: 1. _____ 2. _____ 3. _____
My routine is made up of these movements:

1. _____ 2. _____ 3. _____ 4. _____ 5._____

6._____ 7. _____ 8. _____ 9. _____ 10._____

Optional: (Worth 1 bonus point each) 11. _____ 12. _____

Period _____
Names: 1. _____ 2. _____ 3. _____
My routine is made up of these movements:

1. _____ 2. _____ 3. _____ 4. _____ 5._____

6._____ 7. _____ 8. _____ 9. _____ 10._____

Optional: (Worth 1 bonus point each) 11. _____ 12. _____

Period _____
Names: 1. _____ 2. _____ 3. _____
My routine is made up of these movements:

1. _____ 2. _____ 3. _____ 4. _____ 5._____

6._____ 7. _____ 8. _____ 9. _____ 10._____

Optional: (Worth 1 bonus point each) 11. _____ 12. _____

Period _____
Names: 1. _____ 2. _____ 3. _____
My routine is made up of these movements:

1. _____ 2. _____ 3. _____ 4. _____ 5._____

6._____ 7. _____ 8. _____ 9. _____ 10._____

Optional: (Worth 1 bonus point each) 11. _____ 12. _____

ABOUT "VOLLEYBALL"

Objective:

◆ To work together as a team to score 15 points first.

Essentials:

◆ Gymnasium or outdoors
◆ Volleyballs

How to Play:

1. Serve:
   a. A player is only allowed one serve.
   b. A fault occurs when the ball:
      — Touches the net.
      — Passes under the net.
      — Touches a player on the serving team.
      — Lands outside the line. The line is **good.**
   c. May serve underhanded from any distance that allows success. All overhanded serves are from behind the service line.
   d. A player may only serve three in a row and then must rotate.
   e. Only the serving team may score points.

2. Receiving:
   a. Players must bump the ball when receiving serve.
   b. A team is only allowed a maximum of three hits to return the ball.
   c. No slugging or fist hitting the ball.
   d. The ball must contact only the hands or arms.
   e. The ball may be played off the ceiling on the first or second hit if it returns to the same side that it was hit from.
   f. The ball cannot be played from the ceiling to the other team's court.

3. General rules:
   a. Roll the ball under the net when returning it to the other team.
   b. Return a ball to another court by bouncing it to them.
   c. Rotate in a clockwise manner.
   d. While in play, if a ball hits the net and goes over, it is good.
   e. Players should try to stay in his/her own playing area to hit the ball.
   f. Hitting the ball with open hands is a *carry* and goes to the other team.
   g. Players may not touch or step under the net during play.

Student Tasks:

1. Serve three in a row.
2. Be part of a three-hit combination.
3. Bump or set the ball a certain number of times.
4. Spike the ball.
5. Block a shot.
6. Be a referee.

Variations:

1. Use beach balls in place of regular volleyballs.
2. Allow for a two-hit minimum, four-hit maximum game.
3. Allow for any number of hits on a side.
4. Make large games of 10 to 12 members.
5. Make small teams of two to three players.
6. Use the **Mix 'n Match** format.

FOUR-WAY*

Objective:

◆ To work together as a team to score 15 points first.

Essentials:

◆ Gymnasium or outside court
◆ 2 volleyballs
◆ Score board (optional)
◆ 4 volleyball nets, 5 standards

How to Play:

1. Form four equal teams.
2. All of the rules of regulation volleyball apply.
3. Must be serving to get a point.
4. Serving sequences.
   a. A and B serve at the same time. A serves to D and B serves to C and play each other. (Diagram 1)

Created by Ken Lumsden and Dick Copple, 1991.

b. After both points are played out, C serves to B and D serves to A. (Diagram 2)

c. After both points are played out, A serves to B and D serves to C. (Diagram 3)

d. Next, B serves to A and C serves to D. (Diagram 4)

e. Next, A serves to C and B serves to D. (Diagram 5)

f. Next, C serves to A and D serves to A. (Diagram 6)

g. Players now rotate as in regular volleyball and begin a new sequence.

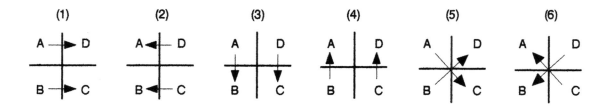

Student Tasks:

1. Serve three in a row.

2. Be part of a three-hit combination.

3. Bump or set the ball a certain number of times.

4. Spike the ball.

5. Block a shot

6. Be a referee.

Variations:

1. Use beach balls in place of regular volleyballs.

2. Make large games of 10 to 12 members.

3. Make small teams of two to three players.

4. Use the **Mix 'n Match** format.

ONE TO THREE

Objective:

◆ To be the first team to score 11 points.

Essentials:

◆ Volleyball court

◆ 1 volleyball per court

VOLLEYBALL

How to Play:

1. Divide the group into teams of three players. One team starts as servers.
2. The other teams alternate receiving.
3. To earn a point for her/his team, the individual server must:
   a. Touch the ball before it hits the floor on her/his side.
   b. Ace the serve.
   c. Have the receiving team hit the ball out of bounds or into the net.
4. *Note:* Only one player, the server, attempts to play the ball on her/his side. This individual should try and return the ball back to the defensive side when possible to keep the ball into play.
5. The receiving team scores a point when they hit the ball back into the serving court without it being touched by the individual server. Rotate to the end of the line after each point. The next group takes the receiving side.
6. First side to score 11 points is the winner.
7. Change serving teams after each game.

Student Tasks:

1. Serve an ace.
2. Return a ball back to the three-player team.
3. Hit the ball into an area where the single server cannot touch it.
4. Come from behind and win the game.

Variations:

1. Play one against six.
2. Play two against four.

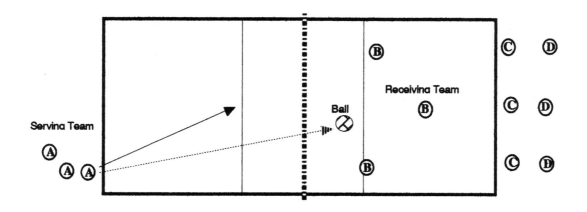

SELF-SERVICE

Objectives:

- ◆ To serve the ball over the net and into the other court of play without a service error.
- ◆ To keep the entire team out of the touch court.

Essentials:

- ◆ Volleyball court
- ◆ 4 to 6 balls at each court

How to Play:

1. Divide into teams of four to six players. Assign a team to each side.
2. Participants begin serving back and forth. A player must go over to the opposite court and sit down if her/his serve:
   a. Goes out of bounds.
   b. Hits the net.
   c. Does not go over the net.
3. Any player sitting may go back to the serve line if she/he can reach out and touch a ball that has been served by her/his own teammates.
4. The game is over when an entire team is sitting down.

Student Tasks:

1. Bring two or more teammates back to the service line.
2. Never go over to the sit-down side.
3. Wind up on the sit-down court only once or twice.

Variations:

1. Base the game on a time limit. The team that has the most servers when time expires is the winner.
2. All serves must be overhanded.
3. Allow students to be on their knees instead of sitting.

© 1996 Parker Publishing Company

All players are sitting down when on the opposite court.

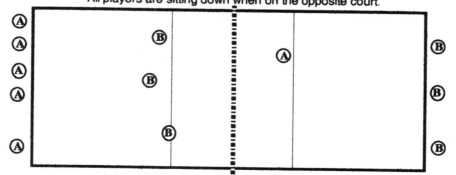

SEVEN UP

Objective:

- ◆ To work the ball up to seven hits and back to zero without a mistake.

Essentials:

- ◆ Volleyball court
- ◆ 1 ball

How to Play:

1. Five or more players are on a team.
2. A team is on each side of the net.
3. Start by tossing the ball to one of the teams. The ball must be returned over the net in one hit. The other side must next hit the ball twice, with the second hit going over the net to the opposite team. The receiving team now must hit the ball three times with the third hit going back to the other team. Attempt to hit the ball one, two, three, four, five, six, seven, six, five, four, three, two, and one without a miss.
4. Rotate positions after a mistake is made and start all over on the count.

Student Tasks:

1. Be one of the hitters on a five, six or seven hit.
2. Make a certain number of sets in a series.
3. Make a certain number of passes in a series.

Variations:

1. Lower the number that the teams must go to and back.
2. Raise the number that the teams must go to and back.
3. Use a beach ball.

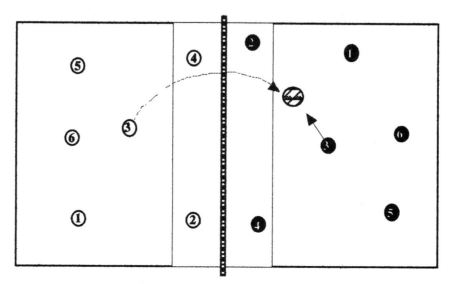

TOP-NOTCH

Objectives:

- ◆ To work to the top position and stay there as long as possible or a set number of times.
- ◆ To not make a mistake.
- ◆ To develop teamwork.

Essentials:

- ◆ Volleyball court
- ◆ 1 volleyball

How to Play:

1. Five or more teams of three players on a team.
2. Each team represents a line on the volleyball court.
3. If any player in a line makes a mistake, that entire team is eliminated and must return to the back of the waiting line.
4. All other teams move up one line to where the eliminated team was positioned.
5. New team that enters the court serves.

Student Tasks:

1. Be part of a three-hit combination.
2. Bump or set the ball a certain number of times.
3. Spike the ball.
4. Block a shot.
5. Stay in the top court three or more times.

Variations:

1. Have two teams compete against the top court which only has one team.
2. Use a beach ball

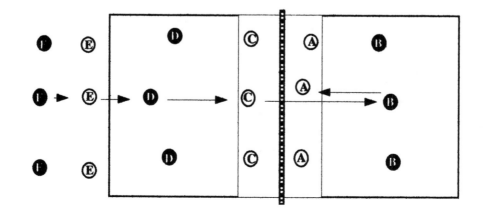

CIRCUIT TRAINING

Objectives:

◆ To move to a new circuit station every couple of minutes to complete a workout.

◆ To learn how to keep records on the self at each of the various stations.

Essentials:

◆ Large room
◆ Circuit station cards posted at each location
◆ Music box
◆ Pencils and clipboards for each student
◆ Circuit scorecards
◆ Circuit maps
◆ Cassette tape with prerecorded whistle blasts every two minutes

How to Play:

1. Stretch and warm the joints and muscles before participation.

2. To start, each student is to go to a **different** station with his/her scorecard, pencil and clipboard, and follow the instructions on the station cards.

3. After two minutes a whistle is sounded (a tape in a recorder works wonders for this task) and all of the students fill in the circuit scorecard with the appropriate data and then rotate one station. If a student is on number eight, for example, he/she moves to station number nine. If she/he moves out of order or to the wrong number, it will mess up an individual who is supposed to be there.

4. Every two minutes, a whistle, bell, alarm or beep alerts everyone to move to the next station. Continue this for the allotted time.

5. Allow time for a cool-down session after the scorecards, pencils, and clipboards have been collected.

6. On day #2, a student should go to the next station from where she/he finished on day #1.

Student Tasks:

1. Show an improvement during the unit.

2. Be able to compute a correct target heart rate.

Variations:

1. Pair up and go to the stations. Allow more time with two people.

2. Allow a student to work out at any station of her/his choice for two minutes. Keep the lines of people waiting for a specific station limited to a small number of participants.

Safety: Use spotters!

SAMPLE CIRCUIT SCORECARD

Name: Bob Smith
Period 3
Target Heart Rate = ___134___ to __176___ Beats Per Minute

No.	Station Name	Day 1			Day 2			Day 3			Day 4			Day 5		
		Lbs.	Rep	Set	Lbs.	Rep	Set	Lbs.	Rep	Set	Lbs.	Rep	Set	Lbs.	Rep	Set
	Sample	90	15	3												
1	**Stair Walk**	4 times														
2	**Rest Station**	X														
3	**Wall Seat**	1:50	sec.													
4	**Pull-Ups**			12												
5	**Military Press**	45	14	1												
6	**Hang**	1:30	sec.													
7	**Seated Rowing**	60	15	2												
8	**Pull Downs**	80	15	1												
9	**Leg Press**	250	15	2												

Directions:

1. Fill in the student information at the top of the page.

2. Looking at the chart on *Target Heart Rate,* have everyone figure out what his/her THR should be and fill in the blanks.

3. On day 1 have the students fill in the required data. Where weights are not being used, time, number of, or just an "X" will be sufficient.

4. Do not write in the day 2 column until it is the second day of the unit.

5. Where weight is used for the exercise, put the pounds of the weight, the number of repetitions done, and the number of set of repetitions performed.

CIRCUIT SCORECARD

Name_____

Period ____

Target Heart Rate = _____to_____Beats Per Minute

No.	Station Name	Day 1			Day 2			Day 3			Day 4			Day 5		
		Lbs.	Rep	Set	Lbs.	Rep	Set	Lbs.	Rep	Set	Lbs.	Rep	Set	Lbs.	Rep	Set
	Sample	90	15	3												
1																
2																
3																
4																
5																
6																
7																
8																
9																
10																
11																
12																
13																
14																
15																
16																
17																
18																
19																
20																
21																
22																
23																
24																
25																
26																
27																
28																
29																
30																
31																
32																
	Start over at #1															

SAMPLE CIRCUIT MAP

Copy and post several of these around the room.

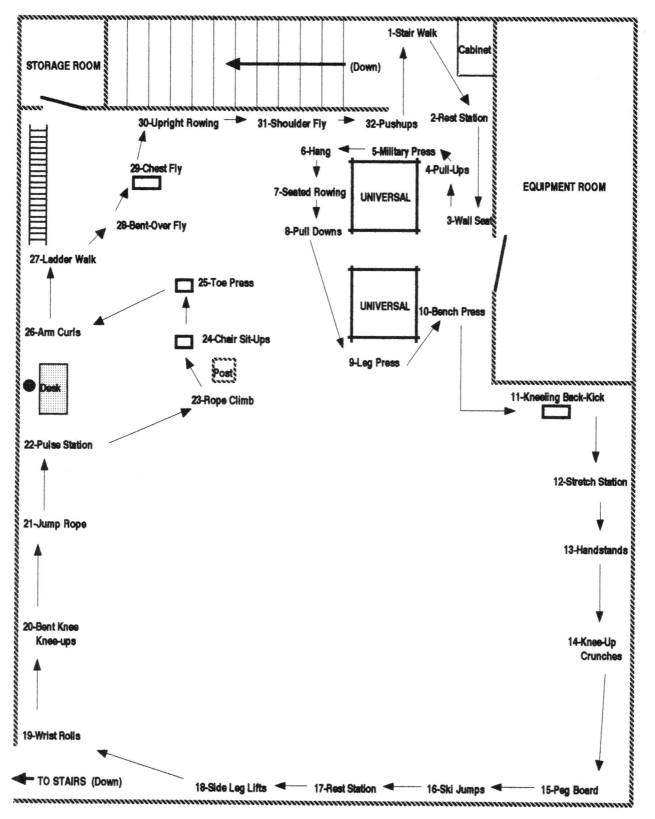

SAMPLE CIRCUIT STATION CARD

Station Number

Sample Circuit Station Card

22

PULL-UPS

BENEFITS: TRICEPS - SHOULDERS

** PALM FACE AWAY ON GRIP.

**DO NOT WHIP OR KICK FEET.

**CHIN MUST GO OVER THE BAR.

**ARMS MUST BE FULLY EXTENDED.

Station Number

ARM CURLS

BENEFITS: BICEPS

** SLIGHTLY TILT THE PELVIS.
**DO NOT USE THE BACK TO LIFT.
**KEEP THE KNEES SLIGHTLY BENT.
**GO SLOWLY IN BOTH DIRECTIONS.

Station Number

BENCH PRESS

BENEFITS: TRICEPS

**BAR COMES DOWN TO MID-LINE OF CHEST.

**KEEP THE BACK FLAT.

**LOWER AND RAISE THE WEIGHT SLOWLY.

**DO NOT SLAM THE WEIGHTS TOGETHER.

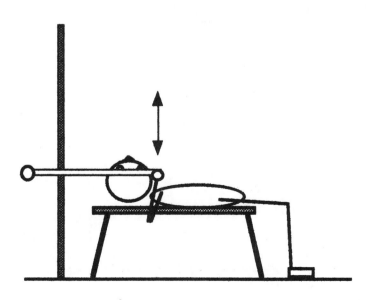

Station Number

BENT KNEE

KNEE-UPS

BENEFITS:　　ABDOMINALS

**LIE ON THE BACK.

**KEEP ARMS AT SIDE.

**BRING KNEES BACK TO THE CHEST.

Station Number

BENT-OVER FLY

BENEFITS: TRAPEZIUS

** KEEP THE BACK PARALLEL TO THE FLOOR.

**LIFT WEIGHTS EVEN WITH THE SHOULDERS.

**BE CAREFUL OF THE FINGERS ON RETURN.

**NOW MOVE YOUR ARMS LIKE A BIRD DOES ITS WINGS.

Station Number

BENT-OVER ROWING

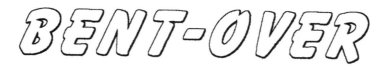

BENEFITS: TRAPEZIUS - LATS - TRICEPS

** KEEP THE BACK PARALLEL TO THE FLOOR
**LIFT WEIGHTS DIRECTLY TO THE CHEST

Station Number

CHAIR SIT UPS

BENEFITS: ABDOMINALS

**TOES HOOK UNDER BOTTOM ROLLER OR BEHIND THE SEAT SUPPORT.

**CROSS ARMS ON THE CHEST.

**LIE BACK PARALLEL TO THE FLOOR THEN SIT UP.

**YOU MAY NEED A SPOTTER.

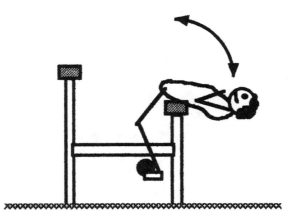

Station Number

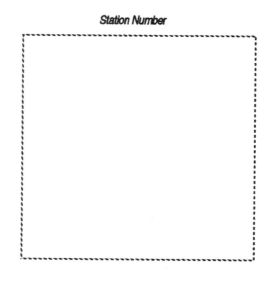

© 1996 Parker Publishing Company

CHEST FLY

BENEFITS: PECTORALS

**LIE WITH YOUR BACK ON BENCH.

**EXTEND ARMS OUT TO THE SIDE AND LIFT OVER CHEST.

**MOVE THE ARMS LIKE A BIRD THAT IS FLYING UPSIDE DOWN.

**BE CAREFUL NOT TO PINCH FINGERS.

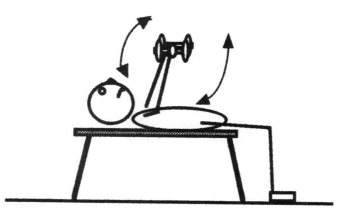

Station Number

HANDSTANDS

BENEFITS: ENTIRE ARM STRENGTH

**MAY DO REGULAR HANDSTANDS ON THE MAT
OR:
**START IN PUSH UP POSITION WITH FEET AT THE WALL, SLOWLY WALK UP THE WALL TO A HANDSTAND THEN WALK BACK DOWN.

Station Number

HANG

BENEFITS: HANDS - LOWER ARMS

** HOW LONG CAN YOU HANG?

Station Number

JUMP ROPE

BENEFITS: CARDIOVASCULAR - LEGS - ARMS - SHOULDERS

**HOW MANY TIMES FORWARD?
**HOW MANY TIMES BACKWARD?

50 ?
100 ?
150 ?

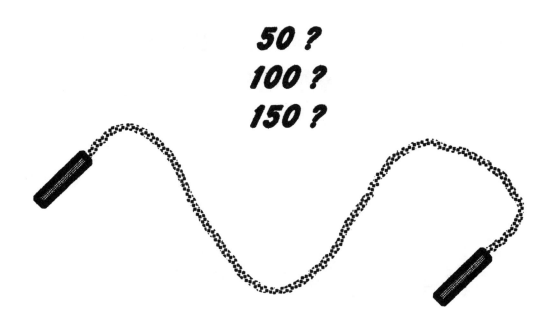

Station Number

KNEE-UP CRUNCHES

BENEFITS: ABDOMINALS

**LEGS GO UP ON THE MAT.

**CROSS ARMS ON THE CHEST.

**LIFT THE HEAD AND SHOULDERS ONLY.

NOTICE: YOU MAY DO THESE AT THE INCLINE BOARD INSTEAD OF HERE.

Station Number

© 1996 Parker Publishing Company

KNEELING BACK-KICK

BENEFITS: ERECTOR SPINAE (LOWER BACK)

** PUT ONE KNEE ON BENCH AND HOLD ON.

**RAISE OTHER LEG STRAIGHT BACK AS FAR AS POSSIBLE.

**DO NOT BEND LEG AT KNEE.

**REPEAT OTHER LEG AFTER 15 TIMES.

Station Number

LADDER WALK

BENEFITS: SHOULDERS - ARMS - GRIPS

**HOW MANY WAYS CAN YOU GO DOWN AND BACK?

1. **GRAB EVERY BAR?**

2. **GRAB EVERY OTHER BAR?**

3. **USE ONLY THE SIDES OF THE LADDER?**

4. **GO BACKWARDS?**

5. **YOU INVENT A NEW WAY USING THE ARMS ONLY?**

Station Number

LEG CURLS

BENEFITS: HAMSTRINGS

** LIE ON BENCH FACE DOWN.

**HOOK HEELS BEHIND ROLLERS.

**BRING HEELS TO THE BUTTOCKS.

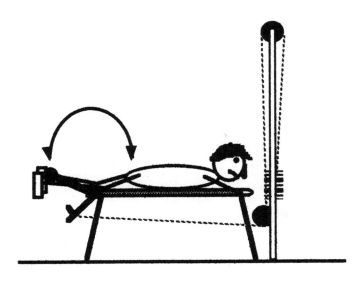

Station Number

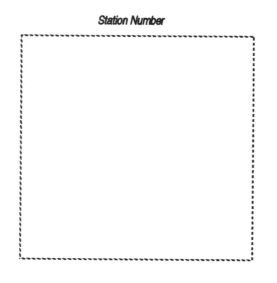

LEG PRESS

BENEFITS: QUADRICEPS - CALVES - ANKLES

**GRASP THE SEAT HANDLES.

**LIFT AND LOWER THE WEIGHTS SLOWLY.

**PLEASE DO NOT SLAM THE WEIGHTS.

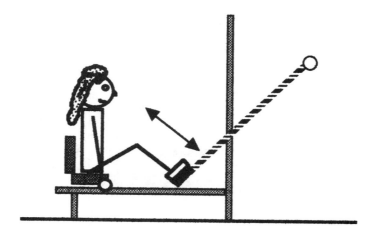

Station Number

MILITARY PRESS

BENEFITS: DELTOIDS - TRICEPS

**SIT ON THE STOOL.

**ARCH AND LOCK THE LOWER BACK.

**LEAN INTO THE BAR.

**LIFT AND LOWER THE WEIGHTS SLOWLY.

**PLEASE DO NOT SLAM THE WEIGHTS.

Station Number

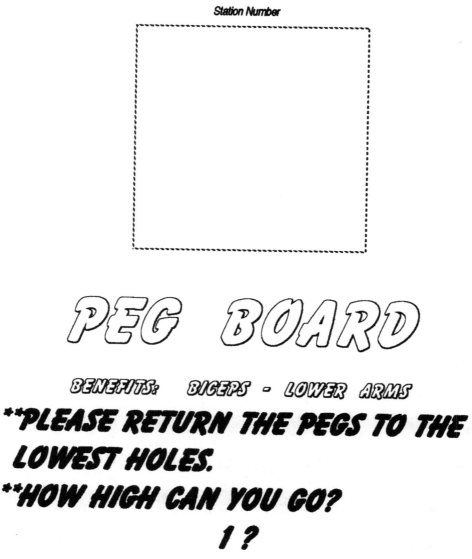

PEG BOARD

BENEFITS: BICEPS – LOWER ARMS

**PLEASE RETURN THE PEGS TO THE LOWEST HOLES.

**HOW HIGH CAN YOU GO?

1 ?

2 ?

3 ?

4 ?

5 ?

6 ?

7 OR MORE ?

Station Number

PULL DOWNS

BENEFITS: LATISSIMUS DORSI (LATS) - BICEPS

**PULL FROM THE KNEES.

**MAY NEED HELP TO HOLD KNEES TO MAT.

**ALTERNATE FRONT AND BACK OF HEAD.

**LIFT AND LOWER THE WEIGHTS SLOWLY.

**PLEASE DO NOT SLAM THE WEIGHTS.

Station Number

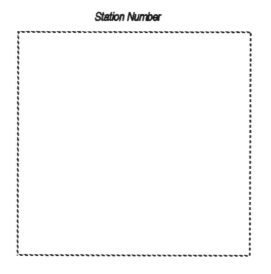

PULL-UPS

BENEFITS: TRICEPS - SHOULDERS

** PALMS FACE AWAY ON GRIP.

**DO NOT WHIP OR KICK FEET.

**CHIN MUST GO OVER THE BAR.

**ARMS MUST BE FULLY EXTENDED.

Station Number

PULSE STATION

BENEFITS: CARDIOVASCULAR

**SIT AND RELAX.

**TAKE YOUR PULSE FOR 1 MINUTE.

**CHECK YOUR TARGET HEART RATE.

TARGET HEART RANGES

AGE	THR
10	136 - 178
11	136 - 177
12	135 - 177
13	134 - 176
14	134 - 175
15	133 - 174
20	130 - 170
25	127 - 166
40	117 - 153
70	98 - 128

© 1996 Parker Publishing Company

Station Number

PUSHUPS

BENEFITS: TRICEPS - DELTOIDS

**KEEP THE BACK STRAIGHT.
**MAY DO THEM FROM THE KNEES.

**CAN YOU SPREAD YOUR LEGS AND DO A ONE ARMED PUSHUP?

Station Number

BENEFITS: SYSTEMS   RECOVERY

**SIT AND RELAX.

**FILL IN YOUR SCORES FROM THE LAST STATIONS.

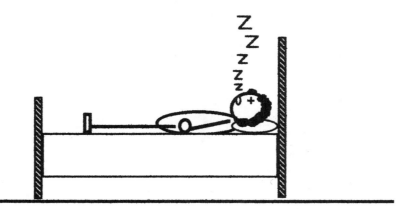

Station Number

ROPE CLIMB

BENEFITS: UPPER BODY

**PLACE THICK MAT UNDER ROPE.
**HOW FAR CAN YOU GO UP?
**HOW FAR BY JUST USING YOUR ARMS?

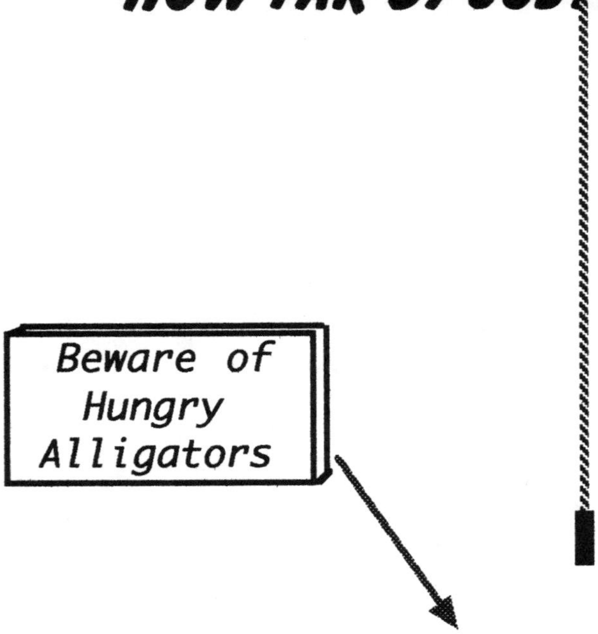

Beware of
Hungry
Alligators

Station Number

SEATED ROWING

BENEFITS: TRAPEZIUS - LATS - TRICEPS

**PULL BAR TO THE CHEST.

**USE ONLY THE ARMS, NOT THE BACK.

**LIFT AND LOWER THE WEIGHTS SLOWLY.

**PLEASE DO NOT SLAM THE WEIGHTS.

Station Number

SHOULDER FLY

BENEFITS: DELTOIDS

** STAND WITH DUMBBELLS AT SIDE.

**BEND THE ELBOWS SLIGHTLY.

**LIFT UNTIL PARALLEL WITH FLOOR.

**NOW MOVE YOUR ARMS LIKE A BIRD
DOES ITS WINGS.

Station Number

SIDE LEG LIFTS

BENEFITS: UPPER LEG - HIPS

**LIE ON SIDE.

**KEEP BOTTOM LEG ON FLOOR.

**TOP LEG IS LIFTED UP HIGH - TOES POINTED.

**SWITCH SIDES AFTER 15 REPS.

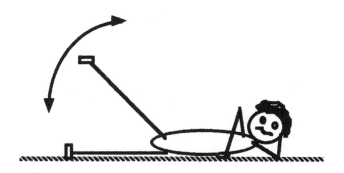

© 1996 Parker Publishing Company

Station Number

SKI JUMPS

BENEFITS: CARDIOVASCULAR - LEGS

**HOW MANY TIMES BACK AND FORTH?
**HOW MANY TIMES SIDE TO SIDE?
**HOW MANY TIMES SCISSOR STEPS?
**HOW MANY 180 DEGREE TURNS?

50 ?
100 ?
150 ?

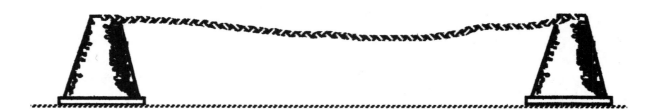

Station Number

STAIR WALKS

BENEFITS: CARDIOVASCULAR - ENTIRE LEGS

**WALK UP AND DOWN THE STAIRS.

**HOLD ON TO THE RAIL.

**1-DOWN, 2-UP, 3-DOWN, ETC.

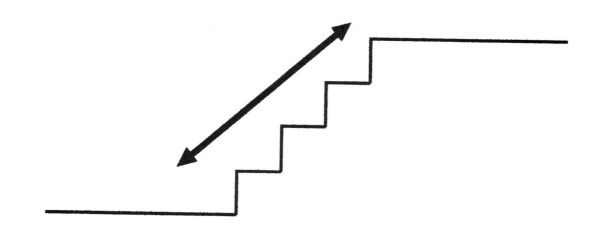

Station Number

© 1996 Parker Publishing Company

STRETCHING

BENEFITS: FLEXIBILITY

**DO THREE DIFFERENT STRETCHES FROM THE CARD THAT IS POSTED ON THE WALL.

Station Number

TOE PRESS

BENEFITS: GASTROCNEMIUS (CALF) - ANKLES

**KEEP THE HIPS UNDER THE WEIGHT.

**LIFT WEIGHT WITH LEGS, NOT THE BACK.

**STAND WITH TOES ON THE RISER.

**DO NOT BEND THE KNEES.

Station Number

UPRIGHT ROWING

BENEFITS: DELTOIDS

**WITH PALMS DOWN HOLD BOTH HANDS TOGETHER.

**RAISE THE BAR TO THE CHIN.

Station Number

WALL SEAT

BENEFITS: QUADRICEPS

**SIT IN THE INVISIBLE CHAIR.

**KEEP HANDS FLAT TO THE WALL.

**MAKE THE QUADS PARALLEL TO THE FLOOR.

Station Number

WRIST ROLLS

BENEFITS: LOWER ARMS AND SHOULDERS

** EXTEND ARMS OUT PARALLEL TO FLOOR.

**ROLL UP THE WEIGHT FORWARD.

**ROLL DOWN THE WEIGHT BACKWARD.

**ROLL UP THE WEIGHT BACKWARD.

**ROLL DOWN THE WEIGHT FORWARD.

TARGET HEART RATE

Copy and post several of these around the room.

HEART RATE DEFINITIONS

1. **Heart Rate:** The number of complete beats in one minute.
2. **Resting Heart Rate:** Your pulse for one minute taken before you get up in the morning. A normal range for youths is 60 to 80 heart beats per minute.
3. **Maximum Heart Rate:** This is the fastest your heart can beat. The maximum for people 20 years or younger is 200 peats per minute. DO NOT EXERCISE AT THIS RATE.
4. **Training Zone:** This is the range in which you must exercise to attain aerobic benefits. This training zone is 65% to 85% of your maximum heart rate. You should work from 20 to 30 minutes in your training zone.
5. **Recovery rate:** How quickly your pulse returns to normal after exercise. To safely stop exercising, it should be 120 beats a minute or less. Ten minutes after exercising it should be less than 100 beats per minute.

HOW TO DETERMINE YOUR TARGET HEART RATE (THR)

220 - AGE = Maximum Heart Rate (MHR)

65% to 85% of (MHR) = Target Heart Rate (THR)

EXAMPLE

```
  220
 -11 (age)
= 209 (MHR)
```

65% X 209 = 136 ⎤
                ⎬— THR = 136 to 167 beats per minute (BPM)
85% X 209 = 167 ⎦

TARGET HEART RANGES

age	THR
10	136 - 178
11	136 - 177
12	135 - 177
13	134 - 176
14	134 - 175
15	133 - 174
20	130 - 170
25	127 - 166
40	117 - 153
70	98 - 128

ARM WRESTLING

Objective:

◆ To put the back of the opponent's hand to the mat.

Essentials:

◆ Mats on large floor area
◆ Knee pads (optional)

How to Play:

1. Pick a partner of about the same size.
2. Lie on the mat facing the opponent.
3. Grasp the thumb of the other person's hand.
4. Clasp other hands between the elbows that are resting on the mat.
5. Players may not raise the elbows from the mat.
6. On the command of "go," both players try to put the back of the other's hand to the mat.
7. Go with the right arm and then the left.
8. Win two out of three matches against an opponent.

Student Tasks:

1. Defeat someone with the right and left arm.
2. Defeat three or more people.

Variations:

1. Arm wrestle from the kneeling position from a desk.
2. Make two or three weight divisions and have a double elimination tournament.

CO-ED WRESTLING

Objectives:

◆ To develop a knowledge of the sport of wrestling.
◆ To learn how to score individually and as a team.
◆ To learn the basic moves and holds.

◆ To understand the safety aspects of the sport.

Essentials:

◆ Large mat room

◆ Knee pads (optional)

How to Play:

1. **NO** all-out wrestling is performed.

2. This unit can be taught in a co-ed setting.

3. It is purely for an educational understanding of the sport.

4. Have the students pair up and spread out on the mats.

5. Allow plenty of room around each couple.

6. Have all pairs face the instructor so that all movements are going in the same direction.

7. The skills are demonstrated and then the students practice them at a slow controlled pace.

8. The various types of wrestling demonstrated are:

   a. Arm

   b. Leg

   c. Sumo

   d. Freestyle

9. Demonstrations cover some of the basic skills for: *(Samples)*

   a. Referee's position: *Upper, lower.*

   b. Take downs: *Single leg, double leg, head and arm.*

   c. Reversals: *Outside arm grab, inside wrist grab.*

   d. Escapes: *Short sit out, long sit out, stand up.*

   e. Pins: *Front cradle, back cradle, head and arm, reverse cradle, durbin.*

   f. Break downs: *Near arm tight waist, head lever, far arm far leg.*

   g. Techniques: *Proper weight displacement, hand holds for falls, etiquette, sportsmanship.*

10. Scoring will be:

Individual	Points	Team	Points
Illegal hold	1	Tie	2
Escape	1	Major = 1 to 8	3
Take down	2	Superior = 9 to 14	4
Reversal	2	Superior Tech = 15 or more	5
Near fall = 3 sec.	2	Forfeit	6
Near fall = 5 sec.	3	Fall or pin	6

11. All highly interested students are encouraged to join a club or go out for interscholastic wrestling.

Student Tasks:

1. Identify and demonstrate some of the moves used in wrestling.
2. Score a match or meet.

Safety:

1. Warm up and stretch properly.
2. Partners should be of near weight, size, and ability.
3. Cover and demonstrate the illegal holds of:
   a. Clasping
   b. Full Nelson
   c. Head holds must include an arm or leg
   d. No arm bars beyond 90 degrees
   e. Safely return partner to the mat when lifting him/her
   f. No single or double finger grabs
4. No jewelry or watches are worn by the participants.

CHICKEN FIGHTS

Objectives:

◆ To be the last person left.
◆ To maintain good balance.

Essentials:

◆ Mats on large floor area
◆ Knee pads (optional)

How to Play:

1. All players spread out over the mats.
2. Each person raises a leg backwards and grabs the foot.
3. Under no circumstances may a player let go of the foot.
4. Everyone hops around on **one** leg trying to push, pull, or bump the others to the mat. The arms of a competitor may be grabbed and held on to when attempting to pull them to the floor.
5. Players may not grab clothing.
6. Players must leave the floor immediately upon falling or letting go of the foot and go directly to the chicken pen.

© 1996 Parker Publishing Company

7. Play five or six matches. Take the top five or six previous winners and have a Grand Championship match where the winner takes all.

Student Tasks:

1. Win a championship.
2. Knock down a past champion.
3. Get into the championship.

Variations:

1. Use the off leg.
2. Have a chicken coop war. This is two different teams going at it until one team is completely eliminated. May need pinnies for identification.
3. Allow players to switch feet during play when the leg gets tired as long as both feet do not touch the floor at once.

IT'S BETTER TO BE A LIVE CHICKEN......
THAN A DEAD DUCK!

DRAG RACES

Objective:

◆ To pull or drag another person across a line on the mat.

Essentials:

◆ Mats on large floor area
◆ Knee pads (optional)

How to Play:

1. Mark two lines about ten feet apart on the mat.
2. Two opponents will **sit** between the lines while facing each other.
3. The grabbing of arms, legs, or torso is allowed.
4. May not grab clothing.
5. First person to drag or pull their rival over the line behind them three times is declared the winner.

Student Tasks:

1. Defeat three different foes.
2. Win by a three-to-zero margin.

Variations:

1. Must be on the knees and shins.
2. Have the students stand.
3. Students must **push** another person across the line.

Safety:

1. Try to have partners fairly close to the same size.
2. All pushing or pulling is either forward or backward, not from side to side, to prevent collisions with other participants.
3. Keep the groups spread out on the floor with plenty of room around them.

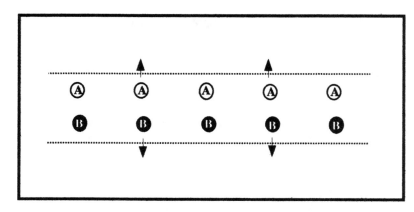

KING CRAB CLASH

Objective:

◆ To cause the other player to touch the mat with something other than the bottom of the feet or hands.

Essentials:

◆ Mats on large floor area
◆ Knee pads (optional)

How to Play:

1. Have all the players spread out over the entire floor.
2. Players get into the crab walk position (chest toward the ceiling) and attempt to push or pull others to the mat.
3. No grabbing clothes.
4. Any player who touches the mat with something other than the hands or feet is out.

Student Tasks:

1. Put three different crabs out.
2. Be one of the top five crabs.
3. Defeat a past King or Queen Crab.

Variations:

1. Make two teams. Try to eliminate the other crabs first. Pinnies may be needed for identification.
2. Have the players flip over and have a bear brawl. The same rules as above are used. Players may not stand up but must remain on all fours.

LEG WRESTLING

Objective:

◆ To cause a partner to leave his/her back and shoulders and do a somersault.

Essentials:

◆ Mats on large floor area
◆ Double elimination form

How to Play:

1. Have the participants pair up and lie on their backs with the head towards the opposition's feet.
2. Next, the wrestlers hook their right arms together at the elbows.
3. On the first **two** commands, both rivals lift their right legs toward the ceiling and touch feet.
4. On the third command, both will lift and hook their legs at the knee, trying to pull the opponent over in a somersault fashion.
5. Two wins constitute a victory.

Student Tasks:

1. Defeat someone with the right and left arm.
2. Defeat three or more people.

Variations:

1. Use the left leg.
2. Make two or three weight divisions and have a double elimination tournament.

Top View

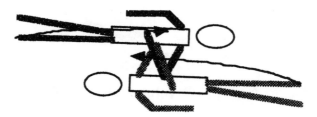

PALM BLASTS

Objective:

◆ To make the other person step in any direction first.

Essentials:

◆ Mats on large floor area
◆ Knee pads (optional)

How to Play:

1. Two rivals stand **one foot apart** and face each other.
2. Each player keeps her/his own feet together and touching at the ankles.
3. Hands are held at the shoulders with flat palms facing their partners.
4. Players may only hit the flat palms of their opponents.
5. Grabbing or hanging on to any part of the adversary is not allowed.
6. A player may use fakes or pull her/his palms out of the way as his/her toe attempts to hit palms.
7. The first participant to cause the other to step or lose balance five times is the winner.

Student Tasks:

1. Defeat a larger person.
2. Win by a three-point margin.
3. Defeat three or more challengers.

Variations:

1. Stand on the left leg only.
2. Stand on the right leg only.

PUSH OR PULL

Objective:

◆ To make the other person step with either foot first.

Essentials:

◆ Mats on large floor area
◆ Knee pads (optional)

How to Play:

1. Two opponents stand while facing each other.
2. Place the right foot so that it is **touching** the outside edge of the right foot of the other contender. (See the diagram for foot placement on next page.)
3. The back foot may be placed anywhere for stability.
4. Players grasp the thumb of each other's right hand like in arm wrestling.

5. Leaning in and pushing with the shoulder is prohibited.

6. First player to cause his/her partner to step with **either** foot, by pushing or pulling with the hands and arms, wins a point.

7. Five points is a game.

Student Tasks:

1. Defeat a larger person.

2. Win by a three-point margin.

3. Defeat three or more challengers.

Variation: Allow players to step and move the back foot freely.

SUMO WRESTLING

Objectives:

◆ To force an opponent out of the circle first.

◆ To force an opponent to touch the mat with something other than the feet.

Essentials:

◆ Mats on large floor area

WRESTLING

◆ Mat with a ten-foot circle drawn on it or a couple of 4 by 8 tumbling mats fastened together side-by-side

How to Play:

1. Divide the class into two or three weight divisions.

2. Two contestants face each other from the opposite sides of the circle. The diameter of the circle should be about eight to ten feet.

3. Action now begins by the opponents trying to push, pull, throw, trip, or trick the other out of the ring or touch the mat with something other than the feet.

4. Grabbing of clothing is not allowed.

5. If both students go out of the circle or touch the mat, the last one to touch is declared the winner. If both touch at the same time, then restart at opposite sides of the circle. The winner stays and takes on a new challenger.

6. Any person who can defeat three other competitors in a row is called a **Grand Master.** This person goes to the end of the line and two new players step into the circle.

Student Tasks:

1. Defeat someone bigger.
2. Win five matches in a row.
3. Become a Grand Master.
4. Defeat a past Grand Master.

Variations:

1. Make the circle diameter around five feet.
2. Allow three players in the circle with everyone for themselves.
3. Put two 2-person teams in the ring.

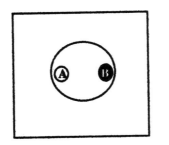

Challengers

Section 2

◆◆◆◆◆

TOURNAMENTS

- ◆ Mix'n Match Format
- ◆ Multiple Activity Format
- ◆ Miscellaneous Formats

INTRODUCTION TO THE MIX 'N MATCH FORMAT

Take a few minutes to look over the information, drawings, and samples listed in this section. It will be time well spent because of the rewards *you* and your *students* will experience.

The history of this unique method of organizing teams was experimented with in the mid 1980's by Ken Lumsden and Don McClure. It was first conceived to solve the problem of absenteeism due to sickness, field trips or other reasons, which could play havoc with teams that were already defined. Six players against nine just didn't fare too well. How could we solve this difficulty? The solution was easy. Make an **extra team** and use those individuals where they were needed. Something so simple, why hadn't we thought of it before?

Well, Don retired, and left me to carry the torch. Still there were problems with time lost in teaching skills, the organization of teams, team make-up, and championship play. Sally and I took the **extra team** concept to a new and higher level by developing class management into the structure, introducing a new formula for more teams, and developing a varied size and activity format. I cannot begin to tell of the many successes that the **Mix 'n Match** has brought not only to our program but to other P.E. instructors who have initiated it. You try it too! Your program, students, and staff will definitely experience a win-win situation when it comes to team activities.

Advantages and benefits of the Mix 'n Match:

◆ Organization is fast, simple and easy to read.

◆ Roll can be taken directly from all of the team form sheets.

◆ Increased student participation and enthusiasm during play.

◆ Decreased boredom during the activity.

◆ Success-oriented task and skill sheets are provided so students can record and monitor their individual goal accomplishments.

◆ Accountability of unit objectives and goals is enhanced.

◆ The "loser" syndrome is lessened since students are **with** and **against** 90% of their classmates.

◆ More time for activity and participation by the students.

◆ Allows for different or multiple activities at the same time.

◆ Allows for variable group sizes.

◆ Referees can be designated without disrupting any team.

◆ Co-ed activities are less of a problem.

◆ Scores are usually closer because of shorter games and multiple rotations.

◆ Allows for the **last** place team to compete in the championship game.

MIX 'N MATCH
SINGLE CLASS INSTRUCTIONS

Organization:

1. Determine the number of teams needed. Formula: (Normal number of teams × 2) + 1 = "Mix 'n Match" required number of teams.

   Example: Normally to play two games of softball, four teams are chosen. With the Mix 'n Match format, though, nine teams are chosen. That is, (4 × 2) + 1 = 9.

2. Select nine teams. (Save time by putting permanent team numbers on the floor.)

3. Record player's name to corresponding team.

4. The skills, tasks or activities for the unit are recorded on the form if desired.

5. Students can practice skills, tasks or activities while in their teams.

Tournament Play: (See example of 9-**Team Schedule.**)

DAY 1

1. Teams are sitting in numerical order.

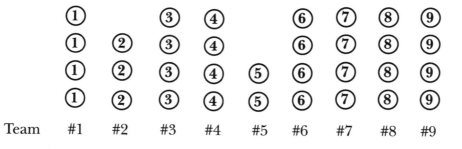

2. Team #1 goes to the front of the class and waits. (*Note:* Day 1 = Team #1)

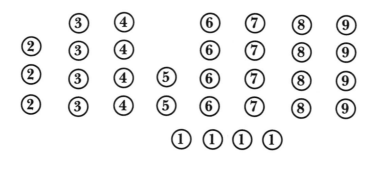

3. Next place #2 behind #3, #4 behind #5, #6 behind #7, and #8 behind #9.

4. Next take team #1 and distribute its players where they are needed. (May be needed for absent players, balancing numbers on teams, or as referees.) *Note:* A team that has one more player than the opponent does not usually dominate. (#6 and #7 + #1 = nine players)

5. Assign the new **combined** teams to their playing areas.

Game 1 = On field "A" (#2 + #3 vs. #4 + #5)
On field "B" (#6 + #7 vs. #8 + #9)

6. If two or more games a day are scheduled, simply circle the teams at the bottom for Game 1 that won, circle both if they tied, then record the wins and ties in the box W or T located by the right side of each individual team.

Game 2 = On field "A" (#2 + #3 vs. #8 + #9)
On field "B" (#4 + #5 vs. #6 + #7)

Game 3 = On field "A" (#2 + #3 vs. #6 + #7)
On field "B" (#8 + #9 vs. #4 + #5)

DAY 2

Same steps as above except Team #2 is asked to come up front and the **Day 2** schedule is followed. Remember that Day 2 = Team #2 is out, Day 3 = **Team #3 is** out, and so on.

Championships (Optional):

1. Tally the standings by giving a win two points and a tie one point.

   Example: Team #3 has: 10 wins = 20 points
                                     3 ties = 3 points
                                     Total = **23 points**

2. Place all teams in their appropriate championship game.

*Gold Medal

1st place + 4th place vs. 2nd place + 3rd place. *Note:* Use the 9th place players in this game when possible.

*Silver Medal

5th place + 8th place vs. 6th place + 7th place.

THESE MEDAL GAMES ARE USUALLY VERY CLOSE SINCE:

   1 + 4 = 5 and 2 + 3 = 5
   5 + 8 = 13 and 6 + 7 = 13

MIX 'N MATCH
DOUBLE-CLASS FORMAT

(Team Teaching)

Combining Teams from Two Different Classes (Team Teaching):

1. Mr. Jones and Mrs. Smith have their classes sit in Teams 1 through 9.

	J1		J3	J4	J5		J7		J9
Mr. Jones's Class	J1		J3	J4	J5	J6	J7	J8	J9
	J1	J2	J3	J4	J5	J6	J7	J8	J9
	S1	S2	S3	S4	S5	S6	S7	S8	S9
Mrs. Smith's Class	S1	S2	S3	S4	S5	S6	S7	S8	S9
	S1	S2	S3	S4		S6		S8	S9

2. Mrs. Smith sends her Team #1 team to line up and sit behind Mr. Jones's Team #1. She next sends her Team #2 to line up behind his Team #3, and her #3 to his #2, her #4 to his #5 and her #5 to his #4, and so on. Since this is DAY 1, Team #1 will be distributed to other teams.

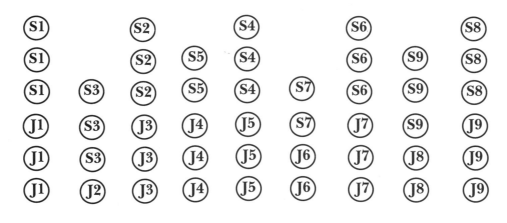

3. They next distribute Team #1 to the teams that will need an extra player(s).

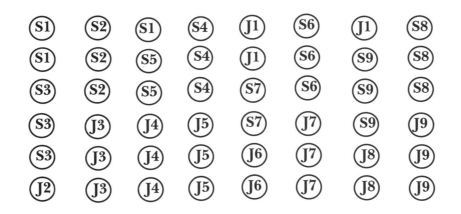

Field Assignments: Assign the various combined teams to the proper field and play a round robin of two or more games during the period.

FIELD DIAGRAMS

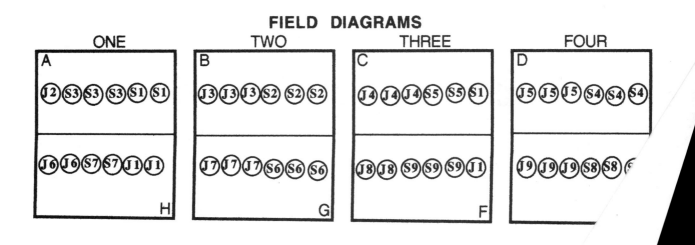

ROUND ROBIN ROTATIONS

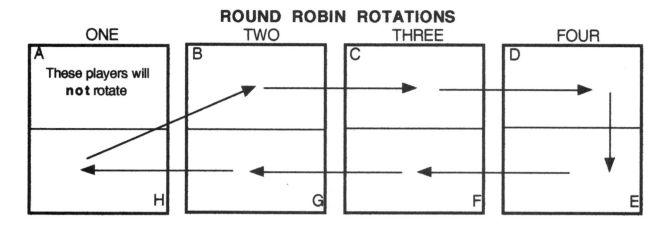

Combined Teams Championships:

1. Tally each class for the final team standings.

2. Combine teams according to the example below.

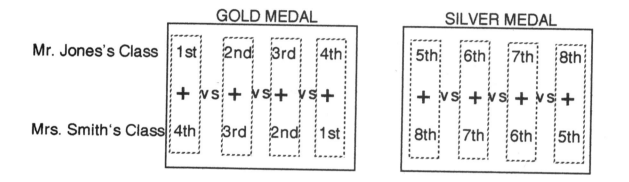

3. Take 9th place team and distribute them in the Gold Medal round if possible.

4. Play a round robin tournament (three games) with each division.

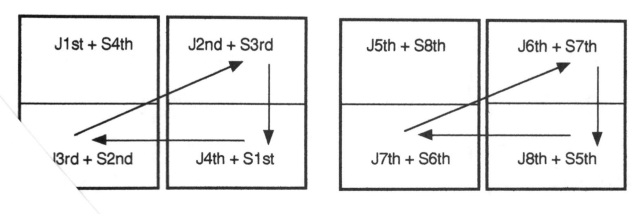

MIX'N MATCH FORMAT

Period: _____
Date: _____
Instructor: _____

Unit:_____

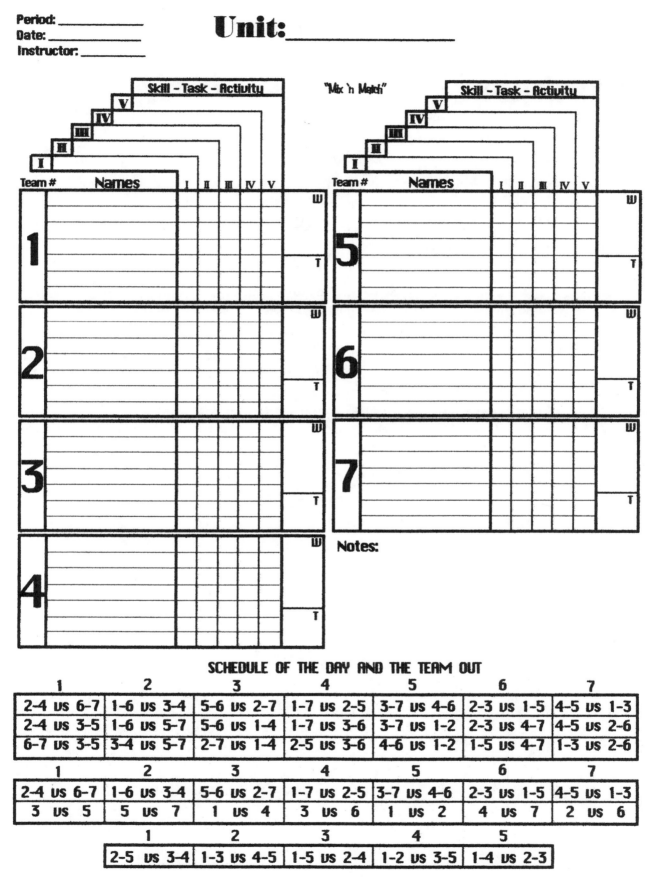

SCHEDULE OF THE DAY AND THE TEAM OUT

1	2	3	4	5	6	7
2-4 vs 6-7	1-6 vs 3-4	5-6 vs 2-7	1-7 vs 2-5	3-7 vs 4-6	2-3 vs 1-5	4-5 vs 1-3
2-4 vs 3-5	1-6 vs 5-7	5-6 vs 1-4	1-7 vs 3-6	3-7 vs 1-2	2-3 vs 4-7	4-5 vs 2-6
6-7 vs 3-5	3-4 vs 5-7	2-7 vs 1-4	2-5 vs 3-6	4-6 vs 1-2	1-5 vs 4-7	1-3 vs 2-6

1	2	3	4	5	6	7
2-4 vs 6-7	1-6 vs 3-4	5-6 vs 2-7	1-7 vs 2-5	3-7 vs 4-6	2-3 vs 1-5	4-5 vs 1-3
3 vs 5	5 vs 7	1 vs 4	3 vs 6	1 vs 2	4 vs 7	2 vs 6

1	2	3	4	5
2-5 vs 3-4	1-3 vs 4-5	1-5 vs 2-4	1-2 vs 3-5	1-4 vs 2-3

9-TEAM (AND MORE) INSTRUCTIONS

"Mix 'n Match"

Directions:

1. Fill in the *Period, Date* and *Instructor* slots.

2. Fill in the student tasks in the *Skill–Task–Activity* section. They are placed in the boxes with the *I, II, III, IV,* and *V.* (This can also be done on the unit grade sheets.)

3. Pick the teams and fill in the *Names* spaces.

4. Stay in the nine teams to practice, do skill drills, talk strategy, and so on.

5. After the drills have been covered, bring the teams together and combine the teams for play. This will be game #1.

6. Remember to distribute Team #1 on Day #1.

7. *Optional:* If time allows for two or three games, simply rotate the combined teams to the next field for a new game.

8. Shorter time allotted games create closer contest scores. This is certain to improve student desire and interest when participating.

9. As a student fulfills a task, allow him/her to place a "+" in the appropriate box. (This can also be done on the unit grade sheets.)

10. At the end of the first game or the end of the period, circle the winners or ties at the bottom of the page. If there is ever any doubt or dispute at a later time, it is very easy to verify any team's record.

11. Fill in the individual team records, when convenient, in the *W* or *T* box.

12. The wins and ties are needed later to determine the final standings.

MIX'N MATCH FORMAT

SAMPLE 9-TEAM

Period: __3__
Date: __Sept. 24__
Instructor: __Mrs. Smith__

Unit: Flash Football

"Mix 'n Match"

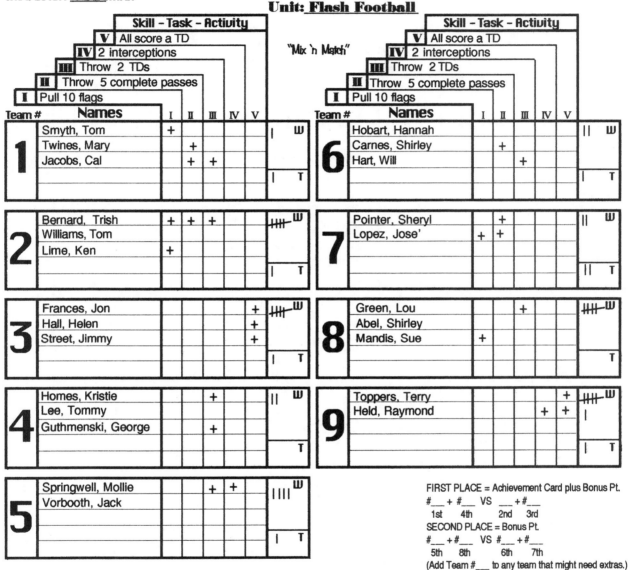

Skill – Task – Activity				
V All score a TD				
IV 2 interceptions				
III Throw 2 TDs				
II Throw 5 complete passes				
I Pull 10 flags				

Team 1 — Smyth, Tom (I +); Twines, Mary (II +); Jacobs, Cal (II +, III +) — I — W — I — T

Team 2 — Bernard, Trish (I +, II +, III +); Williams, Tom; Lime, Ken (I +) — ‖‖ W — I — T

Team 3 — Frances, Jon (IV +); Hall, Helen (IV +); Street, Jimmy (IV +) — ‖‖ W — I — T

Team 4 — Homes, Kristie (III +); Lee, Tommy; Guthmenski, George (III +) — ‖ W — T

Team 5 — Springwell, Mollie (III +, IV +); Vorbooth, Jack — ‖‖‖ W — I — T

Team 6 — Hobart, Hannah; Carnes, Shirley (II +); Hart, Will (III +) — ‖ W — I — T

Team 7 — Pointer, Sheryl (II +); Lopez, Jose' (I +, II +) — ‖ W — ‖ T

Team 8 — Green, Lou (IV +); Abel, Shirley; Mandis, Sue (I +) — ‖‖‖ W — T

Team 9 — Toppers, Terry (IV +); Held, Raymond (III +, IV +) — ‖‖‖ W — I — T

FIRST PLACE = Achievement Card plus Bonus Pt.

#___ + #___   VS ___ + #___
1st   4th   2nd   3rd

SECOND PLACE = Bonus Pt.

#___ + #___ VS #___ + #___
5th   8th   6th   7th

(Add Team #___ to any team that might need extras.)
9th

SCHEDULE OF THE DAY AND THE TEAM OUT

	1	2	3	4	5	6	7	8	9
A	2-3 vs 4-5	1-6 vs 4-8	1-7 vs 5-9	1-5 vs 3-7	1-4 vs 2-6	1-8 vs 4-9	1-9 vs 5-8	1-3 vs 2-5	1-2 vs 3-4
B	6-7 vs 8-9	3-9 vs 5-7	2-8 vs 4-6	2-9 vs 6-8	3-8 vs 7-9	2-7 vs 3-5	2-4 vs 3-6	4-7 vs 6-9	5-6 vs 7-8
A	2-3 vs 8-9	1-6 vs 5-7	1-7 vs 4-6	1-5 vs 6-8	1-4 vs 7-9	1-8 vs 3-5	1-9 vs 3-6	1-3 vs 6-9	1-2 vs 7-8
B	4-5 vs 6-7	4-8 vs 3-9	5-9 vs 2-8	3-7 vs 2-9	2-6 vs 3-8	4-9 vs 2-7	5-8 vs 2-4	2-5 vs 4-7	3-4 vs 5-6
A	2-3 vs 6-7	1-6 vs 3-9	1-7 vs 2-8	1-5 vs 2-9	1-4 vs 3-8	1-8 vs 2-7	1-9 vs 2-4	1-3 vs 4-7	1-2 vs 5-6
B	8-9 vs 4-5	5-7 vs 4-8	4-6 vs 5-9	6-8 vs 3-7	7-9 vs 2-6	3-5 vs 4-9	3-6 vs 5-8	6-9 vs 2-5	7-8 vs 3-4

MIX'N MATCH FORMAT

Period: _____
Date: _____
Instructor: _____

Unit: _____

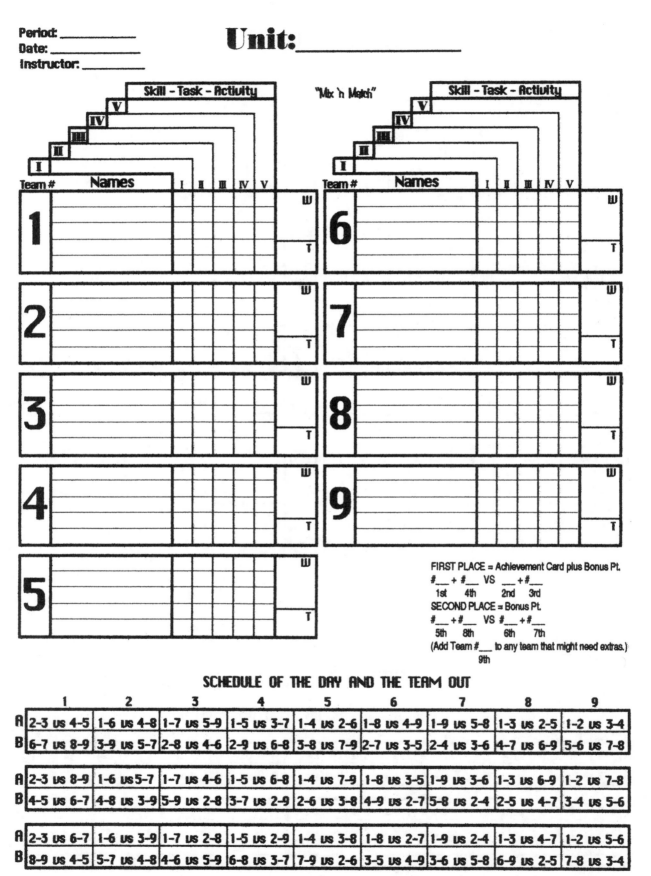

"Mix 'n Match"

Skill – Task – Activity

Team # | Names | I | II | III | IV | V

1 | | | | | | | W / T

2 | | | | | | | W / T

3 | | | | | | | W / T

4 | | | | | | | W / T

5 | | | | | | | W / T

6 | | | | | | | W / T

7 | | | | | | | W / T

8 | | | | | | | W / T

9 | | | | | | | W / T

FIRST PLACE = Achievement Card plus Bonus Pt.
#___ + #___ VS ___ +#___
1st   4th   2nd   3rd
SECOND PLACE = Bonus Pt.
#___ +#___ VS #___ +#___
5th   8th   6th   7th
(Add Team #___ to any team that might need extras.)
9th

SCHEDULE OF THE DAY AND THE TEAM OUT

	1	2	3	4	5	6	7	8	9
A	2-3 vs 4-5	1-6 vs 4-8	1-7 vs 5-9	1-5 vs 3-7	1-4 vs 2-6	1-8 vs 4-9	1-9 vs 5-8	1-3 vs 2-5	1-2 vs 3-4
B	6-7 vs 8-9	3-9 vs 5-7	2-8 vs 4-6	2-9 vs 6-8	3-8 vs 7-9	2-7 vs 3-5	2-4 vs 3-6	4-7 vs 6-9	5-6 vs 7-8

	1	2	3	4	5	6	7	8	9
A	2-3 vs 8-9	1-6 vs 5-7	1-7 vs 4-6	1-5 vs 6-8	1-4 vs 7-9	1-8 vs 3-5	1-9 vs 3-6	1-3 vs 6-9	1-2 vs 7-8
B	4-5 vs 6-7	4-8 vs 3-9	5-9 vs 2-8	3-7 vs 2-9	2-6 vs 3-8	4-9 vs 2-7	5-8 vs 2-4	2-5 vs 4-7	3-4 vs 5-6

	1	2	3	4	5	6	7	8	9
A	2-3 vs 6-7	1-6 vs 3-9	1-7 vs 2-8	1-5 vs 2-9	1-4 vs 3-8	1-8 vs 2-7	1-9 vs 2-4	1-3 vs 4-7	1-2 vs 5-6
B	8-9 vs 4-5	5-7 vs 4-8	4-6 vs 5-9	6-8 vs 3-7	7-9 vs 2-6	3-5 vs 4-9	3-6 vs 5-8	6-9 vs 2-5	7-8 vs 3-4

Period: _____
Date: _____
Instructor: _____

Unit:_____

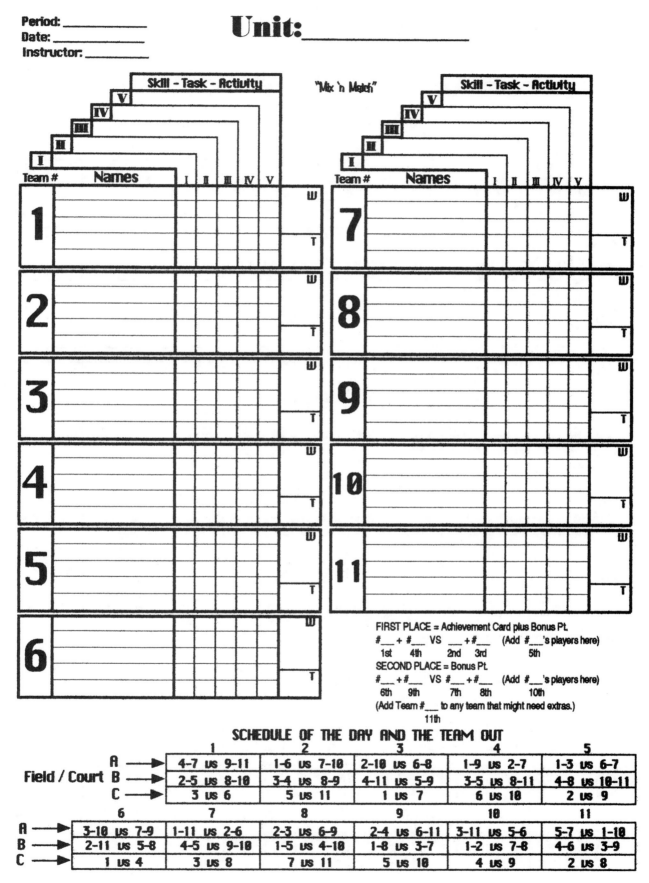

"Mix 'n Match"

Skill - Task - Activity

| Team # | Names | I | II | III | IV | V | W / T |

1
2
3
4
5
6
7
8
9
10
11

FIRST PLACE = Achievement Card plus Bonus Pt.
#___ + #___ VS ___ + #___ (Add #___'s players here)
1st   4th   2nd   3rd   5th
SECOND PLACE = Bonus Pt.
#___ + #___ VS #___ + #___ (Add #___'s players here)
6th   9th   7th   8th   10th
(Add Team #___ to any team that might need extras.)
11th

SCHEDULE OF THE DAY AND THE TEAM OUT

Field / Court		1	2	3	4	5
A →		4-7 vs 9-11	1-6 vs 7-10	2-10 vs 6-8	1-9 vs 2-7	1-3 vs 6-7
B →		2-5 vs 8-10	3-4 vs 8-9	4-11 vs 5-9	3-5 vs 8-11	4-8 vs 10-11
C →		3 vs 6	5 vs 11	1 vs 7	6 vs 10	2 vs 9

		6	7	8	9	10	11
A →		3-10 vs 7-9	1-11 vs 2-6	2-3 vs 6-9	2-4 vs 6-11	3-11 vs 5-6	5-7 vs 1-10
B →		2-11 vs 5-8	4-5 vs 9-10	1-5 vs 4-10	1-8 vs 3-7	1-2 vs 7-8	4-6 vs 3-9
C →		1 vs 4	3 vs 8	7 vs 11	5 vs 10	4 vs 9	2 vs 8

11-TEAM ROUND ROBIN

Units:_____   One to five games a day in round robin format. Mixed activities can be used.

Period: _____

Date: _____

FIRST PLACE = ___ + ___ VS ___ + ___ (Add ___ to this game)
1st   4th   2nd 3rd   5th
SECOND PLACE = ___ + ___ VS ___ + ___ (Add ___ to this game) (Add ___ to any teams)
6th   9th   7th 8th   10th   11th

Day/Team Out

	Game 1	Game 2	Game 3	Game 4	Game 5	Records	
1	4-7 vs 9-11 | 2-5 vs 8-10 — 3-6	2-5 vs 3-6 | 8-10 vs 9-11 — 4-7	8-10 vs 4-7 | 9-11 vs 3-6 — 2-5	9-11 vs 2-5 | 3-6 vs 4-7 — 8-10	3-6 vs 8-10 | 4-7 vs 2-5 — 9-11	Win	Tie
2	1-6 vs 7-10 | 3-4 vs 8-9 — 5-11	3-4 vs 5-11 | 8-9 vs 7-10 — 1-6	8-9 vs 1-6 | 7-10 vs 5-11 — 3-4	7-10 vs 3-4 | 5-11 vs 1-6 — 8-9	5-11 vs 8-9 | 1-6 vs 3-4 — 7-10	Win	Tie
3	2-10 vs 6-8 | 4-11 vs 5-9 — 1-7	4-11 vs 1-7 | 5-9 vs 6-8 — 2-10	5-9 vs 2-10 | 6-8 vs 1-7 — 4-11	6-8 vs 4-11 | 1-7 vs 2-10 — 5-9	1-7 vs 5-9 | 2-10 vs 4-11 — 6-8	Win	Tie
4	1-9 vs 2-7 | 3-5 vs 8-11 — 6-10	3-5 vs 6-10 | 8-11 vs 2-7 — 1-9	8-11 vs 1-9 | 2-7 vs 6-10 — 3-5	2-7 vs 3-5 | 6-10 vs 1-9 — 8-11	6-10 vs 8-11 | 1-9 vs 3-5 — 2-7	Win	Tie
5	1-3 vs 6-7 | 4-8 vs 10-11 — 2-9	4-8 vs 2-9 | 10-11 vs 6-7 — 1-3	10-11 vs 1-3 | 6-7 vs 2-9 — 4-8	6-7 vs 4-8 | 2-9 vs 1-3 — 10-11	2-9 vs 10-11 | 1-3 vs 4-8 — 6-7	Win	Tie
6	3-10 vs 7-9 | 2-11 vs 5-8 — 1-4	2-11 vs 1-4 | 5-8 vs 7-9 — 3-10	5-8 vs 3-10 | 7-9 vs 1-4 — 2-11	7-9 vs 2-11 | 1-4 vs 3-10 — 5-8	1-4 vs 5-8 | 3-10 vs 2-11 — 7-9	Win	Tie
7	1-11 vs 2-6 | 4-5 vs 9-10 — 3-8	4-5 vs 3-8 | 9-10 vs 2-6 — 1-11	9-10 vs 1-11 | 2-6 vs 3-8 — 4-5	2-6 vs 4-5 | 3-8 vs 1-11 — 9-10	3-8 vs 9-10 | 1-11 vs 4-5 — 2-6	Win	Tie
8	2-3 vs 6-9 | 1-5 vs 4-10 — 7-11	1-5 vs 7-11 | 4-10 vs 6-9 — 2-3	4-10 vs 2-3 | 6-9 vs 7-11 — 1-5	6-9 vs 1-5 | 7-11 vs 2-3 — 4-10	7-11 vs 4-10 | 2-3 vs 1-5 — 6-9	Win	Tie
9	2-4 vs 6-11 | 1-8 vs 3-7 — 5-10	1-8 vs 5-10 | 3-7 vs 6-11 — 2-4	3-7 vs 2-4 | 6-11 vs 5-10 — 1-8	6-11 vs 1-8 | 5-10 vs 2-4 — 3-7	5-10 vs 3-7 | 2-4 vs 1-8 — 6-11	Win	Tie
10	3-11 vs 5-6 | 1-2 vs 7-8 — 4-9	1-2 vs 4-9 | 7-8 vs 5-6 — 3-11	7-8 vs 3-11 | 5-6 vs 4-9 — 1-2	5-6 vs 1-2 | 4-9 vs 3-11 — 7-8	4-9 vs 7-8 | 3-11 vs 1-2 — 5-6	Win	Tie
11	5-7 vs 1-10 | 4-6 vs 3-9 — 2-8	4-6 vs 2-8 | 3-9 vs 1-10 — 5-7	3-9 vs 5-7 | 1-10 vs 2-8 — 4-6	1-10 vs 4-6 | 2-8 vs 5-7 — 3-9	2-8 vs 3-9 | 5-7 vs 4-6 — 1-10	Win	Tie

© 1996 Parker Publishing Company

13-TEAM VARIATIONS

"Mix 'n Match"

This is a great form since so many different options can be made available. Use day 4 as an example. Remember that Team 4 is out and will be used as fillers for the other teams.

Option 1: *Mini Teams (6 Games at One Time)* = 3 vs. 5, 8 vs. 13, 2 vs. 6, 10 vs. 11, 1 vs. 7, 9 vs. 12. These 12 teams could also play each other in a round robin format.

Option 2: *Small Teams (3 Games at One Time)* = 3 + 5 vs. 8 + 13, 2 + 6 vs. 10 + 11, 1 + 7 vs. 9 + 12. These 6 teams could also play each other in a round robin format.

Option 3: *Variable Small Teams (3 Games at One Time)* = 3 + 8 + 2 vs. 5 + 13 + 6, 10 + 1 vs. 11 + 7, 9 vs. 12. This works well in volleyball. Remix the teams so that all teams get to play in the smallest court.

Option 4: *Medium Teams (2 Games at One Time)* = 3 + 8 + 2 vs. 5 + 13 + 6, 10 + 1 + 9 vs. 11 + 7 + 12. These four teams can now play each other in a round robin format. The students really like this one.

Option 5: *Variable Large Teams (2 Games at One Time)* = 3 + 8 + 2 + 10 vs. 5 + 13 + 6 + 11, 1 + 9 vs. 7 + 12. Or 3 + 5 + 8 + 13 vx. 2 + 6 + 10 + 11, 1 + 7 vs. 9 + 12.

Option 6: *Large Teams (One Game Only)* = 3 + 8 + 2 + 10 + 1 + 9 vs. 5 + 13 + 6 + 11 + 7 + 12. Or 3 + 5 + 8 + 13 + 2 + 6 vs. 10 + 11 + 1 + 7 + 9 + 12.

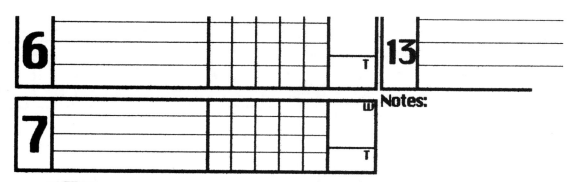

Sample → **SCHEDULE OF THE DAY AND THE TEAM OUT**

1	2	3	4	5	6	7	8	9	10
2-13	1-3	2-4	3-5	4-6	5-7	6-8	7-9	8-10	9-11
5-10	6-11	7-12	8-13	1-9	2-10	3-11	4-12	5-13	1-6
3-12	4-13	1-5	2-6	3-7	4-8	5-9	6-10	7-11	8-12
7-8	8-9	9-10	10-11	11-12	12-13	1-13	1-2	2-3	3-4
4-11	5-12	6-13	1-7	2-8	3-9	4-10	5-11	6-12	7-13
6-9	7-10	8-11	9-12	10-13	1-11	2-12	3-13	1-4	2-5

MIX'N MATCH FORMAT

Period: _____
Date: _____
Instructor: _____

Unit: _____

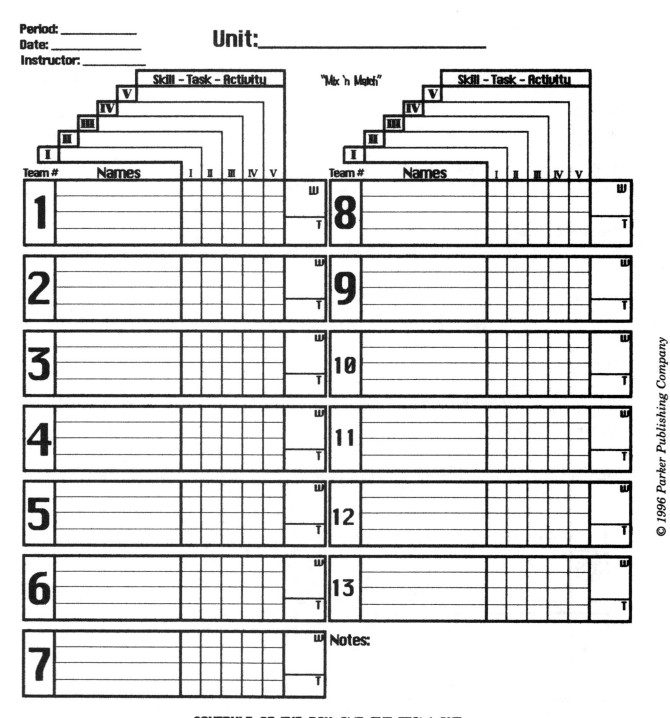

Skill - Task - Activity

"Mix 'n Match"

Skill - Task - Activity

Notes:

SCHEDULE OF THE DAY AND THE TEAM OUT

1	2	3	4	5	6	7	8	9	10	11	12	13
2-13	1- 3	2- 4	3- 5	4- 6	5- 7	6- 8	7- 9	8-10	9-11	10-12	11-13	1-12
5-10	6-11	7-12	8-13	1- 9	2-10	3-11	4-12	5-13	1- 6	2- 7	3- 8	4- 9
3-12	4-13	1- 5	2- 6	3- 7	4- 8	5- 9	6-10	7-11	8-12	9-13	1-10	2-11
7- 8	8- 9	9-10	10-11	11-12	12-13	1-13	1- 2	2- 3	3- 4	4- 5	5- 6	6- 7
4-11	5-12	6-13	1- 7	2- 8	3- 9	4-10	5-11	6-12	7-13	1- 8	2- 9	3-10
6- 9	7-10	8-11	9-12	10-13	1-11	2-12	3-13	1- 4	2- 5	3- 6	4- 7	5- 8

MULTIPLE ACTIVITY INSTRUCTIONS

Multiple Activities:

1. This format allows for two different activities to take place at the same time.

2. It is a great tool for team teaching.

3. One activity usually requires a larger number of participants. An example of this would be to teach volleyball and table tennis together.

4. Another advantage is that students get more individualized instruction, more skill practice, and more game playing in the smaller activity.

5. Use the straight *9-Team Form* and *Dual Activity Schedule* when organizing the units.

Team Distribution Diagram
(Volleyball and Table Tennis Activities)

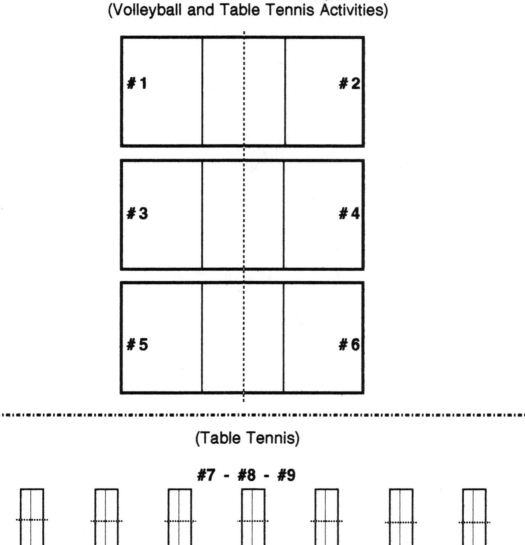

(Table Tennis)

#7 - #8 - #9

MULTIPLE ACTIVITY FORMAT

MULTIPLE ACTIVITY 9-TEAM FORM

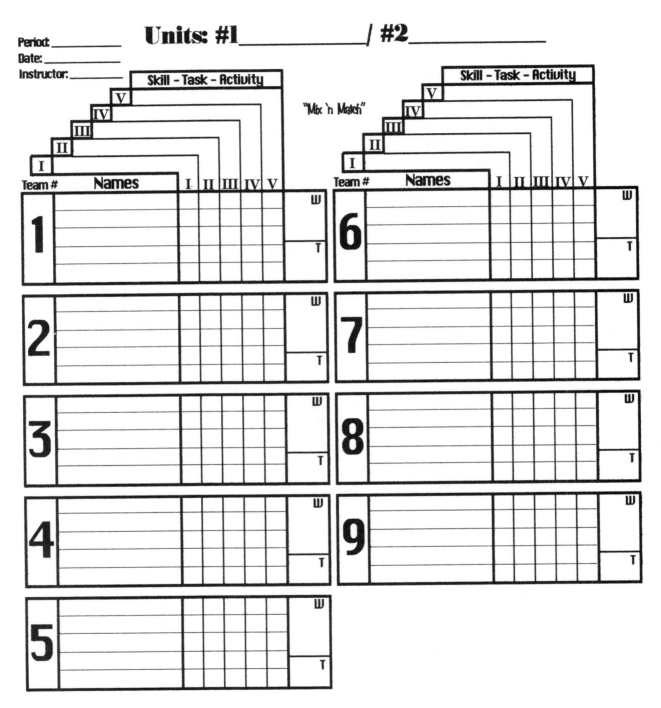

Units: #1_____ / #2_____

Period: _____
Date: _____
Instructor: _____

"Mix 'n Match"

Note: See the next page for the schedule and distribution of teams.

MULTIPLE ACTIVITY FORMAT

SAMPLE MULTIPLE ACTIVITY SCHEDULE AND ROTATIONS

Period:
Date:
Instructor/s:

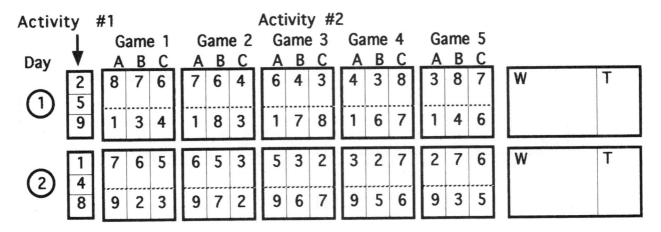

Directions:

1. Fill types of activities, period, date, and instructor's name.

2. The number with the circle around it indicates which day it is for the unit.

3. The three numbers, one below the other and located under the *Activity #1* arrow, indicates which teams are going to go to table tennis. On day ② this would be teams #1, #4, and #8.

4. Under *Activity #2* there are five groups of numbers. These numbers represent a team and in day ②, the first game of the day will have #7 vs. #9 at net **"A,"** #6 vs. #2 at net **"B,"** and #5 vs. #3 at net **"C."** The second game of the day is the next box to the right. Up to five games can be played each day.

5. Notice that the teams rotate one position counterclockwise. The team in the lower left corner does not rotate and remains on that court the entire class period.

6. Record the wins and ties after the games have been recorded with circles. The team number is the same as the day number on the extreme left side.

MULTIPLE ACTIVITY FORMAT

MULTIPLE ACTIVITY SCHEDULE AND ROTATIONS

Period:
Date:
Instructor/s:

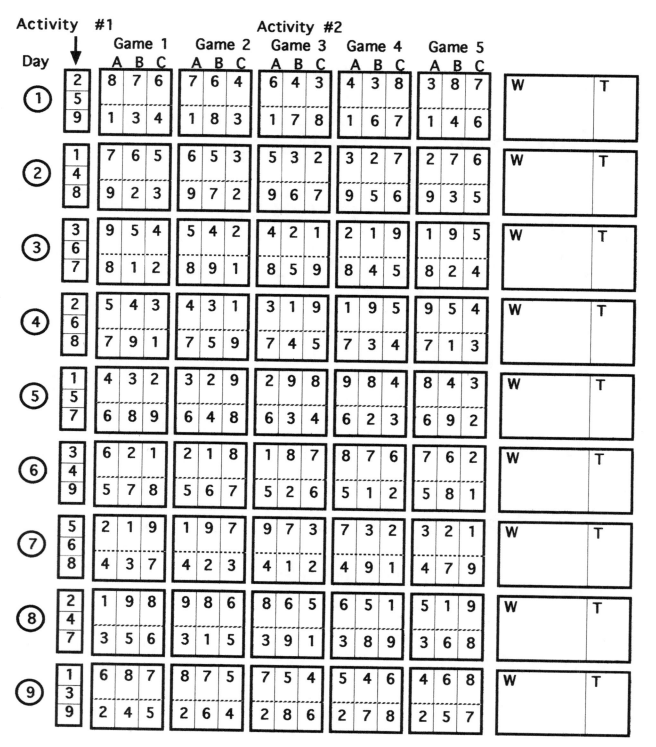

MISCELLANEOUS FORMATS

Double Elimination Bracket: A player or team must lose **twice** to be eliminated from the tournament.

Single Elimination Bracket: A player or team must win to stay in the tournament.

Top Gun:

1. Winners move to the next higher location after a projected **time** or **number** of points have been attained.
2. The vanquished stay at the same spot and take on the next challenger.
3. Once at the "Top Gun" spot, a player or team attempts to win a predetermined number of games **in a row.** This is usually two or three.
4. Any loss at the top spot causes that person or team to go to the bottom spot and start over.
5. When a player or team wins the predetermined number at the top locational, she/he must return to the lowest location and start over.

Total Points:

1. Record the final score of each game played by a team.
2. Tally all the scores of each team.
3. Those teams with the highest cumulative totals are in the Gold Championship bracket. The other teams vie for the Silver.

DOUBLE ELIMINATION

Unit: _____
Period: _____
Date: _____

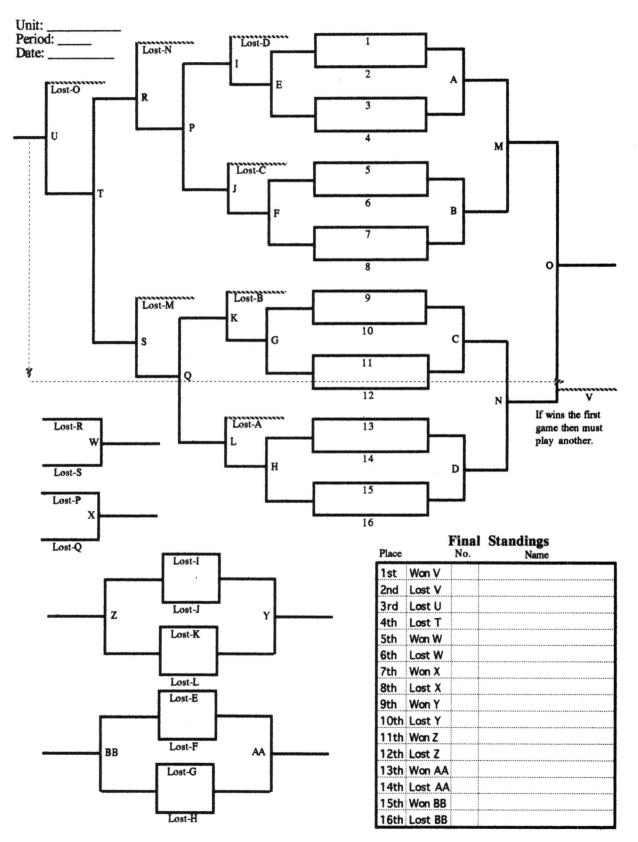

If wins the first
game then must
play another.

© 1996 Parker Publishing Company

Final Standings

Place	No.		Name
1st	Won V		
2nd	Lost V		
3rd	Lost U		
4th	Lost T		
5th	Won W		
6th	Lost W		
7th	Won X		
8th	Lost X		
9th	Won Y		
10th	Lost Y		
11th	Won Z		
12th	Lost Z		
13th	Won AA		
14th	Lost AA		
15th	Won BB		
16th	Lost BB		

SINGLE ELIMINATION

Unit: _____
Period: _____
Date: _____

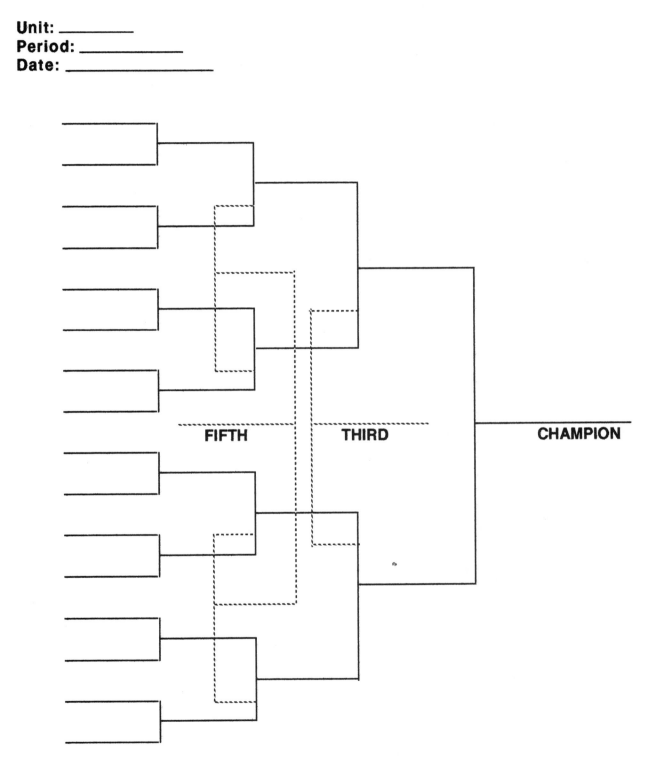

FIFTH   THIRD   **CHAMPION**

Section 3

◆◆◆◆◆

ASSESSMENTS

STUDENT ACCOUNTABILITY FORMAT

Students start with nothing and can earn a maximum total of five points by the end of the class period. Points are never taken away; instead points just are not awarded when undesirable behaviors occur.

How I Got My Grade (Instructor's Key) is presented so that the teacher has an idea of what initials need to be placed on the *Unit Grade Sheet*. Once these are learned, it becomes a snap to record student actions. These also allow quick reference for *Deficiency Reports* and parent conferences.

The student handout for *How I Got My Grade* is given to each student at the beginning of each new term. It is reviewed and desired changes from the students, if any, are made. This allows for no surprises, no gray areas, and lets each student know what is expected of him/her to attain the grade she/he desires. These sheets are collected, revisions made, and then passed out at the beginning of the new grading period.

Students are not graded on how far, how fast, or how high they may jump. When students demonstrate average or above physical skill or interests, they are encouraged to join after-school athletics where the coaches can enhance and polish those skills.

Remember, the instructor does not give each student a grade but only records actions and behaviors, be they good or bad, that are demonstrated by each student during class. These actions will determine their grade.

Final unit grades are then based on a percentage of the total points possible for each student. These total points will differ from student to student due to illnesses, excused field trips, and so on. Some teachers prefer to have students make up those days. That is each instructor's option.

SAMPLE P.E. POLICIES

(These can be handed out to the parents as well as the students.)

Objectives:

- To provide an extensive array of activities with an abundance of opportunities for every student to be successful.

- To create a physical education program where students are totally accountable for their own actions.

- To allow students to give feedback and share ideas that will enhance their program.

- To provide physical activity that will enable each student to monitor desired gains.

- To provide experiences that give release from emotional strain and tension.

- To develop good social behavior with the other students.

- To allow students to experience competitive and non-competitive activities as well as team and individual activities.

- To develop skill, interest and the appreciation for the need of life-long learning, activity, and recreation.

Uniforms:

- All students will dress in shorts and a shirt for activity.

- These must be different from what is worn to school.

- No school clothes, jackets, sweaters, leotards, lycra shorts or thermal underwear will be allowed.

- Clothes will be hemmed, have no inappropriate words or pictures and cover a student well.

- Clothes must be marked with the student's first and last name plus their basket number.

- P.E. clothes are not to be loaned to or borrowed from another student.

- Non-marking tennis shoes with laces are required.

- Sweatshirts and sweatpants may be worn in addition to gym clothes.

Class Participation:

- Everyone is expected to participate in P.E. every other day. Parental excuse notes can be written for a maximum of three (3) days. A doctor's note is required for longer durations. These students may go to the library.

- Students will bring written notes to roll call.

- If a student does not have a note, she/he will be marked as NON-DRESS and can bring a note to the next class.

- If a student is non-dressed and non-excused, she/he may choose to walk during class to improve grade and to still get some exercise.

Baskets and Locks:

- Every student will receive a private basket. Since all clothes are marked with the student's name and basket number, and the area is locked between classes, locks will be optional and supplied by the students (if they desire one).

STUDENT ACCOUNTABILITY FORMAT

Locker Room Behavior:

Dressing Down

1. All students will be in the locker room before the tardy bell rings.
2. After dressing into P.E. clothes, students will go immediately to roll call.
3. Balls will be provided so students can warm-up.
4. The doors to the dressing areas will be locked during class.

Showers

1. Optional for all students.
2. Students must bring their own towel if they desire to shower.

*Locker room conduct—**There will be no:***

1. Waiting for friends.
2. Rough play or fighting.
3. Taking of other's possessions.
4. Vulgar language.
5. Running or chasing others.
6. Lighting matches or lighters.
7. Putting deodorant on others.
8. Food or drink.
9. Destroying school property.
10. Untidiness.

Miscellaneous:

◆ Leave all equipment alone until instructor gives the O.K.
◆ Report all injuries immediately to the teacher.
◆ Discipline problems will be dealt with on an individual basis.
◆ P.E. areas are off-limits during non-class hours.
◆ No dangling or potentially dangerous jewelry shall be worn.
◆ Check with the P.E. office for lost items.
◆ Turn in all found items immediately to the teacher.
◆ Valuables may be locked up in the P.E. office before roll call.

Course Contents:

AERIAL TENNIS	FLOOR HOCKEY	SOCCER
AEROBICS	FRISBEE™ GAMES	SOCKEY
BADMINTON	JUGGLING	SPEED BALL
BASKETBALL	LARGE GROUP GAMES	STUNTS
BODY SHAPING	MAT SOCCER	TABLE TENNIS
CARDIO FITNESS	ORIENTEERING	TEAM HANDBALL
CREATE A GAME	PILLOW POLO	TENNIS
CROSS COUNTRY	PRE-FITNESS TESTING	TRACK AND FIELD
DANCE	POST-FITNESS TESTING	TUMBLING
DARTS	SELF DEFENSE	VOLLEYBALL
FLASH FOOTBALL	SOFTBALL	WRESTLING

Locker Room Conduct

STOP There will be **<u>NO</u>**

** Waiting for friends **

** Fighting or rough play **

** Taking others' possessions **

** Using vulgar language **

** Running or chasing others **

** Lighting matches or lighters **

** Putting deodorant on others **

** Consuming food or drink **

** Defacing school property **

** Being untidy or messy **

Violators will be asked to leave this area <u>immediately!</u>

HOW I GOT MY GRADE

Instructor's Key

I can earn a maximum of five points each day in P.E.

I will earn zero points for:

1. Non-dressed / non-active (ND)
2. Any unexcused absence (U)   Codes for Unit Grade Sheet
3. Being insubordinate (I)
4. Fighting (F)
5. Destroying any school property (DP)

I can only earn a maximum of two points for:

1. Non-dressed / active (ND2) (Walked around field, for example)
2. Cutting class (C)

I can only earn a maximum of three points for:

1. Reduced effort during activity (E)
2. Being tardy (T)

I can only earn a maximum of four points for:

1. Being partially dressed (PD)
2. Performing unsafe acts (US)
3. Showing poor sportsmanship (S)
4. Putting others down (B)
5. Breaking game rules or expectations intentionally (R)
6. Displaying or voicing obscenities (V)
7. Arguing with others (A)

I can earn from one to three extra points for:

1. Showing extra effort (+)
2. Assisting the teacher (+)
3. Performing a predetermined goal or outcome such as a:
   a. Task of (+)
   b. Number of (+)
   c. Routine of (+)
   d. Question of (+)

My grade will be based on a percentage of the total points of each unit.

90% and above	=	A
80% to 89%	=	B
70% to 79%	=	C
60% to 69%	=	D
59% and below	=	Non pass

HOW I GOT MY GRADE

Student Handout

I can earn a maximum of five points each day in P.E.

I will earn zero points for:

1. Non-dressed/non-active
2. Any unexcused absence
3. Being insubordinate
4. Fighting
5. Destroying any school property

I can only earn a maximum of two points for:

1. Non-dressed/active (Walked around field three times, for example)
2. Cutting class

I can only earn a maximum of three points for:

1. Reduced effort during activity
2. Being tardy

I can only earn a maximum of four points for:

1. Being partially dressed
2. Performing unsafe acts
3. Showing poor sportsmanship
4. Putting others down
5. Breaking game rules or expectations intentionally
6. Displaying or voicing obscenities
7. Arguing with others

I can earn from one to three extra points for:

1. Showing extra effort
2. Assisting the teacher
3. Performing a predetermined goal or outcome such as a:
   a. Task of
   b. Number of
   c. Routine of
   d. Question of

My grade will be based on a percentage of the total points of each unit.

90% and above = A
80% to 89% = B
70% to 79% = C
60% to 69% = D
59% and below = Non pass

STUDENT ACCOUNTABILITY FORMAT

SAMPLE TEN-DAY UNIT GRADE SHEET

Unit: Softball
Period: Second
Date: May 6, 1995
Instructor: Mrs. Jones

Activities – Skills

- **I** Assist in two (2) outs
- **II** Pitched two (2) innings
- **III** Caught two (2) fly balls
- **IV** Hit three (3) RBIs
- **V** Violations
- **VI** Violations

No.	Names	1 / 12	2 / 13	3 / 14	4 / 15	5 / 16	6 / 17	I	II	III	IV	V	VI	Number Of Days Present Times Five(5)= Max Points Possible	Total Of Plus And Minus Points	Total Points Attained	Final Unit Grade Change To A Number
1	Alva, Fred	pd	pd	pd	pd	pd		+		+		B A	A S	30	-7	23	C = 5
2	Bettes, Sally			ex					+	+				25	2	27	A = 11
3	Bounds, Frank							+	+		+			30	3	33	A+=12
4	Counts, Billy	nd2	nd2						+					30	-6	24	B- = 7
5	Ellis, Becky								+		+			30	0	30	A = 11
6	Fitzgerald, Bob			nd	pd									30	-7	23	C = 5
7	French, John								+	+				30	2	32	A = 11
8	Gomez, Juan	ex	ex						+	+				20	2	22	A = 11
9	Goodman, Sue	ab				ab		+		+				20	2	22	A = 11
10	Holmes, Sara				t	t			+		+			30	-2	28	A = 11
11	Jones, June								+	+				30	2	32	A = 11
12	Lovett, Ken				nd									30	-5	25	B = 8
13	Mandis, Elaine							+	+	+	+			30	4	34	A+=12
14	Mandis, Sue			nd	nd							A R	R R	30	-14	16	NP = 0

Directions:

1. Fill in the unit name, period, date, instructor's name, and student names.

2. The *Unit Day* section is for taking roll and recording deficiencies such as not dressing down.

3. Write in any skills, tasks, goals, or information needed in the *Activities/Skills* section. When a student has successfully completed a task, let him/her mark it with a "+" or a check.

4. The *Number of Days Present × Five Points* column is used to record the total points possible for each student. If a student was present for six days, she/he could have earned a total of 30 points for the unit.

5. The *Plus and Minus Points* column is used to add all of the bonuses and deficiencies. If a student (see Fred Alva in sample) received five partial dresses (-5), one putting others down (B-1), two argues (A,A,-2) one poor sportsmanship (S-1), and two extra points (+2), this would total to a minus seven (-7). The minus seven would go in this column.

6. The *Total Points Attained* column is determined by adding the previous two columns together. In Fred's case, it would be 30 + (-7) = 23 total points. The number 23 goes in this column.

7. The *Final Unit Grade* column is determined by using the *Unit Grade Scales* sheet. Find the *Day 6* column. Move down it until the number 23 is found. Next move to the extreme right or left *Grade* column and find C = 5. Put the number 5 in this column. Numbers are used since they are much easier to average than letters.

STUDENT ACCOUNTABILITY FORMAT

TEN-DAY UNIT GRADE SHEET

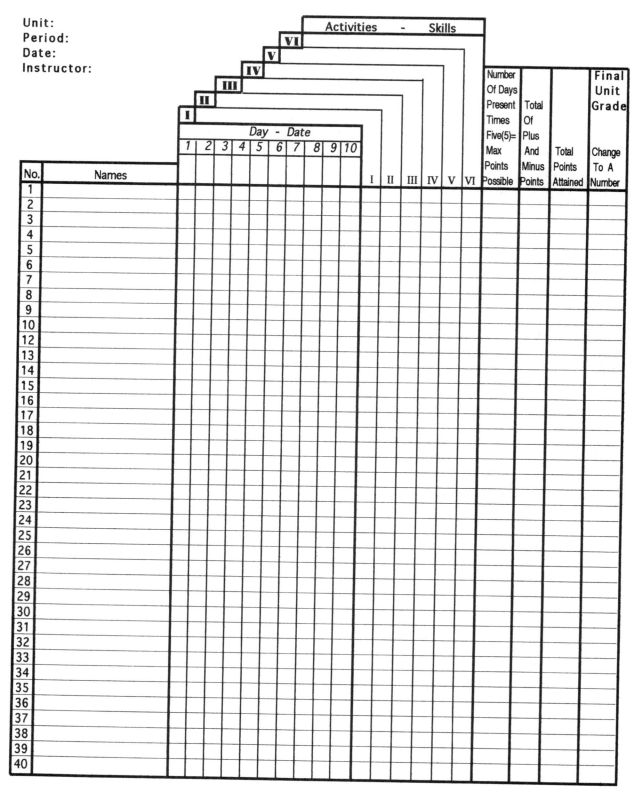

Unit:
Period:
Date:
Instructor:

Activities - Skills

STUDENT ACCOUNTABILITY FORMAT

ABOUT "UNIT GRADE SCALES"

(Five Points A Day)
NUMBER OF DAYS IN THE UNIT

Grade	1	2	3	4	5	6	7	8	9	10	Grade
A+ =12	Student received a certain number of bonus points.										A+ =12
A =11	5	10	15 14	20 19	25 24	30 29 28	35 34 33	40 39 38 37	45 44 43 42	50 49 48 47	A =11
A- =10		9		18	23	27	32	36	41	46 45	A- =10
B+ = 9					22		31	35	40	44	B+ = 9
B = 8			13	17	21	26 25	30 29	34 33	39 38 37	43 42 41	B = 8
B- = 7	4	8	12	16	20	24	28	32	36	40	B- = 7
C+ = 6								31	35	39	C+ = 6
C = 5			11	15	19 18	23 22	27 26	30 29	34 33	38 37 36	C = 5
C- = 4		7		14		21	25	28	32	35	C- = 4
D+ = 3					17		24	27	31	34	D+ = 3
D = 2			10	13	16	20 19	23 22	26 25	30 29 28	33 32 31	D = 2
D- = 1	3	6	9	12	15	18	21	24	27	30	D- = 1
NP	2	5	8	11	14	17	20	23	26	29	NP

Directions:

1. Use this sheet at the end of each unit to easily compute a final grade from the information taken off the *Daily Unit Sheets*. Example is of Billy Counts.

2. Find the *Number of Days in the Unit* column. Slide down that column to find the total points possible that a student obtained.

3. Move to the extreme right or left to determine his or her grade.

STUDENT ACCOUNTABILITY FORMAT

UNIT GRADE SCALES

(Five Points A Day)
NUMBER OF DAYS IN THE UNIT

Grade	1	2	3	4	5	6	7	8	9	10	Grade
A+ =12	Student received a certain number of bonus points.										A+ =12
A =11	5	10	15 14	20 19	25 24	30 29 28	35 34 33	40 39 38 37	45 44 43 42	50 49 48 47	A =11
A- =10		9		18	23	27	32	36	41	46 45	A- =10
B+ = 9					22		31	35	40	44	B+ = 9
B = 8			13	17	21	26 25	30 29	34 33	39 38 37	43 42 41	B = 8
B- = 7	4	8	12	16	20	24	28	32	36	40	B- = 7
C+ = 6								31	35	39	C+ = 6
C = 5			11	15	19 18	23 22	27 26	30 29	34 33	38 37 36	C = 5
C- = 4		7		14		21	25	28	32	35	C- = 4
D+ = 3					17		24	27	31	34	D+ = 3
D = 2			10	13	16	20 19	23 22	26 25	30 29 28	33 32 31	D = 2
D- = 1	3	6	9	12	15	18	21	24	27	30	D- = 1
NP	2	5	8	11	14	17	20	23	26	29	NP

STUDENT ACCOUNTABILITY FORMAT

SAMPLE FINAL TERM GRADE

Qtr/Sem: _2nd_
Date: _Feb. 3._
Period: _4th_
Instructor: _Mrs. Green_

No.	Name	____Units of Instruction____ A: Volleyball, B: Table Tennis, C: Weights, D: Aerobics, E: Square Dance, F:						Add A+B+C+D+E+F for total points	Number of Units	Use "Combined Units Grade Scale" for Qtr./Sem. FINAL GRADE
		A	B	C	D	E	F			
1	Altman, Sara	8	9	NP	6	3		26	5	C
2	Brown, Tony	11	11	11	11	11		55	5	A
3	Byers, Sean	12	11	12	12	11		58	5	A +
4	Clason, Sally	6	7	9	7	10		39	5	B
5	Dooley, Pete	10	9	8	8	NG		35	4	B +

Directions:

1. Fill in all of the student names.

2. In column *A* record their first unit grade of volleyball.

3. In column *B* record their second unit grade in table tennis, and so on.

4. Next, add up all numbers and record in the *Add A+B+C+D+E+F+G for total points* column. **Example:** Sally Clason got a 6 + 7 + 9 + 7 + 10 = 39.

5. Next, record the total number of units that each student received a grade for in the *Number of Units* column. Sally participated in five.

6. Now retrieve the *Combined Units Grade Scales* sheet. Look for the five units column. Go down this column until 39 is found and move to the far right or left *Final Grade* column. The grade that Sally received for the term is a "B."

7. Record the B grade in the *FINAL GRADE* column of the *Final Term Grade Sheet.*

STUDENT ACCOUNTABILITY FORMAT

FINAL TERM GRADE

Period:_____
Qtr/Sem:_____
Date:____
Instructor:_____

No.	Name	Units of Instruction						Add A+B+C+D+E+F for total points	Number of Units	FINAL GRADE
		A	B	C	D	E	F			
1										
2										
3										
4										
5										
6										
7										
8										
9										
10										
11										
12										
13										
14										
15										
16										
17										
18										
19										
20										
21										
22										
23										
24										
25										
26										
27										
28										
29										
30										
31										
32										
33										
34										
35										
36										
37										
38										
39										
40										

Use "Combined Units Grade Scale" for Qtr./Sem.

SAMPLE COMBINED UNITS GRADE SCALE

Final Grade Is Determined From The Average Of The Combined Units

Number of Combined Units For Quarter/Semester

Final Grade	1	2	3	4	5	6	7	Final Grade
			Total Points For Combined Grades					
A+	12	24	35-36	47-48	58-60	70-72	82-84	A+
A	11	22-23	32-34	43-46	53-57	64-69	74-81	A
A-	10	20-21	29-31	39-42	48-52	58-63	68-73	A-
B+	9	18-19	26-28	35-38	43-47	52-57	61-67	B+
B	8	16-17	23-25	31-34	38-42	46-51	55-60	B
B-	7	14-15	20-22	27-30	33-37	40-45	47-54	B-
C+	6	12-13	17-19	23-26	28-32	34-39	40-46	C+
C	5	10-11	14-16	19-22	23-27	28-33	32-39	C
C-	4	8-9	11-13	15-18	18-22	22-27	26-31	C-
D+	3	6-7	8-10	11-14	13-17	16-21	19-25	D+
D	2	4-5	5-7	7-10	8-12	10-15	11-18	D
D-	1	2-3	2-4	3-6	3-7	4-9	5-10	D-
No Pass	0	0-1	0-1	0-2	0-2	0-3	0-4	No Pass

Directions:

1. Use this sheet to determine the final semester or quarter grade.
2. Use the column that determines the total number of different units taught during this semester or quarter.
3. Example is that of Sally Clason.

COMBINED UNITS GRADE SCALE

Final Grade Is Determined From The Average Of The Combined Units

Number of Combined Units For Quarter/Semester

Final Grade	1	2	3	4	5	6	7	Final Grade
			Total Points For Combined Grades					
A+	12	24	35-36	47-48	58-60	70-72	82-84	A+
A	11	22-23	32-34	43-46	53-57	64-69	74-81	A
A-	10	20-21	29-31	39-42	48-52	58-63	68-73	A-
B+	9	18-19	26-28	35-38	43-47	52-57	61-67	B+
B	8	16-17	23-25	31-34	38-42	46-51	55-60	B
B-	7	14-15	20-22	27-30	33-37	40-45	47-54	B-
C+	6	12-13	17-19	23-26	28-32	34-39	40-46	C+
C	5	10-11	14-16	19-22	23-27	28-33	32-39	C
C-	4	8-9	11-13	15-18	18-22	22-27	26-31	C-
D+	3	6-7	8-10	11-14	13-17	16-21	19-25	D+
D	2	4-5	5-7	7-10	8-12	10-15	11-18	D
D-	1	2-3	2-4	3-6	3-7	4-9	5-10	D-
No Pass	0	0-1	0-1	0-2	0-2	0-3	0-4	No Pass

ACHIEVEMENT CARDS

Achievement cards can be given on a regular basis for:

- Being on a winning team.
- Setting a school record in the fitness tests.
- Assisting an instructor.
- Showing extra effort.
- Turning in valuables such as a watch or money.
- Worthy actions or special deeds while in an activity.
- Helping others.

These cards can be printed at a professional print shop. The same size as a business card, these cards can be collected by students for display or scrapbooks.

Sample Achievement Card
(The School Logo Is Printed In The Background)

```
┌─────────────────────────────────────────┐
│ KENNEDY PHYSICAL EDUCATION               │
│        ACHIEVEMENT AWARD                 │
│                 TO                        │
│  _____  │
│                FOR                        │
│  _____  │
│                                           │
│   Date _____   By _____ │
└─────────────────────────────────────────┘
```

BLACK JELLY BEAN AWARD

Black jelly beans can be given on a regular basis for:

- ◆ Being on a winning team.
- ◆ Setting a school record in the fitness tests.
- ◆ Assisting an instructor.
- ◆ Showing extra effort.
- ◆ Turning in valuables such as a watch or money.
- ◆ Worthy actions or special deeds while in an activity.
- ◆ Helping others.

Bought at a local candy store, these jelly beans could be the same color as the school colors. No individual, including a teacher, is allowed to eat a jelly bean unless it is earned.

Students "Eat Em Up"

SAMPLE BEHAVIOR CONTRACT

WILSON MIDDLE SCHOOL

HELEN RICE
Principal

JERRY LANE
Associate Principal

**200 ALKER AVENUE
HIGHLAND, OREGON 97500
(503) 555-6611**

JOHN DOE
Behavior Contract
January 19, 1997

Reason for Contract:

John is exhibiting behavior in P.E. class that puts self and other students in physical danger.

Goal:

To successfully participate in P. E. without putting self and others in danger.

Expectations:

Behave appropriately by:

A. Observing all safety rules.
B. Displaying good sportsmanship.
C. Cooperating and interacting positively with the teacher and peers.
D. No arguing with the teacher.
E. Using positive appropriate language and tone.

Results:

If John meets the above expectations, he will remain in P.E. and receive a passing grade. If John chooses to disrupt, argue and put self and other students in danger, he will be:

1. Sent to the office for the remainder of the period.
2. Serve 30 minutes that day after school in the office.

   If this occurs two times, student will:

1. Miss P.E. for one week and report to the office.

   OR

2. Be suspended from school for any physical assaults, threats and persistent insubordination.

_____   Date _____

Student

_____   Date _____

Teacher

_____   Date _____

Counselor/Dean

_____   Date _____

Associate Principal

STUDENT ACCOUNTABILITY FORMAT

SAMPLE DEFICIENCY REPORT

ASHLAND MIDDLE SCHOOL

". . . Working together to ensure each other's success."

April 22, 1997

Dear Parent,

Please help me make your child more successful. The following is keeping your child from reaching his/her potential:

◆ not dressing down

◆ partial dress

◆ tardy

◆ very little effort given during class

◆ flagrant rules violation

Unit Grades:

a. Large group games	=	D
b. Personal Defense	=	C
c. Cone ball/Colony ball	=	D
	Average =	D+

Please indicate below what you think we should do and return this response to me this week.

Thanks.

Physical Education Instructor

- -

Parent Response

Yes

❑ When necessary, please keep my child after school. Please call to let me know at
_____-_____.

❑ When necessary, keep my child during lunch.

❑ I will work with my child at home.

❑ I would like a conference with you.

Other ideas: _____

_____

_____

STUDENT OF THE MONTH

One student is selected each month that has demonstrated outstanding qualities in physical education. This individual is given a certificate along with a hat/lapel pin.

Sample Lapel Pin
(Actual size is 3/4 inch by 3/4 inch)

The certificates are printed at a printing company on a parchment style paper with the information deemed necessary. The teacher can then fill in the blanks with the proper information.

The pins can be ordered from most any engraving company and are really quite inexpensive.